Prophetic Leadership and Visionary Hope

PROPHETIC LEADERSHIP AND VISIONARY HOPE

New Essays on the Work of Cornel West

Edited by

Barbara Will

PENN

UNIVERSITY OF PENNSYLVANIA PRESS

PHILADELPHIA

Published by
University of Pennsylvania Press
Philadelphia, Pennsylvania 19104-4112
www.upenn.edu/pennpress

Printed in the United States of America on acid-free paper

10 9 8 7 6 5 4 3 2 1

Hardcover ISBN: 978-1-5128-2407-0
eBook ISBN: 978-1-5128-2408-7

Library of Congress Cataloging-in-Publication Data
Names: Will, Barbara, editor.
Title: Prophetic leadership and visionary hope : new essays on the work of Cornel West / edited by Barbara Will.
Description: Philadelphia : University of Pennsylvania Press, [2023] | Includes bibliographic referenes and index.
Identifiers: LCCN 2022043304 | ISBN 9781512824070 (hardcover) | ISBN 9781512824087 (ebook)
Subjects: LCSH: West, Cornel. Race matters. | West, Cornel—Political and social views. | West, Cornel—Philosophy. | United States—Race relations—21st century.
Classification: LCC E185.615 P77 2023 | DDC 305.800973—dc23/eng/20221014
LC record available at https://lccn.loc.gov/2022043304

CONTENTS

Introduction. Cruciform (Almost) All the Way Down 1
Barbara Will

PART I. CORNEL WEST AND HIS INTELLECTUAL GENEALOGY

1. Reading *Race Matters* Again for the First Time 15
Paul A. Bové

2. *Race Matters* and US American Democracy: Cornel West and W. E. B. Du Bois 35
Lucius T. Outlaw Jr.

PART II. BLACK NIHILISM, AFROPESSIMISM, AND PROPHETIC FAITH

3. Nihilism, Pessimism, and Tragic Hope: Black Nihilism Reconsidered 63
Brandon M. Terry

4. Not Nothing: A Mystical Theological Reading of "Nihilism in Black America" 94
Andrew Prevot

5. What Manner of Man Is the Prophet? Cornel West, Abraham Heschel, and the Hebrew Prophets 107
Susannah Heschel

6. Prophetic Fightback: Cornel West, *Race Matters*, and the Black Church 135
Nkosi Du Bois Anderson

PART III. SOCIAL JUSTICE AND HISTORICAL WITNESSING

7. Race (and Love) Matter More Than Ever Now: Affirmative Action, Alliances, and Anti-Asian Hate 161
Matthew M. Briones

8. Soulful Kenosis in Narcissistic Times 178
Farah Jasmine Griffin

Afterword. *Race Matters*: Philosophy in the Funk 193
Cornel West

List of Contributors 201

Index 203

INTRODUCTION

Cruciform (Almost) All the Way Down

Barbara Will

"The object of inquiry for Afro-American critical thought," Cornel West wrote in 1982, is "how to build its language in such a way that the configurations of sentences and the constellation of paragraphs themselves create a textuality and distinctive discourse which are a material force for Afro-American freedom."[1] One can imagine few more illustrious practitioners of this "distinctive discourse" than Cornel West himself, whose own sentences and paragraphs over the course of a prolific half century of writing and speaking have sought in the most inclusive way to articulate the force of African American *mattering.* "Mattering" in the sense of being significant, visible, or legible; of having political weight and bearing; but also, proleptically, in the sense of imagining beyond, of envisioning alternative futures and trajectories for Black Americans and their communities, and indeed Americans of every racial and ethnic background. Articulating how and why Black lives matter is for Cornel West both a political and a prophetic project, equally tied to ongoing pragmatic movements of social justice and ongoing predictive forms of revolutionary critique. It is a project oriented toward exposing injustices, highlighting hypocrisies and shopworn pieties, and celebrating achievements. And it is fundamentally a project of language, of opening minds and hearts through words, of making discourse into "a material force" for the betterment of all.

One of America's preeminent public intellectuals, Cornel West is the author or editor of more than thirty books on subjects ranging from the philosophy of pragmatism to the challenges of multiculturalism to the cultural politics of difference. With teaching appointments at Princeton, Harvard, Yale, Dartmouth, and Union Theological Seminary, West is also a sought-after colleague, an inspiring mentor and teacher, and a celebrated speaker, whose capacity to move audiences through compassionate critique and courageous dialogue is legendary. Few living American intellectuals are so capable of straddling the divide between "academic" and "public." No stranger to controversy, West and his work pose provocative questions in order to promote understanding and action, and, always, to offer a measure of hope and optimism. Described by Marian Wright Edelman as "one of the most authentic, brilliant, prophetic, and healing voices in America today," West holds a unique and cherished position—alongside such prophetic voices as W. E. B. Du Bois, Martin Luther King Jr., Malcolm X, Abraham Joshua Heschel, and Audre Lorde, among so many others—in continually reminding us of the urgent place of racial justice in the unfinished and fragile project of American democracy.

The text at the heart of the present volume is West's *Race Matters*, a slim collection of essays that had a profound and immediate impact on contemporary political discussions on race in America when it appeared in 1993. Part philosophical inquiry, part trenchant sociological analysis, part personal meditation on his own experience with racism during the waning years of the twentieth century, West's book put into words the dreams and frustrations of the post-civil rights era. Published in the wake of the Los Angeles riots of 1992 and the police beating of Rodney King, an event—painfully resonant to this day—that laid bare the rage and fury of communities unwilling to countenance unchecked forms of police brutality, *Race Matters* also spoke viscerally to its immediate historical moment. Like the murder of George Floyd in the summer of 2020, the King beating, and the subsequent acquittal of the four police perpetrators who brutally struck Mr. King fifty-six times, gave rise to a nationwide collective moment of anger and unrest: what West called "justified social rage [toward] . . . the sense of powerlessness in American society" on the part of a wide multiracial and trans-class swath of the population.

When Los Angeles burned, West wrote; and out of his sense of outrage and despair emerged one of the most moving and wide-ranging essays of his career: "Learning to Talk of Race," published in the *New York Times Magazine* in August 1992. "Learning to Talk of Race" was not a departure from what West had been saying all along, in smaller venues, classrooms, and on book tours. But it was the first time West had so clearly articulated, in the pages of a major newspaper, the stakes of America's racial and democratic calculus for a wide audience; the first time that West so publicly took aim at not only the broken promises and structural inequities that defined Black life in the early 1990s, but also "a culture of hedonistic self-indulgence and narcissistic self-regard" that both bisected and transcended race matters and that had led to a deeply American spiritual impoverishment or sense of nihilism. "Learning to Talk of Race" became the introduction for *Race Matters* and the immediate catalyst for the book's publication. It marked the consolidation of an inescapably powerful public voice with a unique ability to speak across classes and registers in the search for a common, morally stringent prophetic activism.

While "Learning to Talk of Race" turned up the volume on West's voice as a public intellectual, the majority of the chapters in *Race Matters* had been published elsewhere in the late 1980s and early 1990s. For years, indeed, West had been writing about a larger set of ongoing issues around Black life in America: the challenge of leadership in a culture marked by the legacy of white supremacy; the limited value of liberal affirmative action programs in promoting the affirmation of Black humanity; the dangerous seductions of African American conservatism and the question of Black self-regard (what West called "black nihilism"); the necessity and difficulty of cross-race solidarity and cross-religious affinity; the need to channel legitimate Black rage over untenable conditions of existence into productive opportunities and viewpoints. The seven discrete essays that dealt with these concerns found clear and lyrical connection when placed side by side in the pages of West's volume. Moreover, a new chapter—"Black Sexuality: The Taboo Subject"—dealt squarely with the "taboo" centrality of the persistent, transgenerational, and toxic myths about Black sexuality for both men and women in this country. Its inclusion in the volume, as West has noted, was necessary to provide "the full dimension of the black experience" in America.[2]

Compelling and accessible, laced with personal insight, *Race Matters* is still one of those rare books that speaks to all. A graduate student in 1993, I remember hearing about this "must-read" book from my academic friends, but also from countless others outside the university walls. *Race Matters* soon became a best seller, lauded for its "ferocious moral vision and astute intellect,"[3] as for its "ability to discern synthesis where others see only chaos and inspire hope in the face of seemingly insurmountable odds."[4] The book page of the *Washington Post* praised the intellectual West for keeping it real: "West understands that ideas cannot be separated from morality and the realities of daily life."[5] Nevertheless, the difficult balancing act West strove for in this book between accessible ideas and intellectual rigor was not universally appreciated. Dissenting opinions struggled with the thinness of West's prescriptions for future action, wishing for less diagnosis and more concrete solutions.[6] Others demanded more pointed analysis of "the interrelations between market mechanisms and white supremacy," which West, particularly in his analysis of Black nihilism, gestures at but never pins down.[7] Even the *New York Times* lamented some of the book's "platitudes" about matters like freedom, democracy, and equality.[8] Almost none of his critics paid attention to the prophetic or Christian resonances behind West's stylistic injunctions and formulations.

In the end, *Race Matters'* easy style and readability belie deeper achievements. The book's erudition, rigorous argument, and cross-hatching connections across matters of race, class, sexuality, gender, religion, politics, and nationality established a new standard for what we now call the public humanities; and the text has only become richer and more relevant to the contemporary moment with each new rereading.

Some twenty-five years later, well into a new century and at the dawn of a new millennium, West's provocative analysis of American democracy inextricably tethered to racial conflict and enduring white racism against peoples of color has not lost its critical edge. Indeed, new threats and new hopes have made this analysis even more urgent today. The supposedly post-racial era of Barack Obama has given way to the white supremacist sloganeering of Charlottesville. The mass incarceration of African Americans at levels unprecedented in American society has created, in the words of Michelle Alexander, a "new Jim Crow." And the Movement for Black Lives, borne into social media through the efforts of three young female activists, has animated a new generation to challenge the complacency of a supposedly color-blind society. *Race Matters*—and its subsequent companion volume, *Democracy Matters*—have served as the key building blocks for understanding the dimensions of these changes in a contemporary moment of struggle, dissension, and debate.

In the summer of 2018, a group of critics, historians, theologians, and philosophers of race came together at Dartmouth College to celebrate the twenty-fifth anniversary republication of *Race Matters* and to ponder anew the questions West's work raises. The three-day event encouraged participants to think broadly about how West's book shaped their development, to place the work within an intellectual genealogy, and to explore its prophetic promise on the horizon of countervailing intellectual currents of the day such as Afropessimism. The event also featured the work of such important and emerging Black artists as Daniel Bernard Roumain, Lisa Armstrong, Enrico

Riley, and two extraordinary Dartmouth students, Thobile Mawewera and Raleigh Nesbitt, to create a memorable weekend of critique, collaboration, and celebration that brought hundreds of participants to Hanover, New Hampshire. As we gathered to reflect on the significance of *Race Matters*, invited contributors from various academic fields used this occasion as a multidisciplinary generative moment to speak both to the text at hand and to the larger issues it raises in the present day. The resulting essays included here offer a wide-ranging account of what Saidiya Hartman calls "the poetics of hope and despair" embedded both in *Race Matters* and in the particular moment of twenty-first-century critical and prophetic race theory.

Given the recent resurgence of racist and xenophobic rhetoric in the political sphere and the continued economic downward mobility of large swaths of American society, as well as the particular havoc wreaked on communities of color by the Covid-19 pandemic, it is not surprising that many of the essays gathered here focus their attention on West's analysis of Black nihilism and the empty promises of political conservatism for persons of color. These are topics that speak directly to the ongoing sense of frustration and helplessness engendered by the national elections of 2016 and the tragic deaths at the hands of police of yet another generation of Black citizens: George Floyd, Breonna Taylor, Ahmaud Arbery, and so many others. At the same time, many also question the binarism of nihilistic thinking and its potential ironically to affirm the very impasse of which it is the critique. The essays in the present volume follow West in refusing to remain in a static or unyielding intellectual orientation, even in the face of deep critical pessimism toward the currents of market-driven neoliberal individualism that continue to dominate twenty-first century American culture. The methodology employed in these essays is one of critical movement and creative imagining through a strong allegiance to the power of language to shape understanding and possibility within non-mainstream communities. The voices collected here are faithful to West's own injunction that courageous thinking requires conceptualizing, feeling, and writing with hope *despite* being fully cognizant of the manifold difficulties embedded in this position. They see their interventions as part of a project of creating "a material force for Afro-American freedom."

This is not to deny the fundamental methodological challenge faced by our writers in addressing—and conveying—the unique expressive fluency and crystalline clarity of West's most trenchant work. Capturing and framing the transformative power of West's own words to the present day requires an ability to think on many different registers at once. There is, first of all, the intellectual tradition within which West is speaking, a tradition that extends back to Plato and weaves through a rich panoply of modern thinkers—from Douglass to Du Bois to Dewey to Hamer to Rukeyser—up to, with great propulsive energy, Martin Luther King Jr. West draws on this vast legacy through multiple acts of intellectual fidelity, both spoken and implicit, inviting his audience on the excitement of this journey as he shares what he calls *paideia*, "deep education." Tethered to this intellectual commitment is West's interest in prophecy, in a multi-strand theological tradition that includes Western religious prophets as well as literary, musical, and comic prophets. For West, the prophetic tradition offers the fullest response to the existential dread of modern life; it is a form of witnessing to disenfranchisement, to the false promises and pieties of modernity, and to the continuance of human suffering despite modern progress. It is also an ethical and political stance rooted in an ongoing search for religious freedom and salvation. "Prophetic pragmatism," what Susannah Heschel describes as "a new path of politics in a religious key," is Cornel West's calling card. Following and flowering out of West's prophetic stance is, finally, his unremitting and capacious critique of social injustice, his refusal to rest with the status quo, his understanding of the urgency of speaking truth to power now, clearly and forcefully, with not a moment to lose. West's Gramscian commitment to intellectual activism embedded in community practice is not unique, of course, but particularly potent in its connection to prophecy and hope.

Each of the contributors in this volume works to capture one or more of these strands of Cornel West's work, while also striving to create distinctions and differences within the legacy that West has forged. While foundational to contemporary African American critical and political thought, West's work is not scripture; its commitment to a "distinctive discourse" is also a commitment to dialogue and debate within the framework of mutual respect, intellectual humility, and what West calls a "love ethic." Such a commitment or call encourages a strong response. The contributors here write in the spirit of *revenants*, continually returning to an urtext that remains haunting and grounding at once, while also departing in critical ways from certain arguments, assumptions, and implied consequences of the terms of *Race Matters*.

Most of the existing scholarship on West's work concentrates on the philosophical, theological, and political frameworks within which he stages his interventions. Among these, the meticulous and probing volume of essays edited by George Yancy, *Cornel West: A Critical Reader* (2001), remains exemplary in its careful explication of key themes in West's writing, including the role of pragmatism and existentialism in his conceptual foundation; the definition of "black nihilism" as either decadence or negative possibility; the sometimes incommensurable tension between philosophical and prophetic world views in West's writings; and the particular constraints and pressures of being an African American public intellectual.[9] (It also must be noted that Yancy's was the first book in US history to engage in its entirety with the work of a living Black American philosopher.) The present volume does not sidestep the analyses of Yancy and his contributors but adds to them through a particular focus on *Race Matters* and its prescient insight into American culture during the turbulent years that followed its publication, particularly the first two decades of the twenty-first century. Reading West across that particular span of time renews one's appreciation for his unwavering commitment to critique as engagement, to writing as a form of inclusion, to speaking as a protestation of what he calls "democratic faith." Years marked by the deadliest terrorist attacks on American soil, the longest war in American history, unprecedented income inequality, the first African American president in US history, and the rise of a resurgent and racist Right have only sharpened the urgency of West's message in *Race Matters* that "we either hang together by combating these forces that divide and degrade us or we hang separately." The contributors to the present volume recognize that ours is "a bleak time of spiritual blackout and imperial meltdown," as West writes in the new introduction for the twenty-fifth anniversary edition of *Race Matters*; nevertheless, their voices seek, in the consistently critical and also hopeful mode of West himself, to "put a premium on courageous truth telling and exemplary action."[10]

This engagement is mobilized through varying critical models in the sections that follow. Organized thematically, each section offers a key point of entry into West's life and work: his deep embeddedness in Black American intellectual traditions; his equally strong allegiance to movements of Black spirituality; his unceasing commitments to social justice movements across many registers and regions. This thematic organization enables critical depth to be brought to bear on specific issues generated by *Race Matters*, or, more generally, by West's own capacious oeuvre and activism as an organic intellectual. At the same time, these specific points of entry traverse one another in crucial ways, and are shot through with common motifs, for example West's searing critique of American racial capitalism, his profound belief in the idea of democracy, and his lyrical invocation of the power of music and literature to secure hope and foster social change. Moreover, given the wide intellectual scope of *Race Matters*, and West's own inclusive and capacious discursive fluency, any interpretive apparatus must perforce reject stark distinctions among intellectual, spiritual, and activist engagements. Notable for the wide-ranging expertise each author brings to her or his analysis, and for the manifold subjects covered across the essays (politics, religion, gender, class, ethnicity, music, literature, education, and the media), this volume seeks to be as comprehensive and inclusive as the figure around whom it centers, Cornel West himself.

Part 1 considers the intellectual genealogy of *Race Matters* through the light of figures central to that text's aim and genesis: James Baldwin, Malcolm X, and W. E. B. Du Bois. In Chapter 1, Paul Bové offers a wide-ranging account of sources central to the model of loving critique promoted by West in *Race Matters*, including Baldwin and Malcom. Referring to West's central concept of a "politics of conversion," Bové traces the lines of connection between this concept and a radical critical tradition steeped in activism, engagement, and an organic connection to communities and movements—a "proper" criticism rather than a "persistent" criticism. Just as Baldwin, Malcolm, Du Bois and others in West's lineage seek to carve out a politics that rises above race exclusiveness, rage, and anger, so too does *Race Matters* outline the ideal qualities of Black leadership sited in an ethical politics of love, a criticism of resistance and inclusion, and a deep investment in the prophetic tradition.

In Chapter 2, Lucius T. Outlaw Jr. probes West's "complicated—even fraught—relationship with the career and legacies of Du Bois," a figure West himself described as "the brook of fire through which we must all pass in order to gain access to the intellectual and political weaponry needed to sustain the radical democratic tradition in our time."[11] Outlaw's essay makes it clear that the trajectory *Race Matters* set in motion for West was precisely that of "wrestling" with Du Bois, a project that initially misses—to Outlaw's mind—a central interrogation with Du Boisian terms of Black peoplehood. For Outlaw, *Race Matters* is a "major, learned, creatively insightful"—but not always successful—counterpoint to the work of Du Bois, a masterful statement of a major public intellectual that nevertheless fails to move forward key insights that Du Bois pioneered decades earlier.

Part 2 engages directly with "Nihilism in Black America," one of West's most important and most controversial chapters in *Race Matters*. Where West in 1993 called for his readers "to face up to the monumental eclipse of hope, the unprecedented collapse of meaning, the incredible disregard for human (especially black) life and property in much of black America," his words occasioned a strenuous debate over agency, victimhood, and the structural conditions of existence for contemporary African Americans.

In an essay that serves as a bridge between Parts 1 and 2, Brandon Terry (Chapter 3) asks how West's attention to this "eclipse of hope" in fact places him in an important lineage of pessimism that extends from Arthur Schopenhauer and Friedrich Nietzsche through W. E. B. Du Bois and up to Walter Benjamin and Hannah Arendt. Terry then draws this debate forward into contemporary debates over Afropessimism, an intellectual movement that theorizes the impossibility of any project of Black political engagement or social renewal as futile, naïve, and always already doomed by and within the unremitting racist mandates of white supremacist American culture. Alongside nihilistic trends within African American expressive culture, Afropessimism, Terry writes, underscores the historical failure of progressivist movements in the twentieth century to erase the legacy of slavery or accommodate a transformative vision of egalitarian racial difference. Yet like West, Terry refuses to rest with the Afropessimist world view in its totalizing sweep. Terry sees this world view as insufficiently attentive to multiple, semi-autonomous strands of oppression that complicate and in some ways resist the conflation of experience into a single totality, thereby sublating the meaning of Black struggle and striving into the "ironic language" of "non-events." For Terry, West's "tragic sensibility" offers a much more powerful mode of critique that locates within failed moments of historical possibility the seeds of future action and social renewal. This sensibility, Terry writes simply, is a mode of keeping faith.

The faith-keeping and prophesying that powerfully lifts up the pages of *Race Matters*, and serves as an antidote to nihilism, is the subject of Chapter 4. There, Andrew Prevot analyzes West's investment in a politics of love and "conversion" as offering a new perspective on the idea of Black nihilism. In a theological tradition that extends back to the medieval Christian mystic Marguerite Porete, West courageously calls out the humanization of peoples denied presence and visibility, or subjectivity—the ironic subjects of nihilistic thinking. Reading West via Porete, Prevot embraces the idea of "conversion" as a mode of demonstrating love in the face of nihilism and preventing the foreclosure of the future in favor of a more exalted future of possibility and hope. Prevot's essay brings spiritual depth and intellectual rigor to the position of the "love warrior."

As West himself has written, "The mark of the prophet is to speak the truth in love with courage—come what may."[12] Susannah Heschel's "What Manner of Man Is the Prophet? Cornel West and the Hebrew Prophets" (Chapter 5) tracks the strong ties between West's theology and philosophy and that of the Hebrew prophets, including Heschel's own father, Abraham Joshua Heschel. The tradition that Heschel reads in West's work is one of heartfelt solidarity with the wretched of the earth, bearing witness, and a "rousing call to justice": words and acts infused by "passion" and "courage" as well as by a strong artistic tradition of call and response. Countering tendencies to pessimism and disavowal through a full-throated, intellectually rigorous blues cry, West speaks "with the spirit of a Hasidic rebbe." West, like the Hebrew prophets, is "a prophetic figure who condemns disavowal, denounces indifference, and proclaims that God is never unmoved but suffers with us." The countertheological dimensions of the prophet's position may be at odds with liberal Protestant tendencies, as well as with market-driven capitalist ideologies and techno-messianic futurity that dictate shallow individualistic wants and desires. Nevertheless, thanks to such figures as West, James Baldwin, Martin Luther King, and Abraham Joshua Heschel the ethical imperative to justice remains strong in this country and offers the best possible antidote to more oppressive and vicious modes of social functioning.

As a fitting close to this discussion of nihilism and prophetic activism, Nkosi Anderson, in Chapter 6, offers a new reading of West's relationship to the Black prophetic Christian tradition as seen through the social justice heritage of the Black church in America. By locating West within this heritage, Anderson dissects the particular form of West's commitments, including his Marxian challenge to recent developments like the prosperity gospel movement and his insistence on the inseparability of spiritual *and* economic renewal in social change. A key historical precedent for West is seen in the historically overlooked figure of George Washington Woodbey, the early twentieth-century Black Socialist, minister, and unrelenting moral exemplar in the fight for social justice, even in the face of enormous odds.

Part 3 opens out to a more general appraisal of Cornel West's voice, writing, and presence as a global public intellectual, social justice advocate, and witness to seminal historical events following the enormous success of *Race Matters*.

In Chapter 7, Matthew Briones considers the substantial impact Cornel West and *Race Matters* have had on a new generation of scholars and activists working as allies on the front lines of social justice matters. From the perspective of an Asian American scholar like Briones, West's book and the tradition from which it hails has offered "a blueprint of promise and possibility in a challenging twenty-first-century racial climate" that affects all Americans. West's acute sensitivity to cross-racial alliances in *Race Matters* and elsewhere testifies to the power of coalition-building in bringing about a more just world.

Farah Jasmine Griffin's concluding Chapter 8 asks, "How [do we] pay tribute to a man who means so much to me, to us, to our struggle, to our history?" Seizing on West's concept of "soulful kenosis," a form of "self-emptying," Griffin points to West's ability to remain humble, disciplined, and obedient in the pursuit of justice and love despite his success and renown. This ability, Griffin implies, is inextricable from the idea of "soul," a feature of Black music and performance in which the performer "gives his all" to the audience and to the tradition of which he is a part. Returning, as do many essays in this volume, to the urtext of Toni Morrison's novel *Beloved,* Griffin places West in a line of soul sisters and soul brothers—writers, artists, musicians, preachers, and prophets—who have consistently "given their all" to the communities, seeking to achieve sustaining hope in times of spiritual blackout.

Cornel West's own afterword to this volume reveals the long arc of an illustrious career within which *Race Matters* serves as a vital touchstone. It is appropriate that West's powerful language would be the last (though by no means final) word in articulating the mattering of his own life and work to himself and his society. Describing his thinking as "cruciform almost all the way down," West reveals the various influences that cross and overlap in his quest to show that race will always matter. Shaped by pragmatic and prophetic commitments, seduced by democratic ideals, caught within a tragicomic sensibility, nurtured by a blues, jazz, and soul tradition, West's discourse lies centrally within the crosshairs of American history, always "wrestling with catastrophe." The struggle, as he showed us in *Race Matters* and continues to show us a quarter of a century later, is one that engages us all.

I would like to close by expressing my gratitude to Dartmouth College, which generously supported the publication of this book as well as the 2018 conference it grew out of. In addition, I would like to extend special thanks to Dr. Maria Cole, whose wisdom, commitment, and creativity inspired this book from beginning to end, and to Sarah M. S. Coulter, without whom neither book nor conference would have come into being. You both embody the best of what it means to be part of a scholarly community devoted to both thinking and doing, as well as the love ethic that Cornel West encourages us all to aspire to.

Notes

1. Cornel West, *Prophesy Deliverance! An Afro-American Revolutionary Christianity* (Philadelphia: Westminster Press, 1982), 15.

2. Cornel West, telephone interview with Barbara Will, April 9, 2022.

3. Michiko Kakutani, "Rage and Reason in the Crisis of Black America," *New York Times*, April 27, 1993, 17.

4. Robert Boynton, "Review of Cornel West's *Race Matters*," *Newsday*, April 25, 1993.

5. David Nicholson, "Race Culture and Morality," *Washington Post*, June 13, 1993.

6. See Richard B. Miller, "Review Essay: Religion and the American Public Intellectual," *Journal of Religious Ethics* 25, no.2 (Fall 1997), 376–79; Kakutani, "Rage and Reason in the Crisis of Black America."

7. David Theo Goldberg, "Whither West? The Making of a Public Intellectual," *Review of Education, Pedagogy, and Cultural Studies* 16, no.1 (1994), 3.

8. Kakutani, "Rage and Reason in the Crisis of Black America."

9. George Yancy, ed., *Cornel West: A Critical Reader* (Malden, MA: Blackwell, 2001). Of particular interest in this volume are the essays by Lewis R. Gordon on Black nihilism ("The Unacknowledged Fourth Tradition"); and Yancy ("Religion and the Mirror of God: Historicism, Truth, and Religious Pluralism").

10. Cornel West, introduction to *Race Matters*, 25th Anniversary ed. (Boston: Beacon Press, 2017), xv.

11. Cornel West, "Black Strivings in a Twilight Civilization," in Henry Louis Gates Jr., and Cornel West, *The Future of the Race* (New York: Knopf, 1996), 68.

12. Cornel West, *The American Evasion of Philosophy: A Genealogy of Pragmatism* (Madison: University of Wisconsin Press, 1989), 233.

PART I

Cornel West and His Intellectual Genealogy

CHAPTER 1

Reading *Race Matters* Again for the First Time

Paul A. Bové

> There is no escape from our interracial interdependence, yet enforced racial hierarchy dooms us as a nation to collective paranoia and hysteria—the unmaking of any democratic order.
>
> —Cornel West, *Race Matters*

The political state of the United States requires that we celebrate those things we do and have done creatively to witness, nurture, and enrich our humanity. Cornel West lays down this rule in *Race Matters*, emphasizing that the love ethic is essential to the creativity of all radical politics and thought. This ethos underlies his career as an activist, intellectual, and friend. "A love ethic," West writes, "must be at the center of a politics of conversion" (19). In saying so, West places himself within a long, effective, and provocative tradition of Black resistance, of calls for an end to white dehumanization of American Blacks. In his *Appeal*, David Walker, for example, indicted the inhumanity of Southern slaveholders and Northern racists in a Christian rhetoric of love that Americans, as Walker calls the oppressors, avoid: "Our divine Lord and Master said, 'all things whatsoever ye would that men should do unto you, do ye even so unto them'" (Walker 38). Walker made Christ's remarks a two-edged sword turned against the hypocrisy of white Christians in the United States while celebrating the dignified moral qualities of Blacks and other who follow and honor the Lord's way. Jesus's love ethic would help clear away the tyranny of racial slavery so that the full humanity of the oppressed could create a new world. Jesus was a revisionist. Proverbs had authorized revenge: "pay them back for what they have done." In Luke 6: 27–35, Jesus exhorts his listeners with the command, "Love your enemies," which means, in the end, "Do to others as you have would have them do to you."

Walker started a tradition to which West belongs. "For I believe it is the will of Lord that our greatest happiness shall consist in working for the salvation of our whole body" (Walker 29). Quickly this belief can become apocalyptic, but it is always utopian: "I assure you that God will accomplish it" (Walker 30). Love, justice, and conversion form one of the earliest expressions of Black resistance and creativity. *Race Matters* celebrates and renews this expression, repeating Walker's hopeful belief in the virtues of Jesus's ethic.

Celebrate is not, however, all that we must do. Celebration is essential, though, because its rituals confirm a commitment to our contemporaries' and predecessors' courageous and generous contributions to the virtues essential to human responsibility for the species and the planet.[1] *Race Matters* remembers and memorializes those who struggled and created in the past, known and unknown. West is a ritualist; his struggles and writings belong to a long and deep tradition that he honors as he draws, reenacts, and relaunches the riches from it.

Cornel West is also a moral teacher, who insists that we must preserve and transport those values as an inheritance, as an essential active record of the creative and courageous moments in Black (and rarely interracial) histories. *Race Matters* is a life guide to the necessity of memory, to the works, events, and styles that make up a permanent palisade against pessimism and despair. *Race Matters* not only enriches life and thought but deeply and creatively embedded in a long tradition guarantees there is reason to work toward a future it helps us imagine.

No book by itself creates a future, not even as a form of necessary preservation and transformation. Human works achieve their desire by acting on others, influencing how they in turn will act in their time and for the future, how they offer the love of criticism. West's struggles against nihilism in *Race Matters* echoes down the long tradition from Walker's address to Blacks to struggle rather than yield or settle. Against nihilism, West proffers Toni Morrison's critical borrowings from the languages of nationalist projects as part of the same tradition and, more important, as evidence that loving disagreement can do more by subsuming negativity. Even in disagreement, but with respect, Morrison's adaptations not only transform the past from which she critically borrows, but it allows her to add to a tradition to help her successors imagine and incarnate—always with others—their own needed alternative futures.

West's efforts are exemplary in the same way. He explains the work a love ethic does in politics and culture. He explains how developments in art and activism result in new formations, new practices, and new languages in which the oppressed create agency. Typically, West makes general claims illustrated by inescapable examples. He introduces Morrison with his own key belief: "A love ethic," West writes, "has nothing to do with sentimental agency or tribal connections."

> Rather it is a last attempt at generating a sense of agency among a downtrodden people. The best exemplar of this love ethic is depicted on a number of levels in Toni Morrison's great novel *Beloved*. Self-love and love of others are both modes toward an increasing self-valuation and encouraging political resistance in one's community. These modes of evaluation and resistance are rooted in a subversive memory—the best of one's past without romantic nostalgia—and guided by a universal love ethic. For my purposes here, *Beloved* can be construed as bringing together the loving yet critical affirmation of black humanity found in the best black nationalist movements, the perennial hope against hope for a trans-racial coalition in progressive movements, and the painful struggle for self-affirming sanity in a history in which the nihilistic threat *seems* insurmountable. (19)

This is characteristic West writing. It is clear, condensed, pointed. The tone catches his cautious understanding of the profound historical problems facing Blacks in the United States while respectfully holding onto the dignified accomplishments of artists, intellectuals, activists, and struggling people striving on terrain mined to harm them. His view of the world situation is wide and deep, and his intelligence brings the complexities of antiracial, anticolonial, sexual resistance to a momentary focus on one object, around one exemplary or metonymic instance of the loving critical creativity upon which, for West, all depends. For all West's visibility as a public intellectual, performing in the lecture hall or meeting room, interviewing on TV, and speaking on podcasts and radio, he is a carefully literate writer, who recognizes the value of writing in the insurgency to which he calls especially Black intellectuals. West is a bluesman, as he calls himself, but in his thinking the Blues, which started in a field, he travels the world and blends with the joy and pain celebration and catastrophe require everywhere. "I became and remain a philosophically trained bluesman who looked to the good news of Jew Christ" (*Brother West* 152–53). This attitude sets careful literacy within the art of the Blues, the history of its emergence, tying orality and writing, organicity and intellectual reflection in a complex insurgent effort, a model to effect and address variously as circumstances admit.

This bluesman says that "*Beloved* can be construed" because it is a construal, a drawing together of various inheritances, not all obviously familial and certainly not all friendly or creative. The fictional construction stands in for what West opens out along the three lines that are essential to his vision: critical affirmation of what has come before, the properly hopeless hope for a biracial coalition to overcome white supremacy, and the affirmation of life and humanity in a world tempted by a rational seeming nihilism. It is against nihilism that *Race Matters* takes it strongest stand. West insists that black nihilism is "*not a philosophic doctrine*" but a matter of lived experience, of the social consequences of white supremacy as the defining function of American formation. Nihilism "*is, far more, the lived experience of coping with a life of horrifying meaninglessness, hopelessness, and (most important) lovelessness*" (*Race Matters* 14). Is West a humanist before he is a bluesman pressing back against the dehumanization of whiteness? The origins of West's humanist commitments are irrelevant. What matters is the preservation and enrichment of Black life and experience against not only repression but despair, especially the manifestation of that despair in intellectual programs and arguments. West belongs to a long tradition of insurgency, but importantly, he understands that tradition also worked "to ward off the nihilistic threat." West's deep humanism recognizes the importance of "structures of meaning and feeling" in communities and persons. His ritualist recall of earlier achievements joins him to those who recognize that "cultures are, in part, what human beings create . . . to convince themselves not to commit suicide," which means that Black intellectuals' insurgent efforts must rest on and advance the struggles and creations of predecessors (*Race Matters* 15). First, of course, comes the joy, dignity, and survival of Black people and communities. Hope against hope however gambles, messianically, on a conversion that remakes the lived world of human experience free of white supremacy, colonialism, and settler murder, but vibrant and nurturing. To the degree that conversion carries this messianic possibility it comes from West's deep Christian humanism, which stands for Christ's universal love, even for oppressors, and hope for an achieved world better for the habitat, for the planet. This part of West's grand vision stands against, for instance, sentiments such as this from Frank Wilderson. When asked to explain why persons should read *Afropessimism*, he responds this way: "With the narrative drive of a captivating novel and the intellectual rigor of critical theory, *Afropessimism* illustrates how black death is necessary for the material and psychic life of the human species. A high-wire act between rage and paranoia, or a breath of sanity?" (5).

West would say, I intuit, that Wilderson's link of rage to the theorized necessity of Black death—a deeply ahistoricized claim when voiced as it is here—is a symptom of the inability of "cultural structures that once sustained black life in America" to "beat back the demons of hopelessness, meaninglessness, and lovelessness" (*Race Matters* 15). Over and against Wilderson's "necessary," then, West poses his own fatal demand: "If one begins with the threat of concrete nihilism, then one must talk about some kind of *politics of conversion*" (*Race Matters* 18).

To be against nihilism and for a politics of conversion obliges intellectuals to engage in self-criticism, to learn their faults, limits, and errors. We have a clear instance of this in West's thinking. In 1991, prior to *Race Matters'* appearance, bell hooks and West published *Breaking Bread: Insurgent Black Intellectual Life*, which aspired to unite antiracism with feminism in an insurgent politics.[2] In public dialogue, hooks and West explained how they came to work together. hooks spoke about disagreements she had with West "over how issues of women's autonomy were connected to Black liberation." hooks and West combined their efforts because each had the same basic goal and vision: unity, liberation, and global vision. hooks explained that "Black women in particular" were ready "to give up on brothers, who feel there's no openness there."

Augustinian moments of conversion are behind *Race Matters*, especially in its critique of nihilism and gender discrimination.

West knows this lesson and his work depends upon it. In response to hooks's request that he explain his evolution on "women's liberation" as an essential element of the social misery of Blacks, West invokes a moment of self-critique as conversion in one of the Black intellectuals central in *Race Matters*, Malcolm X:

> "I think here we really do see how criticism functions in such a way that it leads toward growth and maturity," West replied. "I think the example of Malcolm X is quite exemplary—it was for me in the late '70s and '80s when I was struggling over issues of women and patriarchy. I think Malcolm X is one of the great examples of the claim that the unexamined life is not worth living but the examined life is one of pain, risk, *possibility.* It's not simply having the courage to act on your convictions; at times it's having the courage to criticize your convictions. Think of the young Malcolm and all the convictions he had but in '64 he began to criticize those convictions, which meant he put himself out on a limb. And in the late '70s and early '80s, given loving criticism, I began to move out more and more and recognize that one had to push back patriarchy as well as white supremacy." (Hamilton 2)

West's cultural vision is historical and encompassing, derived from wide reading, listening, and political experience. Before turning to Malcolm, *Race Matters* discusses Toni Morrison's *Beloved* and its style as a single but adequate piece of evidence against nihilism. West chooses this example because it ties together the literate and organicist forms of Black resistance and creativity. The novel's success justifies his evocation of a "hope against hope" for biracial coalitions. That kind of hard but essential hope, so rarely met in US history, finds satisfaction in Morrison's language which merges the Black inheritance of music and high literacy with aesthetic work done by whites, all converging in the new language of Morrison's novel. West does not say the book is a vehicle for hope because of its narrative or because of readers' responses to its tragic story. Its formal success, its historical importance in deploying literate and musical forms of intellectual production is evidence of the forms Black insurgency must take. West points out, however, that Morrison's style had other sources; not only the world of Black oral and literate creation he calls Blues, and but also a white tradition of modernist invention, often bluesy too, that passed from the Great Russians, including West's "beloved Chekhov," via the translations of Constance Garnett to the prose of Virginia Woolf that made modern English a medium for Faulkner's *Absalom!*

Absalom! and finally *Beloved*. The contrapuntal coalescence of Morrison's style sustains the fertilization of crossed traditions, the historical fact of which becomes a metonymy for the hope as well as critical invention that the Black novel conducts as it writes back against the epistemic violence of white literacy.

Morrison's style, the vehicle that creates Sethe, brings the high style of modern English writing within the historical and creative reach of the Blues, changing English language's fiction forever.[3] *Beloved*'s music achieves the cathartic effect of tragedy with the grace and beauty of the Blues, which West beautifully describes as the song of catastrophe taken with dignity (Reed 57). Hortense Spillers objected that in *Breaking Bread*, West had taken the wrong, that is, the predictable organicist path to arouse Black insurgency—invoking Black music and the church sermon—whereas Black writing would better serve "to expose the gaps in Western writing economies" (83).

It is a significant political gesture and sign of his loving critical humanism that West finds the blues among whites, including his beloved Anton Chekhov, to go with Tennessee Williams, Bruce Springsteen, and others. While the blues are everywhere as a potential style of human response to the inescapable catastrophes of human finitude, the Blues as a form of life art as well as art from life belong crucially and vitally to Blacks who cannot for a moment turn away from catastrophe. From within the historical catastrophe of racial slavery and dehumanization, Blacks gave the world what West calls "the most profound interpretation of tragicomic hope in America." Slavery and racialized law, customs, and politics sustain a colonial settler society that shelters whites in their own conscience and consciousness from the dehumanizing catastrophes they inflict, the "normalcy" of which they rely upon until finitude, economic and political injustice, and violence shatter their barriers against catastrophe and occasionally even their inhumane blindness. Even in such moments, white culture turns catastrophe into the consequence of mere nature, of failed socializing, or "fringe actors." Catastrophes such as mass killings and the murders of Blacks resolve themselves into psychologistic narratives. "'I think that mental health is your problem here,' President Trump told reporters on Monday" (Carey). Mainstream white America, West says, conceals catastrophe from itself because it can—to a point. The contingencies of translation and cultural crossings appearing in *Beloved* are reason to believe that the vagaries of history, of human responses to suffering and oppression, deliver to humans each other's needed resources for seeing, understanding, dealing with, and transforming catastrophe into a hope for overcoming of blind cruelty and murderous violence by a coalition of those who know catastrophe, for themselves and all others—who see in it unnecessary elements of common human social life. "There are a number of white brothers and sisters," West says in "Strength in the Blues," "who were willing to deal with the catastrophic with grace and dignity to tell the truth and bare witness" (Uitti).

To tell the truth, to speak truth to power, has become an important goal of progressive thinkers and activists in the United States, with influence among academics—students, faculty, and Leaders—since the publication of *Race Matters*. The US academy has gradually but unequally diversified itself and has recently made "diversity" a kind a normal expression of administrative intent. White official culture yielded long ago to resistant creativity in music, writing, and social style giving up its monopolistic grasp on meaning and exchange, even as corporate power deploys and would constrain Black culture to the market ("*DAMN, by Kendrick Lamar*"). In the academy, the plot twists of this story are well-known.

Under considerable political pressure from social movements, universities grudgingly opened programs and began hiring in African American studies, women's studies, reformed area studies, and more recently under the widely adopted rubric, diversity. Cornel West helps us recall that the state compromises its positions often, if not most often, for its own ends. One motive for the Voting Rights Act was cold war competition with the USSR in Africa. Of course, our histories are never simple or linear; they hold complex forces, multiple struggles, and even contradictory institutional and personal motives. As universities accommodated new areas of study, standing for, and embodying previously excluded peoples, identities, experiences, and creative modalities, these areas flourished anew—not however without challenges, resentment, internal ghettoization, and parasitism. Nonetheless, in part because of this new inclusiveness, research universities especially could more easily and necessarily serve new constituencies ("stakeholders," as Leaders now say) often and increasingly within technical and scientific research areas favored by neoliberal economic distribution. Whatever the complex forces motivating universities' movement away from the rather damning notion of official white culture (perhaps toward a new one?), American academia has become a site of contention and creativity, resulting in it becoming a privileged target of Rightist political action, hoping to disable vital contributors to American culture and to humanity within these newly yet insufficiently diverse and diversified fields of study and teaching.[4]

In November 2016, the Obama administration released a study of US education and inequality of opportunity. Not surprisingly, it noted that "the percentage of faculty of color has gradually increased," but, it goes on to say, "especially for Asians and Hispanics." In 1993 when *Race Matters* appeared, 4 percent of faculty were Black. In 2016, just before Donald Trump took office, 6 percent of faculty were Black. The report concluded that "while the composition of instructional faculty has become more diverse over time, the most progress has been made among non-tenure track and part-time faculty" (*Advancing Diversity and Inclusion in Higher Education* 74). Moreover, most change in the racial composition of tenured and tenure-track hiring occurs in the humanities, education, and social sciences. In the areas of economic and political dominance—handily called STEM—the "underrepresentation" of Black people is still egregious.[5]

These facts sit behind the headlines of racial discrimination at the highest level of academic life, especially at the point where politics and struggle intersect. While newspapers name the forces behind the University of North Carolina's decision to deny tenure to Nikole Hannah-Jones, the nature of the forces denying tenure to Cornel West at Harvard in 2021 are more unnamed.[6] The universities involved lack courage, on the one hand, to stand by their supposed commitments while on the other hand they continue the violence normalized but exposed by the facts displayed in the hiring data about Blacks in academia. Of course, throughout their history, universities follow the mandates of their paymasters, and as the recent turn back to industrial policy by the Biden administration shows, the United States intends to strengthen the ties between knowledge production and the state's aims in great power competition, reforming internal institutions logistically to meet the goals set by the policy aims (Foroohar).

National policy directives align with white violence, the strengthening of Jim Crow politics in the United States, and increasingly marketized cultural formations under the auspices of platforming and algorithmic discrimination. In official culture, it is impossible to find the ethos of humanistic love West demands of us all except in the struggles against these forms of violent repression in BLM and #MeToo and other activist formations, such as those to abolish prisons or end evictions. Celebrating what has been done, as West helps us see, reminds us how much is at stake right now in the United States for those whose work and lives form part of the struggles for justice from hard-earned places within the university. It also reminds us how much responsibility the survivors within the neoliberal university system share in present struggles. West's book reissued reminds us how much so hard won might be disastrously lost.

A white racist straight male politics sees the university as its internal enemy precisely because (until recently) advanced progressive critical and creative intellectuals, scholars, and artists work within and from academia, adopting the university itself as a base for transformation as well as conservation. Among other things, the political Right's supposed free speech noises amount to slandering the university as hateful, racist, and parasitic more easily to defund and suppress forms of knowledge the values in which the Right sees as an obstacle to its authoritarian ambitions. The Right intends to deny independent authority to institutions, peoples, and practices from which challenges to its power might appear. At this point, neoliberal management techniques openly cohere with authoritarian intolerance. Telling the histories of African American and diasporic studies, planning their futures—these actions inherently aim to escape and resist despotism. During the Biden era, the American Right's media attacked the universities for generating critical race theory and exporting it to schools and corporations. For the Right, this silly attack creates a perfect circle: the universities would overthrow the white world by generating critical race theory, itself a doctrine to overthrow whiteness. Two targets for one. Universities under neoliberal management have already done great harm to the disciplines from which critical thinking and insurgency might appear. The latter have no market and must retrench, a fact that Leaders might believe will ease Rightist attacks but will have no more effect on propaganda than any other fact. Nonetheless, weakening the critical possibilities of education and theory serves the interest of a leadership model imposed on the university by the state/market combination even while alleviating, but not, Rightist critiques of the university as birthplace of "woke" anti-culture.

In 1988, Cornel West anticipated much of our situation in a warning tone of a settled fact, "the inevitable expansion of the Academy . . . has made the Academy a world in itself and a caretaker of nearly all intellectual talent in American society" (41). This statement, hyperbolic, invited protests such as Eric Lott's suggestion that "ex-Geto Boy Willie D's [rap] 'Fuck Rodney King,'" (41) was an extramural example of radical, rigorous, and unassimilated "political thinking." To carry the day against *Race Matters*, Lott invokes the much more classically trained intellectual, C. L. R. James, to stand for a much more transformative version of Black agency leading democracy toward socialism than any he could find in West. Set aside that contentious claim to follow Lott's rhetoric as it leads away from James to Stuart Hall and Paul Gilroy. Edward W. Said gave us the valuable concept "traveling theory" (1982), in his analysis of how academic work often absorbs radical work by moving it from a place of vital political struggle to the academy in the United States, France, or the UK.

In 1988, West worried that "even the critique of dominant paradigms in the Academy are academic ones," which break the relation between study and street essential to radical thought. The university's normal internal mechanisms for building careers and fields of study emptied out "the more political and worldly substance of radical critiques" (41). These citations come from West's essay, "The Crisis of Black Leadership." This genre of writing requires not only a critical analysis of its topic but also the formulation of an ideal. In this case, that ideal appears as a compound figure compiled from W. E. B. Du Bois and James Baldwin. Of the former, West writes this encomium: "For Du Bois, the glorious life of the mind was a highly disciplined way of life and an intensely demanding way of struggle that facilitated transit between his study and the streets" (*Race Matters* 40). Having written this, West at once and sharply distinguished Du Bois from professionalized, bureaucratized, and specialized intellectuals. He insists on the distance between Du Bois and the then prominent Afrocentrist scholars who, themselves hoping to avoid the traps of academia, reproduce "similar hierarchies headed by themselves, within a black context." West's charge is part of his critique of those he calls "race-embracing rebels," which has at times met strong objection and resistance. At this point in the essay, however, West is still outlining his image of the proper Black intellectual. Having invoked Du Bois for loving "the glorious life of the mind," for his discipline and integrity, West set aside those counter claims on Du Bois for a "race-embracing politics," while arguing for his own more communal, humanistic, and loving ethical politics.

A problem remained, for West. Where was he to find such a paradigm now, especially given the prominence of academic professionalism? The answer might be, as the mention of Du Bois suggests, in the past, by looking into an active tradition. West worries that academic historicism transforms what might be exempla, what might be living tradition, what might be the fullness of creative work into the academy's self-authorizing practices of "objective inquiry and relentless criticism" (41). West's writing, by contrast, calls to memory tradition that should never detach from life even to authorize the new disciplines called "studies." Two brief sentences catch the problem and the challenge West's thinking poses for all of us: "There are few race-transcending prophets on the current black intellectual scene. James Baldwin was one" (43). The simple present tense of the first sentence—"there are few"—leads away from the present time to the simple but active past, "Baldwin was one." This rhetorical gesture is too precise to be accidental. It thins out and empties that phrase, the few, but it thickens the present again by recalling it to its traditions where its proper exemplars exist. West brings the then and now together so that we see how even in a troubled time, with proper study, proper analysis of circumstance and need, the present can summon what it requires.

To the distinguished, carefully dressed, serious, and intense Du Bois, the avatar of a necessary possibility—for in him, the glorious life of the mind had existed—West adds the "self-taught and self-styled" Baldwin, the genius "fusing the life of the mind . . . with the struggle for justice and human dignity" (43). At this moment in his essay, West makes his definitive judgment clear: "the present generation has yet to produce such a figure." A paragraph that began by conceding "a few . . . prophets" were on the scene, fills in the content of what is needed for prophecy with Baldwin adding to Du Bois, to conclude the paragraph with a dire warning to its readers. "This vacuum," West writes, "continues and the plight of the wretched of the earth deteriorates" (43). With this echo of Fanon in English, West draws together explicitly the deep resources of Black and anticolonial "race-transcending" thinking. He reminds his readers of the always-available strength for struggle in the archive of past thinking and writing. He emphasizes the fundamental importance, created by history, of those prophetic race-transcending intellectuals to Black struggles for justice and dignity, struggles that he often, like Baldwin before him, assigns a redemptive role for human possibility in the face of normative white oppression and cultural poverty.

In 2001, Hilary Putnam made a very forceful judgment on the nature and importance of Cornel West's writing. Putnam had taught West at Harvard and taught with him there in a seminar on Marxism. Before Putnam gives us his judgment of West, he makes sure that we have the proper frame in which to see West's work. Putnam starts this way: West's "agenda is foreign to the way academic reviewers think." (On this point, Putnam likens West favorably to John Dewey, himself a formative figure in one part of West's race-transcending prophetic genealogy.) Putnam very cleverly chooses his evidence for this claim. Richard Rorty, Putnam notes, had written "'that [West's] *The American Evasion of Philosophy* will be widely read and respectfully reviewed, and that it may well become a standard account of the role of Pragmatism in American thought'" (20). Rorty's remarks are professional, and in

Putnam's mind, the result of mere habit, a conventional academic frame. Rorty treats West's writing as a mere academic credential and Putnam implies that Rorty's comment is a good but troubling example of West's persistent warnings about the dangers of academic professionalism to radical intellectuals, to radical life, and to hope. Rorty's professional praise would bring West's work within the academy, in a way that minimizes its own value and ambition, which in turn would obscure the radical contributions of those predecessors West joins in aspiring to achieve common ends. After having set West outside the academic frame, Putnam gives us his final judgment of West's worth—agglutinating Dewey, Du Bois, Antonio Gramsci, and other radical thinkers in West's genealogy, Putnam says, "West's contributions," require that we "*experience the writing as a challenge, a challenge to one's whole mode of life*" (20). *Race Matters* calls for a politics of conversion, aimed not only at Blacks' despair but aimed at all his readers, wherever they are to be found. In *Race Matters*, West writes a sparse, intense, and concrete prose in which nonetheless we must hear and sometimes feel the influence of others who are part of his genealogy.

James Baldwin had famously invoked a saving remnant—by which, he wrote, "I mean the relatively conscious whites and the relatively conscious blacks, who must, like lovers, insist on, or create, the consciousness of others" (346). In these lines, Baldwin echoes and repurposes Du Bois's double consciousness towards a political ethic of loving conversion. When West calls for a politics of conversion, he in turn echoes Baldwin's desire for a conversion of Blacks and whites on all matters of struggle for dignity and justice.

Baldwin raises the pitch of his prose as he ends *The Fire Next Time*. The struggle for conversion is the most critical of all human struggles—on the one hand, the alliance of converted might "change the history of the world," giving us the New World signified by the rainbow, or failing in those efforts, we face an apocalypse—"*the fire next time*" (Baldwin 347). We see the same urgency in West's writing, which makes of Baldwin's vision a politically directed concept—the love ethic for a politics of conversion. *Race Matters* elaborates this concept in terms of its effects upon intellectuals, daily life, struggles for justice and equality, the politics of the body and sexuality, and the critical embrace and education of allies while strongly opposing foes. The ethic of love expresses itself in the daily victories of creative life that support hope while building the relationships that nurture life's enduring struggles to achieve dignity and justice in the forms of radical democracy. In this way, *Race Matters* is the work of an organic intellectual.

Putnam's remarks caught another essential element of West's work, the loving critical engagement with the figures he applauds. West warned against the credentialing function of criticism within the university. "Persistent criticism," as West calls it, is part of the speed up in the Arts and Sciences within the neoliberal university. West is concerned about institutional practices and their effect upon radical thinking. "Persistent criticism" is a professional talisman, which recertifies official academic values—as historicism does—and the ambitions of individual careers formed in keeping with a neoliberal agenda.

Race Matters does not tell us what a proper criticism is; it enacts it. West's critical practice is not sui generis. It shares traits with the best academic critical work while creating a protocol by which to judge the value of all critical and creative work. This is a kind of Nietzschean moment in which West confronts the practical problem, how to judge the value of values or the importance of judgments such as those inhering in persistent criticism. West's own critical models are not only academic. If space allowed, we would analyze the parallels and differences between West's double portrait of Du Bois and Baldwin, and Du Bois's remarkable portrait of Alexander Crummell in chapter 12 of *Souls of Black Folk*. In the space allotted, we can only note West's repetition of Du Bois's compositional technique. In each instance, Du Bois and West recall figures who led complicated lives with often developing or conflicting motives. Most important, these figures produced work that their heirs must keep alive in their own efforts. In this style of intellectual work, West echoes the constellating qualities of Morrison's style in *Beloved*.

West's compound figure of the intellectual ideal maps the lines along which we must do proper rather than persistent criticism. In the spirit of Du Bois, the proper critic revels in the mind, in disciplined broad learning used not only as a resource of values but displayed as a necessary value for creative struggle. The critic moves between study and street to assess the value of concepts in the largest human theater, the "struggle for justice and human dignity." Moreover, like Baldwin—and this is harder given the expansion of the university—the critic must be "beholden to no white academic patronage system" (*Race Matters* 43).

Race Matters exemplifies such criticism by returning to its exemplary figure of self-critical conversion, Malcolm X. The contemporary prophetic intellectual needs the full panoply of analytic skills to go with wide-ranging and intricately detailed grand and local historical knowledge. A love ethic must and alone can guide the intellectuals to make careful necessary judgments while always arguing for the basis of those judgments. Like Gramsci, West argues to be effective, such intellectuals must be in an organic relation to communities and movements. They must, whenever possible, articulate useful concepts and accept democratic accountability. On the question of intellectual and political leadership, West presents a clear difference from a Malcolm sharply portrayed.

West's account of Malcolm is, up to a point, very much like a reading of a figure in a literary work. West begins by discussing Malcolm's style, the aesthetic mode of affective expression, not as the personal expression of subjectivity, but of a people's affect created by, as West says, "the incessant assault on black intelligence, beauty, character, and possibility" (95). In other words, Malcolm is a crisis figure, "unprecedented in American history," who emerged from and spoke to a community with "a boiling urgency and an audacious sincerity" (95). West presents Malcolm as a crisis figure whom we must understand if we are to get an adequate grasp of complex reality and weigh proper lines of thought and action. Malcolm is an emblem appearing from, embodying, and worsening a crisis. As Putnam made clear, West relates to important predecessors and influences with loving critique. He treats Malcolm as an older contemporary. He admires Malcolm's "great love for black people," which "was a concrete connection with a degraded and devalued people in need of psychic conversion" (95). Recognizing Malcolm's love allows West to portray the state of crisis among Blacks constantly assaulted by white racism as the same crisis in their two slightly contrasting times. Since the crisis is the same in kind and even worse in 1993, West has a firm ground for the loving critique that eventually disqualifies Malcolm's thinking as a dangerous political mistake within that crisis.

How is Malcolm a crisis figure? Malcolm was a "prophet of black rage" because he emerged from an assaulted and degraded people with whom he had organic relations. In pathological terms, his rage marked a turning point in the historical state of that people. The people themselves, as we know from West's discussion of Black nihilism and his remarks on Rodney King and the L.A. events, acted out the same rage when crisis verged on the apocalyptic. Baldwin's 1955 essay "Notes of a Native Son" sets the rhythm of life and death—his youngest sibling's birth just moments after their father's funeral—next to the Harlem riot of 1943. The circumstances forced Baldwin to face undesired truths about the tragic facts. He recognized the tragic fatefulness of humanity over and against the hard realities of love and hate in unjust worlds. After a dinner with Elijah Muhammad, Baldwin had written, "I knew the tension in me between love and power, between pain and rage" (321). A younger man in 1943, he might have raged, drunk as he was, but he did not, exhausted by mourning for his hated father. Baldwin began to search out of his personal writerly crisis for a social and political reason to extend his commitment to an ethic of love into a politics and, ironically, he found it in his 1955 reflections on the 1943 riot.

Like Malcolm and West, Baldwin knew Harlem as always in a crisis state, in which he found an entangled and complex but fundamental intelligence about humanity, which justified his love ethic in the politics of the people. "Harlem," Baldwin wrote, "had needed something to smash." In 1943, the streets were tensely disrupted and emotions high because the hatred of white Americans within the Army, where Blacks were serving, made a hard impact on the people at home. In that situation, Harlem needed something to smash. Baldwin's next remark drives home what a crisis is for far too many: "To smash something is the ghetto's chronic need." This echoes Bigger Thomas (the principal character in Richard Wright's *Native Son*) in an essay called "Notes of a Native Son," but his follow-on remarks foreshadow West's much debated claim about Black nihilism—"Most of the time" Baldwin wrote, "it is the members of the ghetto who smash each other, and themselves" (82). Baldwin had already explained that as a young boy he had begun to feel in his contemporaries a "bewildered despair, as though they were now settling in for the long, hard winter of life" (298).

All these echoes in West's writing, the remade presence of his predecessors give us a very thick but slowly emerging figure of Malcolm centered organically within a crisis made by white violence. A crisis is a potential turning point not only for Malcolm's own development but also for the state of his people's place and being—remember Baldwin's paradox that the crisis is chronic. Baldwin's encounter with a sometimes militarized, race-centered rhetoric in Elijah Muhammad preceded West's encounter with Malcolm. Baldwin had written that if the ghetto's need to smash "erupts outward in a more direct fashion," the result would be apocalypse. Looking back on 1943 in 1955, Baldwin asked why the "Negroes"—his word here—did not break down the ghetto's walls. He discovers the truth of his personal and political ethics in the answer to this question. He concluded that the Negro could yield to self-destructive rage and hate. To do so, he said, would mean, "one has to blot out so much of the mind—and the heart—that this hatred itself becomes an exhausting and self-destructive pose" (83). Here is the connection back to Baldwin's frustration with Elijah. Here is Baldwin's version of the love ethic become political. Love is hard and costly because it leaves lovers facing those who not only will not but also cannot love, cannot reciprocate the offer. Love does not live easily because it comes with "gratuitous humiliation" from whites "too ignorant and too innocent for that." Living unloved but loving leaves uncertainties, endless qualifications, and often-conflicting commitments and decisions.

Malcolm was too Manichean for a Baldwin-sympathizing West. Baldwin lived through, thought out, and wrote down the impossible ongoing decisions of love, the equally terrifying risks, and choices between "amputation and gangrene" (83). With Baldwin then not far in the background, West makes Malcolm a crisis figure within a pathological situation for which Malcolm carries the sympathetic signs of suffering and its cause but is himself a kind of catachresis, a misstatement, a sort of error. He uses the wrong words to describe a reality too complex for those words; he himself becomes then the misrepresentation of the real and its misdirection toward an apocalyptic future. West and Malcolm agree on the need for conversion but, as the word tells us, it always opens a question about direction, the next step.

Celebrating Cornel West and *Race Matters* means extolling their virtuous place within our establishments. We should feel uncertainty about this since we are sitting in the much discussed academic world about which we often have doubts—as West's tenure problem with Harvard illustrates. Readers will also realize the persistent gender issues in the book and my representation of it. These are boys' stories, organized as I warned at the start, as a too simple single chapter of our complicated histories. Readers do not need reminding that we need and have other stories, fuller and more active memories, and that stories will resituate this one we are honoring, but we will harm ourselves by forgetting it. The hard-won is under extreme threat in the university and the society in which it sits as a mainstream functional institution. However, we need to do more than circle the wagons. We need to see the potential for loving creativity within our studies and their connections to the world's needs. We need to keep *Race Matters* with us.

Late in his career, Edward Said revised his influential notion of "traveling theory," not because he no longer worried about the academy. In "Traveling Theory Reconsidered," he looked at how heirs to their predecessors' concepts can do more with what they inherit in the act of transformation and adaptation than strict adherence to the original would allow. Rather than see travel as decline, Said came to see travel as expansion and reaffirmation. As an heir to Lukács, he invoked Frantz Fanon, who changed the predecessor's work for the better, who found new concepts and practices organic to his own postcolonial and revolutionary situations. Said moved away from his 1982 account of traveling theory as a reductive depoliticization of the original. He became less formalist, insisted on more complex stories, and urged scholars to trace the workings of radicalization across space, across different geographies, responding to specific needs and opportunities. West's book is another starting point even for those more complex stories we now have. It is a still enabling moment of work within the preservation and creation of values limned in the more complex critical work he developed. We must see academic studies not as Rorty-like assumptions of *Race Matters* into an established order. We must see value in the dispersal of West's book as the late Said came to do with Lukács and others who were remade in a dialectic of criticism and renewal. Like Morrison's *Beloved*, West's book can do its work with its heirs and successors. In the face of their loving critique, he changed the nature of the academy into a place important to loving struggle, to creativity and critique. Had the university not continued that work, had it not been the complex mechanism to preserve, renew, expand, and distribute throughout the society, it would not have the enemies it has had and has still. It is not complete exaggeration to thank Cornel West for our worst enemies.

Notes

1. I read an early draft of this chapter at a conference to celebrate the twenty-fifth anniversary of Cornel West's *Race Matters* on July 14, 2018, at Dartmouth College. Special thanks to Barbara Will, then associate dean, for organizing the event and inviting me to take part.

2. Routledge reissued this book in expanded form in 2017 to celebrate its twenty-fifth anniversary. Its new materials continue West and hooks's dialogue begun before 1991.

3. See "Book Launch Paul Bové's Love's Shadow HUP default." West often describes this development in culture and language from the great Russians, through translation into the English of Virginia Woolf, finding its full voice in Toni Morrison. For West, the blues play a key role in transforming modernism into an instrument for affirming black humanity (Uitti).

4. On July 4, 2018, the Associated Press reported, "The Trump administration said the government would no longer encourage race as a factor in the admissions process" (Tucker) of universities. See also Fortin.

5. See Flaherty. "There has been no change in the share of Black workers in STEM jobs since 2016" (Fry).

6. Robertson suggests that "a powerful donor," Walter E. Hussman Jr., obstructed her tenure. Aware of the fate of Cornel West's tenure at Harvard University, Ms. Hannah-Jones rejected the university's offer of a term contract: "'In light of this information, Ms. Hannah-Jones cannot trust that the university would consider her tenure application in good faith during the period of the fixed-term contract,' according to the letter, which was dated Monday" (Robertson). On the Cornel West fiasco at Harvard, see Nair. The article quotes David L. Carrasco, professor of anthropology, appointed also in the Divinity School: "I support Cornel

West, and the manner of his departure seems to be unmasking something troubling in our beloved university," he wrote. "The question is why is it that from one side of the mouth we hear support for African American studies and scholars while the other side of the mouth refuses to address Cornel West's request and this situation directly" (Nair).

Works Cited

Baldwin, James. *Baldwin: Collected Essays.* Edited by Toni Morrison, Library of America, 1998.

The Bible. New Oxford Annotated Version, 4th ed. Edited by Michael D. Coogan et al., Oxford UP, 2010.

"Book Launch Paul Bové's Love's Shadow HUP Default." *YouTube,* 8 April 2021, www.youtube.com/watch?v=OTSWaaRRI-s&t=954s.

Carey, Benedict. "Are Mass Murderers Insane? Usually Not, Researchers Say." *New York Times,* 8 Nov. 2017, https://www.nytimes.com/2017/11/08/health/mass-murderers-mental-illness.html.

"*DAMN, by Kendrick Lamar.* The 2018 Pulitzer Prize Winner in Music." *The Pulitzer Prizes,* https://www.pulitzer.org/winners/kendrick-lamar, 28 June 2021.

Flaherty, Colleen. "The Missing Black Professors." *Inside Higher Ed,* 22 Aug. 2017, accessed 23 June 2021, https://www.insidehighered.com/news/2017/08/22/study-top-public-universities-finds-limited-faculty-diversity-and-yet-signs-progress.

Foroohar, Rana. "America (finally) gets an industrial strategy." *Financial Times,* 28 June 2021, https://www.ft.com/content/52d1d810-75ed-4c32-b2cf-565a6d6e71b7.

Fortin, Jacey. "'Access to Literacy' Is Not a Constitutional Right, Judge in Detroit Rules." *New York Times,* 4 July 2018.

Fry, Richard et al., "STEM Jobs See Uneven Progress in Increasing Gender, Racial and Ethnic Diversity." *Pew Research Center Report,* 1 Apr. 2021, https://www.pewresearch.org/science/2021/04/01/stem-jobs-see-uneven-progress-in-increasing-gender-racial-and-ethnic-diversity/.

Hamilton, Amy. "Insurgent Black Intellectual Life: bell hooks and Cornel West break bread." *Off Our Backs,* vol. 23, no. 7, 1993, pp. 1–3.

hooks, bell and Cornel West. *Breaking Bread: Insurgent Black Intellectual Life.* South End Press, 1991.

Nair, Meera S. et al., "Harvard Reversed Course and Offered Cornel West Consideration for Tenure After Public Outcry, He Says." *Harvard Crimson,* 11 Mar. 2021, https://www.thecrimson.com/article/2021/3/11/cornel-west-tenure-reversal/.

Putnam, Hilary. "Pragmatism Resurgent: A Reading of *The American Evasion of Philosophy.*" *Cornel West: A Critical Reader,* edited by George Yancy, Oxford UP, 2001, pp. 19–37.

Reed, Roxanne. "The Restorative Power of Sound: A Case for Communal Catharsis in Toni Morrison's *Beloved.*" *Journal of Feminist Studies in Religion,* vol. 23, no. 1, spring 2007, pp. 55–71.

Robertson, Katie. "Nikole Hannah-Jones Says She Won't Join U.N.C. Faculty Without Tenure." *New York Times,* 23 June 2021. https://www.nytimes.com/2021/06/23/business/media/nikole-hannah-jones-university-of-north-carolina-tenure.html. Accessed 23 June 2021.

Said, Edward W. "Traveling Theory Reconsidered." *Reflections on Exile and other Essays.* Harvard University Press, 2000, pp. 436–52.

Spillers, Hortense. "The Crisis of the Negro Intellectual." *boundary 2,* vol. 21, no. 3, autumn 1994, pp. 65–116.

Tucker, Eric. "Government Blesses Omitting Race from Admissions, Enrollment." Associated Press, 4 July 2018, apnews.com/article/north-america-ap-top-news-courts-supreme-courts-jeff-sessions-aa1ca62495714553b83dd8881507654a.

Uitti, Jacob. Interview with Cornel West. "Strength In the Blues—An Interview with Cornel West." *Monarch Review: Seattle's Literary and Arts Magazine*, 9 Sept. 2012, http://www.themonarchreview.org/cornel-west-strength-in-the-blues/.

United States Department of Education, *Advancing Diversity and Inclusion in Higher Education*. Government Printing Office, Nov. 2016, http://www2.ed.gov/rschstat/research/pubs/advancing-diversity-inclusion.pdf, p. 74.

Walker, David. *David Walker's Appeal*. 1829. Hill and Wang, 1965.

Wilderson, Frank. Interview with John Williams. "In 'Afropessimism,' a Black Intellectual Mixes Memoir and Theory." *New York Times*, 27 Apr. 2020, p. 5.

West, Cornel. *Race Matters*. Beacon Press, 1993.

West, Cornel. *Brother West: Living and Loving Out Loud, a Memoir*. SmileyBooks, 2010.

CHAPTER 2

Race Matters and US American Democracy: Cornel West and W. E. B. Du Bois

Lucius T. Outlaw Jr.

I

The invitation to participate in the twenty-fifth anniversary commemoration and reconsideration of Corn (as Cornel is known to relatives and close friends) West's *Race Matters* (1993) has been an honor and a compelling reason to re-engage with this historic text, a small book of articulations that has had enormous impacts and helped set the trajectory by which Corn became, and remains, one of the most significant public intellectuals of the twentieth and twenty-first centuries who is based in and focusing attention on US America (and on countries and regions beyond our national borders). The honor of this reengagement is all the more significant since Corn remains a very close and special friend of forty-plus years, who is friend as well to wife Freida and "Uncle Cornel" to our three sons.

For this reengagement I returned to a copy of *Race Matters* (1993) given to me and Freida by Corn with a handwritten note to us on the title page along with his signature, "Bro' Corn." Freida has spent time with this gift book and returned to it from time to time over the years, leaving traces of her engagements with the text with her underlines and recognizable handwritten marginal notations. This book also includes "L. Outlaw" on the inside of the front cover, written by the firstborn of our sons. Throughout the book, also, are his underlines and marginal notations, and mine. Moreover, when the firstborn son graduated from his university, Corn was the commencement speaker and handed our son his diploma while my then eighty-year-old father witnessed from the audience and marveled at Corn's commencement address. Afterward, my father insisted that I buy him a copy of *Race Matters*. I did.

Over subsequent years when I visited my father in the family home in Starkville, Mississippi, *Race Matters* was on prominent display. Thus, this gift, and gifted, book became and remains a family treasure and, for these reasons, *Race Matters* deserves my (and my family's) commemoration.

Nonetheless, for this formal commemorative reengagement, in addition to recounting that, and how, *Race Matters* came to have family significance, I needed to determine what, for me, are the significance of the agenda for, and the significance of the writings that comprise, the book. It was in pursuit of these significances that I gave myself over to an immersive rereading of the copy of *Race Matters* that was Corn's gift (not the twenty-fifth anniversary edition, a copy of which I did not have at the time of my initial reengagement to prepare my conference presentation).

Clearly, *Race Matters*, and Corn, have acquired substantial significance since the book's publication, anecdotally and as evidenced by the anniversary republication with a new introduction. My aim, however, is not to endeavor to account for and assess this significance. Rather, it is to acquire, from a close rereading, a renewed understanding of Corn's agenda for the book. (I will leave aside whether anyone in addition to Corn contributed to deciding on the production and publishing of a book on race matters, to the selection of the particular articulations—and not others—by him to make up the book's chapters, and on the ordering of the essays as chapters. No doubt a full account of the history of how the selected articulations came to be published as a book with the title *Race Matters*, with the involvements of whom, would be a worthwhile addition to twenty-fifth anniversary considerations.)

II

In settling on a critical reengagement with Corn's apparent agenda for *Race Matters*, I have taken as my guide what Corn set out in his preface (ix–xi). First, there is his disclosure that Plato and Du Bois "posed the most fundamental challenges to my basic aim in life": on the one hand, the challenge of "Plato's profound—yet unpersuasive—critique of Athenian democracy as inevitably corrupted"; on the other, the challenge of "Du Bois's deep analysis of the intransigence of white supremacy in the American democratic experiment" (*Race Matters* x). On my reading, Corn's general concern is the US American democratic nation-state and civilizational projects that have given rise to world-historic challenges to humane human existence and to the well-being of virtually all life on this planet, challenges that have emerged out of the dialectic of articulations and practical efforts with regard to democracy-making in a historically distinctive context of invidiously hierarchically racialized and class-conflicted encultured populational diversities—i.e., "races." More focal concerns for Corn have to do with the well-being—particularly the lack thereof—of most Black folk in US America. Challenged by his sense of Plato's diagnosis of democracy as inevitably corruptible, and his sense that, for Du Bois, the Western civilizational, and the particularities of the US American nation-state instantiation of, projects of White Racial Supremacy are intransigent, Corn, in *Race Matters*, engages with a number of critical issues having to do with "what *race* matters have meant to the American past " and "how much race *matters* in the American present" (x, emphasis in original). (It is still rewarding, more than twenty-five years later, to savor the conceptual jiujitsu dexterity at play in Corn's forging of a richly multivalent and provocative title for this challenging book.)

Now, though Corn declares in his preface that he encountered a "fundamental challenge" to his life's aim in having to contend with Plato's critique of democratically structured polities, issues regarding democracy are less of an articulate focus in *Race Matters*. Rather, these issues are the focus of what he has characterized as the sequel to *Race Matters*: his *Democracy Matters* (2004), wherein the focus on race matters in the US American context is broadened to wrestle with international matters generated by the global involvements of imperialistic US capitalism. Consequently, in keeping with my focus on *Race Matters,* I shall not trace and assess the arc of Corn's engagements with matters of race and democracy across these two books but shall explore how Corn confronts the "fundamental challenge" he encountered in contending with writings and other efforts, and the legacies of the same, of W. E. B. Du Bois, particularly Du Bois's engagements with matters of race. Since Corn prefaces *Race Matters* with the disclosure of a Du Boisian challenge, I am led to conclude that the book as a project, and/or the chapters of the book, stand in part as an effort by Corn to meet that challenge. At issue for me, first, is the matter of what, precisely, is the challenge that Du Bois poses for Corn; and, second, the matter of assessing how well Corn meets the challenge in *Race Matters.*

The Du Boisian challenge, Corn declares, comes by way of "Du Bois's deep analysis of the intransigence of white supremacy in the American democratic experiment" (x). How is it, why is it, that Du Bois's probing analyses and critiques of White Racial Supremacy pose a challenge *to Corn*?

He does not say.

The task, then, is to work initially with what Corn does provide in the prefatory and introductory texts (as well as in the chapter-essays) to fashion a critical hermeneutical understanding of the Du Boisian challenge, and of Corn's response(s) to it.

Corn informs us in his preface that his "basic aim in life" is "to speak the truth to power with love so that the quality of everyday life for ordinary people is enhanced and white supremacy is stripped of its authority and legitimacy" (x). This is quite an ambitious aim, indeed: to "speak" publicly and with such efficacy as to "strip white supremacy of its authority and legitimacy"—that is, to be especially noteworthy as a person of great efficacy among historic expressive "public intellectuals," i.e., "persons of letters for whom words are a vehicle for political action and their own participation in political movements" (Gates xii). This is a helpful characterization of a "public intellectual," a nom de guerre, so to speak, that Corn has long accepted as an appropriate characterization of much of his life's work.[1] Accordingly, it is not an inappropriate imposition, but altogether proper, I believe, to critique his performance as a "public intellectual" by way of his *Race Matters* project.

To be noted, at no point does Corn set out how "speaking" in general, his "speaking" in particular, can and will disrupt the centuries-long, institutionalized, socially (politically, economically, culturally) constructed effects of the dialectics of articulations and praxes of projects of White Racial Supremacy, so much so as to render such projects without authority and legitimacy. In neither his preface nor his introduction to *Race Matters* does Corn offer an account of how the articulations comprising the book constitute political actions, nor an account of his involvement(s) with any particular social-political movement(s), or how the combination of speaking and involvements would be efficacious in contesting—let alone stripping authority and legitimacy from—White Racial Supremacy while enhancing the quality of life of the unidentified "ordinary people" on whose behalf he positions himself as being of service.

These absences make Corn's expressed ambition—his "basic aim in life"—all the more striking, and problematic, as a commitment to be taken seriously. While he seems to regard Du Bois's critically minded engagements with conceptions and projects of White Racial Supremacy as having, as it were, run aground on the intransigence, thus the persistence, of racist racial supremacy, Corn's apparent aim is to succeed where Du Bois failed: to overcome the intransigence and further to "strip white supremacy of both its authority and its legitimacy" while enhancing the quality of life "for ordinary people"—all by the efficacy of his "speaking" "the truth to power."

Now, in my judgment, this aim is inflated by ambition that carries Corn 250 miles on the wrong side of humility and is not informed by tempered self-understanding, which leaves Corn deep in the badlands of hubris. Drawing on the growing-up experiences of adolescence among my male peers in my hometown, Starkville, as we contested our overly inflated senses of our developing Negro masculinity, I am compelled to conclude that Corn's declaration of his aim amounts, as we used to say, to his "writing a check with his mouth that his ass can't cash" (translation: declaring oneself as having much more capability than can actually be brought forth). Less colloquially, I offer that Corn's declaration of his aim requires, to invoke an appropriate admonition of the legendary revolutionaries James and Grace Lee Boggs, that Corn be subjected, and subject himself, to *serious* criticism! Having declared his aim, Corn owed the readers of *Race Matters* at least a promissory account of how his "speaking" might be socially and politically efficacious and, as well, be an efficacious contribution to some identifiable, viable social-political movement(s) contesting White Racial Supremacy.

Such an account is missing.

Again, why are Du Bois's analyses of white supremacy a "formidable challenge" to Corn? On one interpretation, perhaps, because Du Bois and his analyses are inspirations and models to be followed while facing up to the realization that Du Bois's efforts are more than a bit challenging because of the towering statue of his legacies of engagements, intellectual productions, organizational involvements, and leadership as a lifelong engaged critically minded scholar and public intellectual *par excellence* who was devoted to lifting up and securing the humanity, and the flourishing, of folks African and of African descent, and of other peoples. Moreover, on another interpretation, because, I believe, Corn's "basic aim in life" is fueled by a deeply felt motivation to be better than Du Bois, and more successful, in confronting the intransigency of white supremacy since it decidedly was not "stripped of its authority and legitimacy" by Du Bois's efforts.

Corn, I am convinced, has a complicated—even fraught—relationship with the career and legacies of Du Bois, a matter that I have addressed at length in a previous writing ("On Cornel West"). I refer you, Dear Reader, to what for me is the seminal text by Corn in which this fraught relationship is made manifest, "Black Struggle in a Twilight Civilization" (53–112), regarding which Corn declared: "If all of my writings but one had to disappear, this essay is the one piece I hope would survive." (This declaration is set forth in an introductory note to the republication of "Black Strivings" in *The Cornel West Reader* [1999], which was published three years after the essay was prepared for and first published in *The Future of the Race* [1996].) This was a joint venture by Corn and Henry Louis Gates Jr.; each contributed an essay ("Parable of the Talents," by Gates; "Black Strivings," by Corn), to which was added an appendix made up of an essay by Gates on Du Bois's "The Talented Tenth," Du Bois's 1903 "The Talented Tenth," and Du Bois's significant revisiting of his essay in his 1948 "The Talented Tenth Memorial Address." Regarding the "Black Strivings" essay, Corn reveals that "this essay is my first and only sustained encounter with the greatest of all black intellectuals—Du Bois" (*Cornel West Reader* 87).

What prompted Corn to take up this "sustained encounter" with Du Bois? Apparently, the effort grew out of several years of conversation in which he and Gates had been engaged as colleagues in the Department of Afro-American Studies at Harvard University, during which the two of them, and their colleagues, wrestled with what they took to be the professional, departmental, and personal responsibilities to a mission "to analyze, and reinterpret for our generation, the great writings of the black past, showing how they continue to speak to us today," in the process endeavoring "to ground our understanding of the present in the germinal thought of our collective past" (*Future of the Race* vii–viii).

> One such effort has produced this book, in which we two "grandchildren" of the group of intellectuals Du Bois dubbed "the Talented Tenth" have sought to think through—and critique—Du Bois's challenge of commitment to service that, we deeply believe, the formally educated owe to all those who have not benefited from the expanded opportunities afforded by the gains in civil rights and its concomitant, the programmatic attempt to fulfill America's commitment to equal opportunity, popularly known as "affirmative action." (viii)

So although he was somehow challenged by Du Bois prior to, or by way of, the production of the essays that came to be included in, and the preparation and publication of, *Race Matters*, several years passed before Corn gave himself over to a sustained consideration and critique of Du Bois, producing an essay in which he "investigates the nature of Du Bois's life and thought and the tensions inherent between them . . . analyzes Du Bois as a thinker, focusing particularly on his political and philosophical ideas," and "explicates Du Bois's thought by situating him in the context of his times and within the limitations imposed by his social, political, and intellectual milieu." (*Future of the Race* viii–ix).

Given the framing and occasioning of *The Future of the Race* that Gates and Corn set forth in their preface, at the forefront of their shared concern was a critical reengagement with Du Bois's articulation of the responsibilities of the most "talented" portion of Black folk in US America in order to determine what was required and appropriately best desired for the historical, civilizational development of Black folk, the majority of whom—90 percent in Du Bois's estimation—had been systematically prohibited and prevented, for *centuries,* from gaining appreciative knowledge of these requirements and proprieties by enslavement and oppression otherwise, and prohibited and prevented from acting on such knowledge in systematic, cross-generational fashion. The "talented" 10 percent, Du Bois reasoned, having gained such experience-enriched knowledge, were to discern and lead accordingly.

Du Bois's reasoning was drawn from his assessment of the history of human civilizational development: "Was there ever a nation on God's fair earth civilized from the bottom upward? Never; it is, ever was and ever will be from the top downward that culture filters. The Talented Tenth rises and pulls all that are worth the saving up to their vantage ground" (*Souls of Black Folk* 847). It is this conviction (surely debatable), combined with his lived experiences and social scientific investigations, that, on my reading, provide the motivations for Du Bois's endeavoring to think out, and to offer as a persuasive rationale for, the need for a "talented ten percent" of Black folk to lead the cultural development that, if taken up by substantial numbers of the 90 percent, would effect the civilizational development of folks of African descent in US America. Hear, once again, the first and second paragraphs that open "The Talented Tenth":

> The Negro race, like all races, is going to be saved by its exceptional men. The problem of education, then, among Negroes must first of all deal with the Talented Tenth; it is the problem of developing the Best of this race that they may guide the Mass away from the contamination and the death of the Worst, in their own and other races. Now the training of men is a difficult and intricate task. Its

> technique is a matter for educational experts, but its object is for the vision of seers. . . . Three tasks lay before me; first to show from the past that the Talented Tenth as they have risen among American Negroes have been worthy of leadership; secondly, to show how these men may be educated and developed; and thirdly, to show their relation to the Negro problem. (842)[2]

At issue, then, for Gates and Corn as professional educators and scholars: whether they, too—given their having become cultivated "talents," to significant extents by way of formal modes of education and experience for which such education is required currency as well as a likely consequence, and quite of the kind Du Bois experienced in his own becoming one of the "talented" minority of Black folk—were called to the responsibilities set forth by Du Bois; whether and how they might ought to take up these responsibilities in the late twentieth century; on what terms and to what ends—or not might or should they do so.

To be sure, there are insights aplenty to be gained from a close consideration of Corn's "first and only sustained encounter" with Du Bois (up to 1996), especially in light of the significance that Corn gives to this particular essay among all that he had written up to the time of its republication in 1999. It is, in many respects, a challenging essay, one in which he both praises and condemns Du Bois, not just critiques him. However, the essay is troubled in many respects, among these by frequent use of evaluative terms with which Corn characterizes Du Bois while expending little effort to define and/or otherwise fully account for (such as, for example, denouncing Du Bois as a "mild elitist"), as if readers will understand and concur with his usages and characterizations. Further, while the essay is something of a seeming tour de force in learned erudition by way of the very broad range of genres of works, and the names of figures, invoked in the text and footnotes (frequently qualified by a generous use of superlatives to characterize the persons and works celebrated), there is a stunning lack of self-awareness on Corn's part of the extent to which this display of erudition does not distinguish him, if at all, from the supposed "elitism" for which he criticizes Du Bois.

Quite the contrary. For Corn's erudition is the result of decades spent in the most elite of historically and predominantly white institutions of higher education, immersed in enriching the life of his mind while mastering modes of sociality characteristic of life in such institutions as he added his own flavor and flair drawn from the rich cultural lifeworlds of Black folks in which he was socialized across his life from childhood through his high school years. In short, Corn has even more of what might well be characterized as an "elitist" educational pedigree, and an academic career situated *only* in "elite" institutions of higher education, than was ever true of Du Bois. The latter began his academic career at Wilberforce University, spent years engaging in wide-ranging historical and sociological research and teaching while on the faculty of Atlanta University. This followed a stint in Philadelphia, conducting in-person, detailed sociological research in the city's Negro-populated Seventh Ward that was published as the groundbreaking *The Philadelphia Negro* (1899), research that was followed and complemented by research trips to Virginia undertaken to explore conditions of life and labor from which many in the Seventh Ward had migrated. Also, to be remembered, and appreciated: during the decades of his intellectual productions and social engagements, where else could Du Bois have been employed as an academic, and he and his family have lived and socialized, except in segregated Negro institutions and sections of whatever their city of residence, quite contrary to the situations of work and residency Corn has chosen and enjoyed that have become available to grandchildren of the Talented Tenth of Du Bois's generation?

How stunning, then, the even more damning judgment by Corn that Du Bois suffered an "inability to immerse himself fully in the rich cultural currents of black everyday life" (*Future of the Race* 56):

> Du Bois's inability to immerse himself in black everyday life precluded his access to the distinctive black tragicomic sense and black encounter with the absurd. He certainly saw, analyzed, and empathized with black sadness, sorrow, and suffering. But he didn't feel it in his bones deeply enough, nor was he intellectually open enough to position himself alongside the sorrowful, suffering, yet striving ordinary black folk. . . . He was reluctant to learn fundamental lessons about life—and about himself—from them. . . . Du Bois's Enlightenment worldview . . . prohibited this kind of understanding. Instead, he adopted a mild elitism that underestimated the capacity of everyday people to "know" about life. In "The Talented Tenth," he claims, "knowledge of life and its wider meaning, has been the point of the Negro's deepest ignorance." In his classic book *The Souls of Black Folk* there are eighteen references to "black, backward, and ungraceful" folk, including a statement of his intent "to scatter

> civilization among a people whose ignorance was not simply of letters, but of life itself." . . . Du Bois—owing to his Puritan New England origins and Enlightenment values—found it difficult not to view common black folk as some degraded "other" or "alien"—no matter how hard he resisted. (*Future of the Race* 57–59)

I have quoted Corn at length in order to highlight what I take to be a seriously problematic critique of Du Bois that raises questions not only about the Du Boisian challenge Corn feels, but about Corn's own career as well. First, Corn doesn't inform his readers how to determine whether or not Du Bois *felt* something appropriate "deep in his bones" regarding Black folk, whether he did so "deeply enough," nor how the feeling should have been made evident. Certainly, Du Bois thought otherwise about his relationship to Black folk, speaking to just this matter in the closing paragraph of "The Forethought" to *Souls of Black Folk*: "Before each chapter, as now printed, stands a bar of the Sorrow Songs,—some echo of haunting melody from the only American music which welled up from Black souls in the dark past. And finally, need I add that I who speak here am bone of the bone and flesh of the flesh of them that live within the Veil?" (359–60).

Clearly, in this declaration Du Bois endeavors to establish his recognition and appreciation of the suffering and sorrow of Black folk who endured enslavement, and more, who structured and expressed their feelings and wisdom gained in song—"sorrow" songs, as Du Bois characterized them. Moreover, Du Bois endeavors to establish his identification with these folk, in biblical terms, as one who was "bone of their bone" and "flesh of their flesh." Did Corn miss this? Or did Corn simply not believe Du Bois, not take Du Bois at his word, and go on to displace Du Bois's declaration with a characterization of Corn's own making?

Further, Corn claims that Du Bois was "reluctant" to learn lessons of life from "sorrowful, suffering, yet striving ordinary black folk" because Du Bois "underestimated the capacity of everyday people to 'know' about life." Here, too, I believe, Corn is simply wrong: Du Bois did not underestimate these Black folks' *capacity* to know. Rather, on my reading it was Du Bois's judgment that their capabilities for knowing had not been fully and properly cultivated *during centuries of enslavement*! That enslaved, even freed (yet still oppressed in many respects by way of invidious racism), Black folk suffered from many forms of *imposed ignorance* of certain knowings (provided, for example, by formal education) cannot be denied. Nor that, in addition to restrictions and intimidations of various kinds and intensities, violence leading to death was employed routinely in order to try and ensure (though far short of complete success) that motivating and guiding understandings of possibilities for modes of life in keeping with notions of and aspirations for the most developed forms of civilized living heretofore achieved not be cultivated and taken up by Black folk to the detriment of their enslavement and oppression otherwise. And, at the heart of these efforts were those devoted to convincing all folks, white and Black, that Black folk were by nature incapable, and unfit, to achieve and enjoy, let alone produce, such modes of "civilized" life. The systematized projects of White Racial Supremacy were designed and implemented in order to enforce the racist judgment that Black folk were not fully human and, among other ends, the projects were deployed to ensure the ignorance and degradation of Black folk in every possible way while enslaved, and after. Of course, then, there were millions of severely brutalized Black folk who were not in various ways graceful *as a consequence*, though there were more than a few who forged new forms of gracefulness within the crucibles of enslavement and oppressive "freedom" as Du Bois came to learn and would celebrate in *Souls* and elsewhere.

Corn says of Du Bois that his "Enlightenment naïveté" misguided him in terms of his belief that education was an antidote to imposed ignorance, an error that was compounded by his adopting "Victorian strategies." Among these was assigning leadership responsibilities to the "Talented Tenth" whose service, Du Bois believed, would involve "shaping and molding the masses by managing educational and political bureaucracies (e.g., schools and political parties)" and involved, Corn asserts, Du Bois's belief that "the effective management of these bureaucracies by the educated few for the benefit of the pathetic many promotes material and spiritual progress" (*Future of the Race* 64–65).

What are we to make of this criticism—of the negatively infused tone in the choice of words: "educated few . . . pathetic many"—by Corn, who continues to be fully ensconced in elite, historically predominantly white educational institutions; who continues to be engaged in educational praxes serving "the exclusive few" admitted to these institutions in which he continues to be engaged in the services of teaching, mentoring, learning, scholarly productions, and administrative work? Where is critical self-awareness on Corn's part, especially in light of what he offers a few pages further on, seemingly approvingly, as a characterization of the proper public intellectual that was noted earlier: "The fundamental role of the public intellectual . . . is *to create and sustain* high-quality public discourse addressing urgent public problems *which enlightens and energizes fellow citizens, prompting them* to take public action. This role requires *a deep commitment to the life of the mind* . . . which serves *to shape the public destiny of a people*" (*Future of the Race* 71, emphasis added). How are these specifications not of a kind with what Corn has criticized as "Enlightenment" and "Victorian" commitments?

Furthermore, where is the appreciation by Corn of the concrete historical conditions and forms of life of Black folk during the long and trying decades from the end of formal enslavement to the turn of the twentieth century? To be remembered: Du Bois began his career in the historic conditions of transitions of the late nineteenth century, thirty years after the end of the Civil War. Emancipation from enslavement, such as it was, was but decades old. Du Bois would devote considerable effort to historical and sociological studies of the actualities of life for Black folk after the war and supposed emancipation. Forms of ignorance were prevalent among Black folk, by design and implementation. The degradations consequent to White Racial Supremacy had made more than a few Black folk utterly morally degraded "other" and "alien" to most white folk—and to some Black folk, for some even to themselves—some of whom (Black folk) were carriers of the memories of times-before-white-folk when folks African and of African descent thrived in gracefulness in many ways. Moreover, Corn seems to have slept his otherwise acute appreciation of the different roles and responsibilities that come with divisions of labor and other structurings of the social world that give rise to different modes and extents of the cultivation of modes of being that facilitate some (few) doing well compared to others (many) who, their lives and souls curtailed and/or distorted, do less well, or don't even try.

Du Bois recognized the conditions and causes of dehumanization and prohibited gracefulness, in part due to his immersing himself in the lifeworlds of "common black folks," starting during summers of his undergraduate years at Fisk University when he went to the hills and hollows outside Nashville, Tennessee. Teaching, residing with and gaining firsthand knowledge of the lives of Black families and their individual members of whom he writes poignantly, for example, in "Of the Meaning of Progress," the fourth chapter of *The Souls of Black Folk* (405–14).[3] He was immersed in Black life and living again when conducting research in Philadelphia's Seventh Ward. After leaving the very rich and enforming Black family, institutional, and communal life he was born into for undergraduate studies at Harvard, when since, if ever, has Corn lived such communal Black life other than as a commuter? Not at all, I hazard to say, certainly not as an academic professional and public intellectual, as did Du Bois, though Corn endeavors mightily to "keep the spirit," as it were, but on terms and in ways he deems quite different from Du Bois.[4]

To be noted, in "Black Strivings" Corn praises Du Bois as "the towering black scholar of the twentieth century," a "great titan of black emancipation" (*Future* 55). Still, Corn declares that Du Bois "falls short of the mark" due to "his inadequate interpretation of the human condition and his inability to immerse himself fully in the rich cultural currents of black everyday life. His famous notion of the Talented Tenth—including his revised version—reveals this philosophic inadequacy and personal inability" (*Future* 56). Corn goes to great length to identify and diagnosis what he takes to be the causes of Du Bois's shortcomings: "His interpretation of the human condition—that is, in part, his idea of who he was and could be—was based on his experiences and, most importantly, on his understanding of those experiences through the medium of *an Enlightenment worldview* that promoted *Victorian strategies* in order to realize an *American optimism* . . . three basic foundations of his perspective" (*Future* 57). Corn continues with a lengthy explication of what he takes to be the crippling shortcomings and implications of these ascribed perspectival "foundations."

Corn's diagnosis and critique are aided by what he takes to be nineteenth- and twentieth- century counterexamples of intellectuals who succeeded where Du Bois failed: in particular, Leo Tolstoy, who, Corn asserts, dealt with "soul-starved Russians a generation after the emancipation of the serfs in 1861"; and Franz Kafka, who wrestled with "anxiety-ridden central European Jews a generation before the European Holocaust in the 1940s" (*Future* 96, 75). It is within this context of comparison that Corn locates Du Bois's major failing: "Indeed, my major intellectual disappointment with the great Du Bois lies in the fact that there are hardly any traces in his work of any serious grappling with the profound thinkers and spiritual wrestlers in the modern West from these two groups—major figures obsessed with the problem of evil in their time" (*Future* 75–76).

Why does Corn require that Du Bois have "grappled with" such thinkers and the subjects (peoples) and foci of their writings, with the "problem of evil" as they conceived it, especially? There was no shortage of concern on the part of Du Bois with the evils of White Racial Supremacy, or even with those evils internal to shared Black life that were conditioned by invidious race matters yet were thought by him to be within the orbit of responsibility for attenuation by Black folk. At no point does Corn raise the question whether his "major figures" wrestled with "the problem of evil" that included the dehumanizing enslavement and oppression otherwise of folks African and of African descent, even in Europe; nor does he hold his "major figures" accountable for not wrestling with these evils. Du Bois fell short, for Corn, because his (Du Bois's) critical judgment and vision for just social renovations were not enriched by immersing himself in the works of the likes of Tolstoy and Kafka. Yet Corn makes no effort to determine whether Tolstoy (1828–1912) or Kafka (1883–1924) enriched their concerns and visions by reading works by Du Bois, say his *Souls of Black Folk* (1906), which was in print and available for their consideration during their lifetimes. In addition to critical perspective gained on the likes of Tolstoy and Kafka among other "great figures" lifted up by Corn, there is even more critical insight to be gained regarding Corn by a deeper probing of his taking the measure of Du Bois by Tolstoy/Kafka yardsticks, by the yardsticks of the lives of folks other than Black folk. Why is it that writings by Tolstoy and Kafka in which they do not contend with the conditions of unjust suffering imposed on Black folk are taken by Corn to be *the* measures by which unjust suffering is addressed by a properly engaged "public intellectual"?

Corn does not say.

I would be required to leave the context of *Race Matters* entirely in order to engage in a deeper, critical probing of "Black Strivings" (*Future of the Race*). An excursion into this text has been taken in order to draw on (and to direct attention to) a very pertinent and revealing essay by Corn in order to forge a hermeneutical hypothesis regarding why Corn declares in *Race Matters* that he is challenged by Du Bois yet does not offer reasons why in this book, though he does devote substantial attention to Du Bois in "Black Strivings," published three years *after* the publication of *Race Matters*.

It is difficult to determine whether—and if at all, to what extent—Corn's understanding and assessment of Du Bois were as well-formed during the 1993 production and publication of *Race Matters* as they came to be articulated in the 1996 publication of "Black Strivings." Nor can I account for the apparent development of this understanding and assessment of Du Bois during the intervening years (1993–96) that are set forth as the critique that constitutes much of "Black Strivings." This apparent development is not a matter that I have discussed with Corn; nor am I aware of any articulation by him in which he has accounted for such development other than what is offered in the preface to *The Future of the Race*, authored jointly with Henry Louis Gates Jr. (vii–xvii).

It would be intellectually inappropriate, and unethical, then, to impose upon the earlier *Race Matters* an interpretation of Corn's fleshed-out assessment of Du Bois from the later "Black Strivings." However, I do believe that it is quite appropriate, even necessary, from the vantage point of the twentieth-fifth anniversary reconsideration of the publication of *Race Matters* to, first, take note of the significant milestone of the 1996 production and publication of "Black Strivings" in a book devoted to critical self-assessments in the light of Du Bois's career and legacy, and of the call to service that Du Bois issued to the "Talented Tenth"; to take note of the significant milestone of the 1999 republication of "Black Strivings" in a large collection of fifty of his writings (*none* of the essays in *Race Matters* are included!) in which this particular essay is singled out by Corn as his "first and only sustained encounter" with Du Bois and the *only* one of his essays he would have survive if all others were to disappear. Having singled out "Black Strivings" as of such significance to him, I believe that while reassessing *Race Matters* twenty-five years after its publication we are compelled to ask of Corn: "Why was it the case that on neither of those milestone occasions of scholarly production and publication, then republication (of "Black Strivings"), did you take stock of your earlier efforts in *Race Matters* in light of the ambitious aim that you announced? Has your critique of Du Bois in "Black Strivings" been followed by equally strenuous *self-critique*?

I will hazard the hermeneutical possibility already offered: namely, that at the time of the production of *Race Matters* (1993) Corn was both inspired and challenged by Du Bois's legacies of effort but bothered by what he thought to be Du Bois's shortcomings. However, it was only when prompted by Gates[5] to give his attention to a critical engagement with Du Bois that Corn did so for inclusion in what we now have as *The Future of the Race*. I will offer a conclusion that I reached in preparing my 2001 assessment of the 1999 republication of "Black Strivings": that the upshot of Corn's critique of Du Bois was *to establish himself as a much more successful successor to Du Bois* in "hitting the mark" in contesting White Racial Supremacy as a public intellectual devoted to the affirmation of the humanity of Black folk and devoted to the renovation of the conditions, practices, and aims characterizing their living such that Black folk would enjoy sustained, cross-generational flourishing ("On Cornel West").

III

How well, then, does Corn meet the Du Boisian challenge(s) in the *Race Matters* effort? Each of the essay-chapters provides rich and provocative considerations. They are, as well, evidence of Corn's love-infused, self-sacrificing expenditures of gifted and broadly and deeply informed critical intellectual energies in developing piercing critical diagnoses of what he takes to be some impactful conditions and practices affecting the lives and living of Black folk—"nihilism"; "racial reasoning"; a "crisis of black leadership"; "new black conservatism"; investments in pursuits of "affirmative action"; relations between Black and Jewish folks; tabooed subjects in discussions of Black sexuality; "black rage"; the significance and legacy of Malcolm X. Nonetheless, I question how well the discussions meet what Corn has identified as Du Boisian challenges.

Not very well, in my judgment. And, for a number of reasons . . .

First, because *Race Matters* (1993) is crippled, in several very significant ways, by a number of profound, even astounding, instances of *evasion* (a term of critique that Corn employs with great skill in his *The American Evasion of Philosophy* [1989]). At no point in *Race Matters* does Corn endeavor to wrestle with "race" or *race*, neither conceptually nor empirically, as did Du Bois across the itinerary of his quite lengthy career: for example, most prominently early in his (Du Bois's) career in the seminal "The Conservation of Races" (1896) prepared for and presented as the second occasional paper during an 1897 meeting of the American Negro Academy; again, during 1940, in *Dusk of Dawn*; and, near the end of his life as he continued his career as a public intellectual, in "Whither Now and Why" (a presentation, three years before his death in 1963, to the 25th Annual Conference of the Association of Social Science Teachers meeting in Charlotte, North Carolina [published in *Quarterly Review of Higher Education Among Negroes*, vol. 28, July 1960, 135–41]), in which Du Bois argues for the critical need for sustaining, forging if need be, institutionalized means by which to preserve and enhance the production of the forms of culture definitive of the past and ongoing evolutionary development of folks of African descent in US America, in particular.[6] All of Corn's invoking of "race" in *Race Matters* is without any historical, conceptual, or empirical grounding or contextualization—neither philosophical, sociological or anthropological, cultural, nor biophysical.

Yet another striking evasion: wrestling with "white supremacy," to which he refers quite frequently, Corn offers no account of what this heavily weighted, quite significant, critical term and concept refers to; what constitute its realities; how it came to be; how projects ordered by commitments to establishing and/or sustaining white racial hegemony have been and are legitimated and gain authority; how such racial supremacy is perpetuated across generations and centuries. How, then, to work at countering its authority and legitimacy? For all of his otherwise acute and astute learnedness, missing in *Race Matters* is anything in the way of critical insights from such important works as Peter Berger and Thomas Luckmann's seminal *The Social Construction of Reality* (1966) or the Smedleys' important work *Race in North America* (2012). These are glaring omissions that amplify Corn's evasion of "race"/*race* and of the constructions and maintenance of the social realities of White Racial Supremacy.

That Corn evades the challenges—and the moral and intellectual responsibilities—of engaging with "race"/*race* is all the more striking since such engagements had become prominent among academics and public intellectuals, among others, in the years prior to, during, and after the publication of *Race Matters* in 1993. And, it is safe to say, more than a few of those engagements were focused on wrestling with Du Bois's "Conservation " and, most especially, in response to a particular engagement with this Du Boisian text: namely, Kwame Anthony Appiah's influential "The Uncompleted Argument: Du Bois and the Illusion of Race," which first appeared in a special issue of *Critical Inquiry* in 1986 and was subsequently included as a chapter in his widely read, highly acclaimed, and fiercely challenged *In My Father's House*, published the same year as *Race Matters*. Simply put, *Race Matters* was published during a historical moment when explorations of "race"/*race* were both extensive and intensive, a context that, I do believe, enhanced the significance of what has come to be regarded as Corn's signature contribution to the heated discussions in which a very broad range of persons and groupings, lay and professional, were, and continue to be, engaged, nationally and internationally. Thus, the significance of *Race Matters* twenty-five years and running, notwithstanding Corn's evasive failure to take on "race"/*race* directly.

One of the dire consequences of this evasion is that in *Race Matters* Corn offers no account of the possibility, let alone the viability, of a coherent and viable, historically and geographically salient, notion of Black *peoplehood* even though he speaks repeatedly of Black folk as though constituting a distinctive grouping, at the very least experientially and *culturally.* In speeches and writings elsewhere, as in "Black Strivings " *(Future*), Corn readily engages in affirmations of Black folk sharing distinctive, commendable experiences that have been and are culturally productive (of distinctive forms of music, literature, religious experience and worship, of dance and speech), so much so that he readily embraces and seeks soul-nourishment from the productions of various creative figures (of the music of blues, gospel, jazz, funk, and R & B; of various genres of Black literature and of Black religiosity, for example) who have been especially adept at creating and expressing structured meanings and feelings definitive of lifeworld experiences that have made for Black folks' endurance through determined "clinging to 'a hope not hopeless but unhopeful'" (*Future of the Race* 112) while being forcibly subjected to projects of White Racial Supremacy, endurance that is the outcome distinctive of what Corn characterizes as Black *strivings.*[7] And his critiques of various forms of Black nationalism in *Race Matters* leave unaddressed the question whether *any* notion of a Black *nation*—of a Black *peoplehood*—can, should, or needs to be made viable.

The questions are not even posed.

Du Bois wrestled with these vexing issues throughout his long career. And in "Whither Now and Why" he argued forcefully that in gaining full citizenship rights in US America Negroes should not "simply adopt the ideals of Americans and become what they are or want to be" and have in this process "no ideals of our own," which would mean "we would cease to be Negroes as such" ("Whither" 149). Again, Du Bois: "I am not fighting to settle the question of racial equality in America by the process of getting rid of the Negro race, getting rid of black folk, not producing black children, forgetting the slave trade and slavery, and the struggle for emancipation; of forgetting abolition and especially of ignoring the whole cultural history of Africans in the world. . . . No! What I have been fighting for and am still fighting for is the possibility of black folk and their cultural patterns existing in America without discrimination; and on terms of equality" ("Whither" 150).

Now, let us note that, though Corn's pronounced "basic aim in life" is to confront and dispose of white supremacy, all of the essays in *Race Matters* (1993) have Black folk as their thematic focus, *not* White Racial Supremacy! Let us note, as well, that in the book's "Introduction" Corn speaks of a growing "pervasive spiritual impoverishment," concluding that "The collapse of meaning in life—the eclipse of hope and absence of love of self and others, the breakdown of family and neighborhood bonds—leads to the *social deracination* [my emphasis] and *cultural denudement* [my emphasis] of urban dwellers, especially children" (*Race Matters* 5). These critical diagnoses are very much in line with those of Du Bois as expressed in both his "The Conservation of Races" and in "Whither Now and Why." Decidedly different, however, is that Corn makes no effort to affirm the needs for and benefits of family life, neighborhood bonds, etc., that he takes to be shared by and definitive of cultural life that, in turn, is definitive of the cultural *lifeworld* and *identities* of Black folk. Of quite serious consequence for Corn's *Race Matters* intellectual project-made-public on behalf of Black folk is that *he offers no explanation* why "deracination" and "cultural denudement" are not to be desired, why these processes should not be ignored or even accepted as constituting "progress."

Simply put, missing is any case for "conserving" the raciality of Black folk on any terms of understanding "race"/*race*. There is no effort exerted in Corn's *Race Matters* that is of a kind with Du Bois's efforts in "The Conservation of Races," which efforts continue to compel intellectual engagements and reengagements nearly a century and a quarter after its production was made public. I, for one, remain convinced that Du Bois's efforts, his notion of "conservation" especially, are both viable and worthwhile, though bolstering the viability and worthiness of the notion, and of his efforts, requires careful work that is tempered by attending to ongoing developments in several fields dealing with the historic emergence, development, migrations, genomic constitution and evolution, etc., of human population groups long considered—sometimes erroneously, too often invidiously—as "races" (Outlaw, "'Conserve' Races?"; "Race and Solidarity").

There are other serious consequences of Corn's evasion of an affirmative account of *race* on behalf of a notion of Black peoplehood. One of the more acute consequences is his apparent reliance on an unacknowledged, thus seemingly uncritically accepted, abstract, individualist philosophical anthropology by way of which he can speak of US America using such terms as "us," "our," a "common history," a "shared public square," of "the common good that undergirds our national and global destinies" (*Future of the Race* 6) without any apparent need to explain the viability of such referencing that prescinds from any pertinent distinguishing anthropological characteristics, whether racial, ethnic, gender, cultural, and so on, thus without having to wrestle with the vexing anthropological diversities continuing to bedevil the US American democratic project conceptually and politically. Here, again, more evasion, even as he takes note of the challenging need to "generate new leadership" to "help Americans determine whether a genuine multiracial democracy can be created and sustained in an era of global economy and a moment of xenophobic frenzy" (*Future of the Race* 7–8). What is a viable counter to xenophobia? Denial of "real" ethnic and/or racial differences on behalf of an affirmation of the "essential" sameness of all human individuals that should be recognized and embraced as trumping all "accidental" differences such as raciality and ethnicity? What is the viability, conceptually and politically, of a 'multi*racial*' democracy? Corn offers neither resources for conceiving, nor guidance in how to conceive and work productively toward, such an anthropological structuring of democratic life at any level of a US American polity composed of many peoples, not just of unaffiliated, abstract "individuals."

To be fair, Corn's evasion is not complete, for he knows, all too well, that the US American democratic project began as, and has largely remained, what he (and others) have characterized as a herrenvolk project, a concept that embraces and invokes notions of hegemonic racialized nationalism. Corn has, as well, given himself over to an immersive, critical engagement with Alexis de Tocqueville's monumental account of the development of this project in *Democracy in America* (1835), especially the in some ways penultimate chapter 10 of volume 1: "Some Considerations on the Present State and Probable Future of the Three Races That Inhabit the Territory of the United States" (302–96).

Engaging with Tocqueville's richly complicated account is of critical importance, for he regarded *democracy* not as a matter of abstract principles, but as a fundamental idea/ideal—"equality of conditions"—made manifest in the "passions, habits, and sentiments" of the quotidian life of white folks from Western Europe, Anglo-Saxons especially. And of particular importance, Tocqueville was convinced that democracy-making in US America, while a divinely ordained venture, was inextricable from the raciality of Anglos-becoming-Americans. Thus, the need for him to consider the challenges of the presence of *three* races in the midst of the historic project.

I know from our discussions that Corn has a deeply read critical understanding of this Tocquevillian account, further evidenced in his (Corn's) critical characterization and critique of the herrenvolk structuring of the US American venture. But here's the rub: recognition and critical understanding of the herrenvolk nature of the US American democratic project *should* explode the ideological subterfuge of the masquerading ideology of an abstract, raceless (classless, nongendered) "liberal individualism" as the nation-state's grounding philosophical anthropology, an ideology that has long served illicitly as a backward-looking explanatory, rationalizing, norm-setting, and legitimating schema for the hierarchical systems of racialized, class, and gendered social structurings of the ordering schema/project of US America's White Racial Supremacy.

Thus, Corn should have been much more diligent than is the case in *Race Matters* (1993) in invoking affirmatively such notions as "*we* . . . as a people"; "*our* common destiny"; "*our* interracial interdependence" while not taking up the challenging Du Boisian work of providing scientifically (sociologically, anthropologically, and historically) refined notions and accounts of biocultural populations heretofore regarded as "races." This is in no way an effort on my part to minimize or disregard the politically important embracing, inclusive, solidarity-cultivating effort at work in invoking the rhetoric of "we" and "our" by a prominent public intellectual such as Corn. However, neither listeners nor readers should be misled by the apparent naïveté latent in such rhetoric when it is unsupported by clarified understandings of demographic diversities that are far from being minor sources of political challenge in the US American context and elsewhere. Neither retreats from nor appeals to either "conservative" Right or liberal" Left versions of classical nineteenth-century abstract notions of "individualism" that have long masked the racist racialism of White Racial Supremacy are viable resources for contending with invidious race matters in the present, nor for guiding us into a future of more fully realized interracial and multiethnic democratic equity and justice.

Du Bois saw through the masking:

> Turning to real history, there can be no doubt, first, as to the widespread, nay universal, prevalence of the race idea, the race spirit, the race ideal, and as to its efficiency as the vastest [*sic*] and most ingenious invention for human progress. We, who have been reared and trained under the individualistic philosophy of the Declaration of Independence and the laisser-faire [*sic*] philosophy of Adam Smith, are loath to see and loath to acknowledge this paten fact of human history. . . . We are apt to think in our American impatience, that while it may have been true in the past that closed race groups made history, that here in conglomerate America *nous avons changer tout cela*—that we have changed all that, and have no need of this ancient instrument of progress. This assumption of

> which the Negro people are especially fond, can not be established by a careful consideration of history. ("Conservation of Races" 817)

Of course, one need not be persuaded by Du Bois's reasoning. However, if one is committed to affirming the peoplehood of Black folk, not just our individuality as persons, then the especially difficult work of forging a viable philosophical-anthropology, and more, in support of the struggles to sustain Black folk and to undergird our flourishing in democratic cooperation and sharing with other peoples must not be evaded. Rather, to contend with race matters requires contending with "race"/*race*. And if, in doing so, we Black public intellectual "grandchildren" of those to whom Du Bois attributed heavy responsibilities as a "Talented Tenth" will, indeed, "ground our understanding of the present in the germinal thought of our collective past" (*Future of the Race* vii–viii), then we *must* take particular care in how we engage with, and continue, the life and legacy of W. E. B. Du Bois while interrogating his assignment of responsibility, and those responsibilities we assign ourselves.

Corn has not fulfilled his responsibility in this regard, in my judgment, though he has made a noteworthy, learned, creatively insightful attempt. But it is an attempt that is flawed (though not quite fatally) by hubris born of a crippling lack of disciplined, critical self-awareness that affects important aspects of both his intellectual work and his living. Having devoted this writing to some of the former, a brief, delicate word about the latter, that is, Corn's living.

From passages already quoted, we have texts to explore further ("Whither Now and Why" in particular) just how, and with what significance, Du Bois conceived of Black folk as a distinctive people, and conceived of how crucial families, married life, the raising and education of children, among other matters, are to the conservation of Black peoplehood. What about Corn? Is his life beyond his "speaking," compared, say, to the life of Du Bois fully considered, exemplary of one who lives with principled commitment to intimate relationships, of marriage and family-making if one joins in such relationships, that are conditioned by appropriate forms of solidarity to peoplehood writ small and particular, and to US American nationhood writ large and democratic? For in such relationships, once engaged in, there are *major* responsibilities.

How should taking up and living these responsibilities be understood to align with the responsibilities of being a public intellectual who addresses shared social and political life? If we think family life and shared communal and political life are dialectically related and, at their best, mutually supportive and nurturing, then we are compelled to assess not just the guidance regarding a polity offered us by politically concerned public intellectuals, but as well their advice *and the example of their living* regarding family and shared communal life. Further, we must be resolute and principled in requiring those offering such advice to show us, convincingly, that the example of their living is a most important test of the veracity of their lived commitments as well as of their advice; that their lived relations are principal and principled sources of what wisdom they have earned and seek to share by which we might enhance family and shared sociopolitical life. Otherwise, on what basis could or should we give credence to their advice?

In this regard, the personal life of my dear friend Corn West comes up short, as those of us close to him know all too well. Du Bois, flawed though he and his living were, was still better at the living in important respects than has been Corn, I venture to say, which enriches Du Bois's offerings with more experienced wisdom and thus gives much more salience to his offerings, no matter how misguided Corn's disparaging mischaracterization of important instances of Du Bois's values and commitments as, in part, "Victorian."

Take note, Bro' Corn . . .

Notes

1. Note, for example, the following characterization of a proper public intellectual by Corn that he sets forth in a writing devoted to a critical engagement with Du Bois that was published three years after the publication of *Race Matters*: "The fundamental role of the public intellectual—distinct from, yet building on, the indispensable work of academics, experts, analysts, and pundits—is to create and sustain high-quality public discourse addressing urgent public problems that enlightens and energizes fellow citizens, prompting them to take public action. This role requires a deep commitment to the life of the mind—a perennial attempt to clear our minds of cant (to use Samuel Johnson's famous formulation)—which serves to shape the public destiny of a people. Intellectual and political leadership should be neither elitist, nor populist; rather it ought to be democratic, in that each of us stands in public space without humiliation, to put forward our best visions and views for the sake of the public interest. And these arguments are presented in an atmosphere of mutual respect and civic trust ("Black Strivings" 71). There is more to be said regarding this characterization, which I take to be self-characterizing for Corn, and, of particular importance, regarding the writing in which it is offered.

2. Corn interprets Du Bois's consistent reference to "men" when speaking of the Talented Tenth in *The Souls of Black Folk* as obvious indications that Du Bois's consideration of leadership is hampered by patriarchal commitments. To the contrary—when, in the third paragraph, Du Bois proceeds to identify examples of "the educated and intelligent of the Negro people" who, "from the first . . . have led and elevated the mass . . . ," note the first person

named: "In colonial days came Phillis Wheatley . . ." (842–43)! This is not the only instance in "The Talented Tenth" where Du Bois lifts up Black women as examples of leaders.

3. It should be noted that it was at Fisk that two persons also studied who met and began a love-infused relationship that led to marriage and the subsequent birth of Cornel!

4. "[Du Bois] and I are birds of very different feathers. My freestyle, California spirit stands in stark contrast to his austere, New England soul. My Chekhovian Christian sensibilities rooted in gut-bucket blues and jazz dispositions violently clash with his Enlightenment and Victorian sentiments based on his Fisk, Harvard, Berlin, Atlanta, and New York experiences. To put it bluntly, I am much closer (and proudly so) to the funk of a James Brown or George Clinton, the soul of a Curtis Mayfield, Richard Pryor or Aretha Franklin than he. Yet we remain soul mates in our struggle for oppressed peoples, especially black humanity" ("Black Strivings" 87). Du Bois moved to Ghana during 1961, and died there in 1963. How, then, could he have been as "close" to these artists as Corn, who was but ten years old when Du Bois died, artists whose careers were ascendant *after* his death?!

5. "I thank my close friend and brother Skip Gates for suggesting I write this essay on Du Bois and modernity" ("Black Strivings" 87).

6. "Any statement of our desire to develop American Negro culture, to keep up our ties with coloured people, to remember our past is being regarded as 'racism.' I, for instance, who have devoted my life to efforts to break down racial barriers am being accused of desiring to emphasize differences of race. This has a certain truth about it. As I have said before and I repeat I am not fighting to settle the question of racial equality in America by the process of getting rid of the Negro race" ("Whither Now and Why" 149–58, 150).

7. "Black strivings are the creative and complex products of the terrifying African encounter with the absurd *in* America—and the absurd *as* America. Like any other group of human beings, black people forged ways of life and ways of struggle under circumstances not of their own choosing. They constructed structures of meaning and structures of feeling in the face of the fundamental facts of human existence—death, dread, despair, disease, and disappointment. Yet the specificity of black culture—namely, those features that distinguish black culture from other cultures—lies in both the *African* and *American* character of black people's attempts to sustain their mental sanity and spiritual health, social life and political struggle in the midst of a slaveholding, white supremacist civilization that viewed itself as the most enlightened, free, tolerant, and democratic experiment in human history" ("Black Strivings" 79).

Works Cited

Appiah, Kwame Anthony. *In My Father's House: Africa in the Philosophy of Culture*. Oxford UP, 1993.

Appiah, Kwame Anthony. "The Uncompleted Argument: Du Bois and the Illusion of Race." *"Race," Writing, and Difference*, edited by Henry Louis Gates, Jr., U of Chicago P, 1986, pp. 21–37.

Berger, Peter L., and Thomas Luckmann. *The Social Construction of Reality: A Treatise in the Sociology of Knowledge*. Doubleday, 1966.

Du Bois, W. E. B. "The Conservation of Races." *W. E. B. Du Bois: Writings*. Library of America, 1986.

———. "Dusk of Dawn: An Essay Toward an Autobiography of a Race Concept." "Writings," Library of America, 1986, pp. 549–802.

———. "The Souls of Black Folk." *Writings*. Library of America, 1986.

———. "Whither Now and Why." *The Education of Black People: Ten Critiques, 1906–1960*, edited by Herbert Aptheker, U of Massachusetts P., 1973.

Gates, Henry Louis, Jr. Series Introduction. "The Black Letters on the Sign: W. E. B. Du Bois and the Canon." *The Oxford W.E.B. Du Bois: Black Reconstruction in America*. Oxford UP, 2007, pp. xi–xxiv.

Gates, Henry Louis, Jr., and Cornel West. *The Future of the Race*. Knopf, 1996.

Outlaw, Lucius T., Jr. "'Conserve' Races? In Defense of W. E. B. Du Bois." *Critical Social Theory in the Interest of Black Folk*. Rowan & Littlefield, 2005, pp. 139–62.

———. "On Cornel West on W. E. B. Du Bois." *Cornel West: A Critical Reader*, edited by George Yancy, Blackwell, 2001, pp. 261–79.

———. "On Race and Solidarity: Reconsiderations." *The Routledge Companion to Philosophy of Race*, edited by Paul C. Taylor, Linda Martín Alcoff, and Luvell Anderson, Routledge, 201, pp. 423–45.

Smedley, Audrey, and Brian D. Smedley. *Race in North America: Origin and Evolution of a Worldview*. Westview Press, 2012.

Tocqueville, Alexis de. *Democracy in America*. 1835–1840. Translated by Harvey C. Mansfield and Delba Winthrop, U of Chicago P, 2000.

West, Cornel. "Black Strivings in a Twilight Civilization." *The Future of the Race*, by Henry Louis Gates, Jr., and Cornel West. Knopf, 1996.

———. "Black Strivings in a Twilight Civilization." *The Cornel West Reader*, by Cornel West. Basic Civitas, 1990, pp. 87–118.

———. *Democracy Matters: Winning the Fight Against Imperialism*. Penguin, 2004.

———. *Race Matters*. Beacon Press, 1993.

———. *Race Matters*, Twenty-Fifth Anniversary. Beacon Press, 2017.

———. *The American Evasion of Philosophy: A Genealogy of Pragmatism*. U of Wisconsin P, 1989.

PART II

Black Nihilism, Afropessimism, and Prophetic Faith

CHAPTER 3

Nihilism, Pessimism, and Tragic Hope: Black Nihilism Reconsidered

Brandon M. Terry

> Nihilism is standing at the gate: from where does this uncanniest of guests come to us?
>
> —Friedrich Nietzsche

Black Nihilism as a Species of Nihilism

Amid Cornel West's vast and inimitable corpus, perhaps his most (in)famous and controversial attempt to plumb the existential depths of suffering and the ethical stakes of struggle came toward the end of the last century in his opening essay from *Race Matters* (1993): "Nihilism in Black America." The familiarity this essay has accrued in the years since its publication, especially among black intellectuals and other commentators on African American life, somehow does not dull its ability to unsettle with rereading. "The most basic issue now facing black America," West stridently declares, is "*the nihilistic threat to its very existence*" (*Race Matters* 12). This specifically *black* nihilism, West ventured, is a "*lived experience of coping with a life of horrifying meaninglessness, hopelessness, and (most important) lovelessness*" born from the bitter alchemy of rapacious market capitalism, social anomie, and enduring racial domination (*Race Matters* 14).

In raising these ethical-existential questions of nihilism, pessimism, and hope, West revisits terrain powerfully explored by the nineteenth-century

German philosopher Arthur Schopenhauer. Surveying the suffering, boredom, and anxiety of human beings with awareness of their impending demise, Schopenhauer came to dark conclusions about the value of our species' existence. "If we picture to ourselves roughly as far as we can the sum total of misery, pain, and suffering of every kind on which the sun shines in its course," Schopenhauer contends, "we shall admit that it would have been much better if it had been just impossible for the sun to produce the phenomenon of life on earth."[1]

This judgment, Schopenhauer argued, followed from bravely confronting the hard truths of human existence without recourse to any of the easy but misguided consolations at our disposal. He especially mocked most attempts at theodicy, suggesting that creation myths that treat the world as God's mistake, the clash of competing deities, or the work of an evil being were more plausible than the Christian story of God looking upon *this* world and judging it "good." "I suppose I shall have to be told again," Schopenhauer wrote, "that my philosophy is cheerless and comfortless simply because I tell the truth, whereas people want to hear that the Lord has made all things very well. Go to your churches and leave us philosophers in peace!"[2]

Friedrich Nietzsche, who arguably took Schopenhauer's challenge more seriously than any other prominent thinker, argued that "what actually arouses indignation over suffering is not the suffering itself, but the senselessness of suffering," or, as he put it elsewhere in *On the Genealogy of Morality*, "the fact that there was no answer to the question [man] screamed, 'Suffering for *what*?'"[3] On Nietzsche's elitist account, average people—the so-called "herd"—are primarily seduced away from confronting this "terrible truth" of metaphysically meaningless human suffering by distractions (e.g., work and entertainment), ritualistic habits, and naïve religious faith.[4]

Nietzsche also argued, however, that Christian doctrines of compassion and their political analogues (e.g., egalitarianism) could *deepen* the threat of nihilism in particular directions. In a world where human suffering invites emotional and ethical investment due to compassion and egalitarianism or demands *justification* on similar grounds, the question of whether the world is amenable to justice or at least the amelioration of undeserved suffering becomes urgent.[5] When no justification, legitimation, or redemption of suffering appears forthcoming or even possible, this raises suspicion about whether life under such burdens is even worth living.

As West suggests, this may seem *especially* true if the authors and agents of such burdens are frail, fellow persons, who disproportionately and arbitrarily impose misery upon some rather than others. Ironically, discontent and despair may grow deeper when hopes engendered by ostensibly liberal, egalitarian ideals sit disappointingly contradicted by the fact of oppression. For West, this disappointment undergirds the dilemma that New World slavery fastened upon the modern world, what West calls "the ignoble paradox of modernity."[6]

West conceives of nihilism as, in part, a problem of *despair* and an accompanying spirit of life-negation. Nihilism, on this account, is not only a question of disorientation or disenchantment concerning values. One's judgment that "the world is necessarily or essentially inhospitable to the realization of his values" can also engender nihilistic dispositions.[7] Although not consistently recognized, this pessimism is also related to one of Nietzsche's accounts of nihilism. "A nihilist," he writes, "is a man who judges of the world as it is that it ought *not* to be, and of the world as it ought to be that it does not exist."[8] It is the conviction, to put it plainly, that our highest ideals and values are impossible to achieve in this or any other world, including an "afterlife."[9]

For West, nihilism is a *perpetual* and *widespread* challenge that is *uniquely imposing* for African Americans, given their location at the center of this ignoble paradox and amid the broader cultural patterns of the West. "Nihilism is not new," he writes, and even "the initial black struggle against degradation and devaluation in the enslaved circumstances of the New World was, in part, a struggle against nihilism." Indeed, West goes so far as to declare that this "loss of hope and absence of meaning" is "the major enemy of black survival in America" (*Race Matters* 23).

Unfortunately, as with many inquiries into the ethical life of black peoples in the New World, the reception of West's argument has largely been misguided and confused. The shallow, albeit persistent, criticism insists that West, in naming a *black* nihilism, inadvertently bolsters the neoconservative and even racist ideology of black pathology.[10] For such critics, describing a sizeable cohort of black ghetto denizens as having "a numbing detachment from others and a self-destructive disposition toward the world," or "a cold-hearted, mean-spirited outlook," was to reproduce the terms of racist discourse and pathologizing stigma that undergird antiblack stigma in the post-Jim Crow era (*Race Matters* 14).

Yet any attempt to reduce West's argument to unwitting conservatism fails in two respects. First, it fails to read the essay alongside West's longstanding neo-Marxist analysis of the interpenetrating structural, ideological, and aesthetic foundations of racial and economic domination.[11] As he briefly reiterates in "Nihilism in Black America," his views on these matters are in stark opposition to conservative social theory. To describe a condition of "black nihilism" is not to endorse an *explanatory social theory of black disadvantage* that gives causal priority to abnormal cultural patterns that prevail in the ghetto. Nor does it deny the causal or ethical significance of the "basic structure" of society, with its historically cumulative and unjust patterns of group-based inequalities.[12] Nor, moreover, does West's worry that the decline of civic associations and social institutions helps engender nihilism commit him to the argument, made famous by Robert Putnam among others, that an objectionable spirit of individualism and technology-enabled withdrawal is chiefly responsible.[13] Instead, West points the blame for social fragmentation at the effects of economic inequality and the intensifying privatization and marketization of all spheres of human life. Such forces destabilize neighborhoods and institutions, with profit imperatives proving particularly corrosive to the ethical ideals of churches, schools, and other domains once more insulated from such pressures (*Race Matters* 24–25).

Second, it is incumbent upon such critics to clarify whether they think that nihilism of *any* sort is possible. If so, we might ask whether such a phenomenon could have *any* meaningful social consequence or whether it is possible to *diagnose* it through any extant form of cultural criticism or social theory.[14] While West's attempt to connect the interpretation of some range of self-undermining or objectionable practices that were apparently increasing or intensifying in black communities (e.g., violence, drug addiction, and suicide) to the broader philosophical literature on nihilism was indeed novel, the claim that forms of hopelessness and meaninglessness embedded in particular practices or stances toward the world represent an existential threat to the flourishing of some members of the group is a familiar one in black letters.

James Weldon Johnson, for example, wrote of a "general spirit . . . of hopelessness or acquiescence" amid the wake of Reconstruction's defeat and the "triumphant materialism of the age."[15] Mary Church Terrell, at the end of the Great Depression, lamented how the "colored man . . . resigns himself to his fate" in "a sort of stoical despair" created by "the helplessness and the hopelessness of the situation in this country."[16] James Forman likewise complained that in Mississippi, before the civil rights insurgency, "years of terror, economic intimidation, and a total, grinding, day-in, day-out white racism had created a black population numb with fear and hopelessness."[17]

The psychologist Kenneth Clark despaired, in the 1970s, of the "racial prisons of America's ghettos" and argued that the "frustration, despair, and a sense of hopelessness" forged by such domination is manifest in drug abuse, crime, and other behaviors.[18] Perhaps most stridently of all, Malcolm X argued that a clear-eyed assessment of ghetto conditions "is primarily responsible for the ever-increasing sense of frustration and hopelessness that exists" and is manifest in substance abuse, violent crime, and other vices. "We are trapped," Malcolm warned, in "a vicious cycle of economic, intellectual, social, and political death. . . . Giving birth to children who see no hope or future but to follow in our miserable footsteps."[19]

The persistence of such claims does not dissolve, of course, the reasonable debate over what behaviors or dispositions might persuasively express, enact, or embody "nihilism" in particular contexts. Nor are such voices, despite their admirable commitments to black liberation, immune by default from the habituated contempt toward the poor or the fear of deviance characteristic of so much modern social thought. We should treat charges of "nihilism," therefore, in a spirit of receptivity and fallibility. Assessing such judgments should obligate us to produce or reconstruct comprehensive accounts of what our interlocutors think constitutes flourishing and dignity, rather than enervation and degradation. Perhaps even more important, nihilism-talk must remain open to revision and reformulation in response to arguments advanced in defense of the practices or dispositions described in such fashion.[20]

Nonetheless, the accumulated weight of this tradition amounts to a view that critics of nihilism-talk would do well to take seriously. Forms of hopelessness and the threat of meaninglessness have proved so persistent in the face of intergenerational oppression that they may not be waved away by triumphalist romanticism about "resistance" or rationalist evasion of the darker currents of psychic life. This is because, in part, they reflect genuinely reflective ruminations on whether life is worth living in the face of suffering and evil.

Nihilism and the Nineties

Still, some critics, perhaps picking up on West's palpable sense of crisis, have sought to assimilate *Race Matters*' charge of "nihilism" to the 1990s-era surge of conservative and neoliberal commentary on ghetto denizens as an "underclass" degenerating into unprecedented pathology and predation.[21] Such criticisms, however, misunderstand the sweeping historical scope in which West situates the challenge of nihilism and the philosophical complexity of the intervention. Indeed, the speed with which these critics move from a dismissal of West's "politics of conversion" to the familiar call for a radical, multiracial, leftist social movement to uproot the foundations of capitalism and racism betrays a certain naïveté.[22] West's argument tries to unmask how such clarion calls often presuppose or themselves must carefully nurture enduring practices and dispositions of hope, faith, perseverance, and the will to sacrifice among individuals reasonably pessimistic about the prospects of struggle or the worth of its likely costs.

Where West's intervention finds urgency in a 1990s milieu, however, is from the collision between two of late-twentieth-century America's most unique and unexpected cultural-political developments. The first was the apparent collapse of viable left and independent black political alternatives in the face of a consolidating neoliberal consensus.[23] The second was the popularity, especially within African American expressive culture, of art that unabashedly expressed nihilistic themes.

The Crisis of the American Left

West's historical narrative of black progressive politics echoes, in some sense, Nietzsche's unsettling insight that social misery is not itself necessarily sufficient to engender nihilism. Even severely oppressed peoples are often capable of enduring profound hardship when they share a judgment that their suffering is *meaningful* or intrinsically related to some worthwhile goal. But when "the aim is lacking" and the "'why?' finds no answer," as Nietzsche put it, the threat of nihilism intensifies.[24] Nietzsche argues that we tend to first arrive at nihilism by seeking "a 'meaning' in all events that is not there," then becoming "discouraged" and "ashamed" by "the recognition of the long *waste* of strength, the agony of the 'in vain,' insecurity, the lack of any opportunity to recover and to regain composure . . . as if one had *deceived* oneself all too long."[25] For Nietzsche, "disappointment" in the failure of certain moral ideals (e.g., "the moral world order," "the growth of love and harmony," "the gradual approximation of a state of universal happiness," etc.) or the shattered faith in an underlying unity (e.g., the nation, the race, humanity) or transcendent, "universal" values are especially likely to lead to nihilism.

While for Nietzsche, this is part of the reason to disavow such commitments, for West, the catastrophe of the defeat of such egalitarian ideals is a tragedy to mourn. As early as *Prophesy Deliverance!* (1982), West decried the "marginality of Marxism in American life" and lamented a long-standing failure to build a powerful social movement within the "progressive" Left.[26] By *Race Matters*, written after the collapse of the Berlin Wall and the Soviet Union, West lamented that the Left was pushed so far into retreat by a virulent conservative reaction that even the legitimacy of Keynesian liberalism was in crisis (*Race Matters* 77). Indeed, West goes so far as to deride the period's ascendant bipartisan enthusiasm for "the elimination of nearly every federal benefit program for the nonelderly poor," as providing ideological cover for policies with "genocidal effects on the black poor" (*Race Matters* 87).

West's early attention to the "paradox of the Afro-American rebellion" and subsequent diagnosis of the "crisis in black leadership" is also crucial. Highlighting the class dynamics of postwar black politics, West argued that "liberal" legislative victories (e.g., the Civil Rights Act of 1964) and the "petit bourgeois" aspirations of many civil rights leaders (e.g., access to public accommodations, desegregation of higher education, residential integration) could not deliver on, or adequately domesticate, the political demands of the black poor. For West, the Black Power movement that followed, despite its radical posture, fared even worse. The amenability of black nationalist rhetoric to usurpation by black petit-bourgeois entrepreneurs in politics, academia, and the marketplace, contributed to the collapse of interracial progressivism. It also intensified the costs of patriarchal subordination upon black women and untethered black freedom movement organizations from their earlier organic relationships to black communities through churches and other organizations. The collapse of the emancipatory hopes of black progressivism amid the contradictions of these movements and the broader sociopolitical transformations of the late twentieth century led, in West's account, to the growth of a culture of cynicism, irony, and solipsism. The late twentieth century saw the political freedom dreams of the past calcify into the monumental ruins of our present.[27]

Things Done Changed: Black Expressive Culture and Nihilism

Like Nietzsche, West also treats expressive culture and its reception as an important site for reflection on the problem of cultural nihilism.[28] The traumatic character of ghetto poverty amid the aforementioned structural changes and eclipse of viable egalitarian political movements had become one of the vital thematic preoccupations of African American art by the 1990s, especially in the ascendant genre of hip-hop.[29] While black artists had long offered critical reflections on ghetto life, the wave of music and film of the 1990s contained currents dramatically distinct from the realist and naturalist protest novels of the mid-twentieth-century ghetto (e.g., Richard Wright's *Native Son*, Ann Petry's *The Street*, and Chester Himes's *If He Hollers Let Him Go*) or the elegiac blues lamentations so influential in 1960s and '70s-era rhythm and blues (e.g., Marvin Gaye's "Inner City Blues," Curtis Mayfield's *Superfly*, Bobby Womack's "Across 110th Street," Stevie Wonder's "Living for the City," and Donny Hathaway's "The Ghetto"). These older works of art, in part because of their resilient hope in political, social, or personal transformation, or because their underlying ethical commitments lead them to take a third-person narrative stance, faced difficulty fully inhabiting and interrogating the most thoroughgoing forms of ghetto despair.

The divergence in these musical genres also reflects a *qualitative* difference in the character of the mid-twentieth-century American ghetto versus its counterpart as we approached the turn of the twenty-first century. During the last decades of the twentieth century, ghetto neighborhoods saw a rapid decline in middle-class residents and married households and an enormous increase in chronic joblessness and incarceration. They also were on the front lines of an exceedingly violent underground drug economy undergoing radical expansion and the collapse of traditional community institutions (e.g., small businesses, large churches, civil society groups, etc.).[30] West connected these changes—especially the expansion of the underground drug economy, urban violence, and state repression through incarceration—to "contempt for black people" and the project of "pacifying" ghetto rebellion and discontent.[31] These forces, in particular, West argued, accelerated the flight of working- and middle-class blacks from inner cities, creating "terrains of human bondage to the commodity form [via] enslavement to the buying and selling of drugs." "For the first time in African American history," West argues, "fear and trepidation among black folk toward one another [became] pervasive."[32] Violence, of course, loomed ominously over *Race Matters*, with 1993 marking the peak of recorded US gun homicides and the highest murder rates for black girls (13.1 per 100,000), black male teenagers (79 per 100,000), and black males aged 18 to 24 (195.9 per 100,000) in American history.[33]

West's sense that these changes somehow destroyed important sources of meaning and solidarity while providing ample reasons for profound despair was echoed widely in art, with hip-hop music and film providing the most sustained interrogations of nihilistic threat under such conditions. For West, hip-hop in that era represented a "paradoxical cry of desperation and celebration of the black underclass and poor working class, a cry that openly acknowledges and confronts the wave of personal coldheartedness, criminal cruelty, and existential hopelessness in the black ghettos of Afro-America." Uniquely in the tradition of black music, West argued, many hip-hop artists "radically call into question" the "roots of transcendence and opposition," the impulse toward hope, and the assumption that care is redemptive or even authentic.[34]

The Hughes brothers' *Menace II Society* (1993), arguably the greatest of the early '90s "hood" films, depicts the protagonist Caine, played by Tyrin Turner, as thrown into the anomie and alienation that West laments. Named to evoke both "crack" cocaine *and* the biblical figure who fails to show proper reverence to God and fraternal duty by slaying his brother Abel, Caine is orphaned by his father's murder and his mother's fatal drug overdose. On the cusp of high school graduation, we find him adrift, living with his grandparents in a relationship that grows fractious and fearful before our eyes. Both parties grasp the grandparents' impotence as effective guardians in the face of broader social forces pulling Caine away from school and toward gangsterism, nihilism, and hedonism.

This depiction is allegorical. In the grandparents' age, familial role (grandparents stepping in as parents), and unheeded insistence on Christian piety, the grandparent-grandchild relation narratively represents a broader social disruption in the continuity of black institutions, cultural strivings, and authoritative traditions that once served as a buffer against despair and anomie.[35] Caine's grandparents represent not only a past that lacks authority in the present but past strivings and hopes that cannot find secure footing or redemption in the present. Caine's murderous and sociopathic best friend O-Dog (Larenz Tate), more of a specter than a well-developed character, is meant to symbolize the consequences of this crisis of authority and the nihilism it makes possible.[36]

The two most crucial scenes in the film echo each other to dramatize this overarching theme. When Caine's grandfather attempts, shortly after Caine survives a carjacking and shooting, to turn his grandson and O-Dog away from street violence, he appeals to God's commandments, the salvific future of the hereafter, and the moral worth of all persons, no matter their earthly station. Refusing such claims, O-Dog responds by invoking the suffering of the ghetto and the race *writ large*. "I don't think God really cares too much about us, or he wouldn't have put us here," he proclaims, later lamenting privately to Caine that "Black people got too much damn religion as it is." Unable to exercise any authority, biblical or parental, Caine's grandfather plaintively asks the teenager as he leaves home whether he cares to live or die. Caine's response is devastatingly noncommittal and passively nihilistic. "I don't know," he says quizzically before agreeing to kill a crew of rivals, ostensibly in retaliation for the murder of his cousin.

This scene foreshadows the one that ends the film. While Caine is preparing, with great hope, to leave Los Angeles with his girlfriend, Ronnie (Jada Pinkett), and her son, he is fatally shot in retaliation for an assault committed earlier in the film as part of a paternity dispute.[37] As Caine gasps for his last breaths, the viewer hears his voice, which has been omnisciently narrating throughout the film. We realize as Caine dies before us that this narration may have been posthumous. The film concludes with the dying Caine revisiting his grandfather's question once more and changing his answer to "Yeah, I do." At the precipice of death, Caine is led back to affirm the will to life, but it is, tragically, too late.

More unflinching than even *Menace II Society* is the Notorious B.I.G.'s *Ready to Die* (1994). The album is perhaps known best for the triumphalist radio hits (e.g., "Juicy" and "Big Poppa" respectively) orchestrated by its producer, Sean "Puff Daddy" Combs, but it begins, however, with the diagnostic "Things Done Changed." In this song, Biggie (aka Christopher Wallace) describes, from his vantage, the collapse in hope, community trust, and familial solidarity stemming from the cumulative burdens of ghetto poverty and the escalating violence within these neighborhoods.

"The streets are a short stop," he summarily declares, "either you're slinging crack rock, or you got a wicked jump shot." Remarking on the phenomenon of parents and guardians, at their wits' end, calling the police on their children, he proclaims: "Back in the days, our parents used to take care of us / Look at 'em now, they even fuckin' scared of us/callin' the city for help because they can't maintain/Damn, shit done changed." The decline of social bonds amid structural and interpersonal violence is crucial here. Still, the depth of despair and hopelessness cannot be understood without grasping the sense that an imagined future of social progress, communal continuity, and genuine flourishing appears foreclosed while still melancholically haunting any assessment of whether life is worth living. If we read the album's sequence as a narrative arc, its flirtations with hedonism, gangsterism, and braggadocio are all superseded, in the last instance, by a kind of nihilism that leads Biggie—after weighing the worth (or lack thereof) of his attachments to his mother, his children and their mother, religion, and morality—to commit suicide at the album's end.

West's discussion of suicide in "Black Nihilism" responds to these broader cultural currents. It takes seriously their resonance with Albert Camus' famous contention that suicide is the "one really serious philosophical problem" and "deciding whether or not life is worth living is to answer the fundamental question in philosophy" from which "all other questions follow."[38] What West shares with the Left existentialist tradition is this sense that underneath any call for the oppressed to suffer the risks inherent in collectively struggling against their oppression, or even counseling them to endure such suffering at all, lie fundamental *ethical-existential* questions. These existential dilemmas wrestle with the specter of pessimism and its relation to nihilistic judgments or dispositions toward our sense of the *value* of life and the *worth* or *point* of striving across the full range of human activities (e.g., politics, intimacy, art, etc.), especially given the likelihood of failure.[39]

Nihilism and Pessimism

From a particular vantage, however, nihilism may contain something laudable. In its "active" form, at least, nihilism rejects the "lies we should like to tell ourselves" about the depth, certainty, or significance of human suffering. It breaks with the forms of "self-narcotization" (e.g., distraction by entertainment, nostalgia, *ressentiment*, fanaticism) by which we evade the terrible truths of our condition or descend into "passive" despair.[40]

A particularly deceptive and self-deluded myth, Nietzsche argued, by which the most "level-headed are led astray," is the idea of "Progress," where both time and everything in it marches forward toward developing the highest human ends or goods together.[41] In Nietzsche's view, the past is "a tremendous experimental laboratory in which a few successes are scored, scattered throughout ages, while there are untold failures, and all order, logic, union, and obligingness are lacking."[42]

For West, the vital rejoinder to *romantic* notions of progress is not the cultural degeneration that animated Nietzsche's aristocratic radicalism, but instead "the pervasive evil of unjustified suffering and unnecessary social misery in our world," and the ghastly wreckage of past injustice.[43] In this sense, West shares much in philosophical orientation with the well-known passage from Walter Benjamin's "Theses on the Philosophy of History," where the latter describes the mythos of "Progress" through the image of Paul Klee's painting, *Angelus Novus*, which:

> shows an angel who seems about to move away from something he stares at. His eyes are wide, his mouth is open, his wings are spread. This is how the angel of history must look. His face is turned towards the past. Where a chain of events appears before us, he sees one single catastrophe, which keeps piling wreckage upon wreckage and hurls it at its feet. The angel would like to stay, awaken the dead, and make whole what has been smashed. But a storm is blowing from Paradise and has got caught in his wings; it is so strong that the angel can no longer close them. This storm drives him irresistibly into the future, to which his back is turned, while the pile of debris before him grows toward the sky. What we call progress is this storm.[44]

An "active" nihilism, then, may at least pave the way for a more clear-eyed recognition of the extent of human suffering, now and in the past. Yet this raises for West an immediate question. How can this honest confrontation help us *overcome* nihilism and find redemptive meaning and value in the resistance, travails, and disappointments we inevitably confront as finite beings pursuing our goals? After all, judgments of pessimism about the ability to overcome or redeem such suffering can lead to despairing skepticism or ironic condescension on the value of *any* particular political program and the worth of politics, collective agency, and even life itself. Without some form of *hope* or a sense that the sufferings and strivings that constitute African American life have import and value, West sees no opening for struggle, resilience, and reverence for the dignity of the oppressed. Without these, it becomes impossible to keep the *possibility* of "hard-won progress" in particular domains alive.[45] A courageous confrontation with the abyss of suffering, in other words, may lead some to a judgment that misery and despair are inevitable and treat this fact as a condemnation of the world or life itself.

Against this temptation, those like Nietzsche and West seek orientations to the world that are "life-affirming." Since some degree of suffering is inevitable, as a fact of the human condition and as part of any struggle to improve it, this practice of philosophy champions modes of being that create redemptive meaning within and through suffering. It is incumbent upon us not to flee from the pain and disappointment germane to human life but to *transfigure* it as best we can.

For Nietzsche, such transfiguration would not, for example, affirm the excellences, ideals, or values of creative geniuses who create *despite suffering* but also affirm *even* the suffering and resistance that *occasioned* or *constituted* such creativity.[46] While West shares with Nietzsche an interest in genius cultivators of artistry and creativity that transfigure the value of suffering rather than deepening it, his distillation of nihilism's threat is ultimately sparer and more egalitarian.[47] West's concern to convert people away from nihilism is not primarily about cultural vitality as a way of life or radical aristocratic perfectionism. It is, fundamentally, about refusing to allow despair the last word over whether the lives of oppressed peoples are worth living, whether their traditions and exemplary instances of fortitude and moral courage are worth celebrating and sustaining, and whether it is worthwhile to struggle and strive in pursuit of justice and good.[48]

In confronting these questions of hope, pessimism, and nihilism in *Race Matters* and the brilliant essay, "Black Strivings in a Twilight Civilization" (1996), it is apt that West invokes W. E. B. Du Bois's *Souls of Black Folk* (1903) since Du Bois memorably faces this problem through reflections on the inheritance of tradition and the death of his son.[49] For Schopenhauer, no person in full grasp of the depth of human suffering would rationally choose to reproduce, given the sentence to which they would condemn their offspring. In *Souls'* "Of the Passing of the First Born," Du Bois invests this abstraction with the concrete horror of the death of his own child, Burghardt, as well as the terror that any black child he would bring into this world would come of age in a racist society organized to cruelly crush her aspirations, degrade her self-respect, and steal her life, over the arbitrary myth of "race."[50]

Riding home from his infant son's funeral, Du Bois narrates his drift into a pessimism worthy of Schopenhauer. As he recalls his state of mind: "there sat an awful gladness in my heart. . . . No bitter meanness now shall sicken his baby heart till it die a living death, no taunt shall madden his happy boyhood. Fool that I was to think or wish that this little soul should grow choked and deformed within the Veil! . . . Better far this nameless void that stops my life than a sea of sorrow for you."[51] The language and imagery of the "nameless void" are crucial here. In deploying a rendering of death as nothingness so absolute that it negates even the venture of anticipatory description, Du Bois underscores the terrible truth of life on the underside of the "Negro problem" by refusing to seek refuge in the consolation and comfort of blissful heaven.

In *Darkwater* (1920), Du Bois returns to this Schopenhauerian challenge, inflected by racial oppression in the United States. There he conveys that "the mothers and fathers and the men and women of my race must often pause and ask . . . Ought children be born to us? Have we any right to make human souls face what we face today?"[52] Du Bois answers in the affirmative, but it is an answer with great consequence because, as he writes, it is "in the treatment of the child [that] the world foreshadows its own future and faith." It is the child, he writes, that represents "that vast immortality and the wide sweep of infinite possibility" that underwrites hope in justice and the good.[53]

Here, Du Bois's gestures are resonant with Hannah Arendt's treatment of "the fact of natality," which she treats as the ontological root of human action. Arendt contrasts this emphasis on contingency, possibility, and a shared world beyond any individual life with the necessity, regularity, and fatality of "natural processes."[54] The distinctive character of human being-in-the-world is precisely the power to bring forth something *new*, either in initiative-taking with others or by revealing our individuality through communicative action in public. Building upon Saint Augustine's concept of *initium* and romanticism's distillation of the sources of originality and genius, Arendt treats "the fact of natality" as the ontological ground of this capacity. Natality, "the birth of new men and the new beginning, the action they are capable of by virtue of being born," continuously introduces not only the possibility of "interrupting" forms of life as they presently exist, but also the possibility of trying to sustain them through storytelling and solidarity as well.[55]

Given that natality presupposes that we are born into a world alongside others that precede us and that we live alongside others who will, in all likelihood, survive us, natality is perhaps best understood as a way of speaking intelligibly about a kind of human freedom. This is the freedom to cooperatively and collaboratively make judgments about what forms of life we want to disavow or preserve—the latter being the shared ground of Arendt and Du Bois's invocations of "immortality."[56] This, Arendt sweepingly proclaims, is "the miracle that saves the world, the realm of human affairs, from its normal, 'natural' ruin." It is natality that "can bestow upon human affairs faith and hope" because it allows for the unmaking of ignoble worlds, the forging of new bonds of solidarity in pursuit of the good, and the discovery of new forms of meaning by which to make sense of our fate together—none of which can be fully anticipated or determinate.[57] This indeterminate hope, as West's former teacher and fellow John Dewey-inspired pragmatist, Richard Rorty, puts the point, involves "the ability to believe that the future will be unspecifiably different from, and unspecifiably freer than, the past."[58]

For Du Bois, the most pressing hope was that the human capacity to create something new would find realization in the transfiguration or revaluation of the ignoble inheritance of chattel slavery and Jim Crow. In grasping the "shameful" evil of white racial domination, and the "glory" and "lofty ideal" embodied in the intergenerational struggles against it, he argues that we may furnish our children's children with a grand "life motive"—"a power and impulse toward good," put to service in the "great battle of human right against poverty, disease, and color prejudice."[59]

Afropessimism and the Revolt Against Hope

Such ideas—that the capacity to initiate or found something new through solidaristic action, that the transfiguration of black suffering is possible, that a naturalistic theodicy encompassing racial justice might sustain practical faith or even that nihilism rather than hope should be kept at bay—have all been increasingly subjected to severe skepticism in our contemporary era, a century after *Darkwater.* These arguments, often advanced under the name "Afropessimism," insist that these possibilities are always already foreclosed given the foundations of the modern world in racist ontology and domination.[60]

On the Afropessimist account, the fact that "blackness" accrued its meaning in the crucible of slavery and the slave trade as a *negation* of the human (and its various constitutive determinants, e.g., the rational, beautiful, civilized, etc.) means that blackness and negation, or blackness and abjection are inextricably linked and compulsively enforced. Since blackness and black subjects are themselves creations of antiblack violence, and "blackness" lacks any prior positive ontological content that could be reclaimed or used to resist abjection's totalizing erasure, Afropessimists insist that attempts at the "*affirmation* of blackness prove to be impossible without simultaneously affirming the violence that structures black subjectivity itself."[61] As Calvin Warren expounds, "the very structure of meaning in the modern world—signifier, signified, signification, and sign—depends on anti-black violence for its constitution."[62] On this argument, the crisis of "meaninglessness" that West identifies just *is* the self-apprehended, lived experience of blackness' enduring function as the constitutive other of the most fundamental ontological and metaphysical categories of modernity—including, especially, "the human," which Afropessimists contend is fundamentally inapplicable to black "non-being." Warren, in particular, indicts West for not grasping "black nihilism" as a wise response to the terrible truth of our inheritance.

Black nihilism is intimately entangled with a sense of history, imbued with what Jürgen Habermas describes as the "time-consciousness" of modernity.[63] For Habermas, modernity's unique relationship with time lies in its "open, expectant stance to the future," which keeps "perpetually open the promise of a future different from the past."[64] However, this stance toward the future can engender feelings of pressure, urgency, and anxiety that invite ideological accounts of the future: neoliberal theories of modernization, liberal notions of progress, dogmatic Marxian philosophies of history, or exceptionalist myths of ethnoracial ascendancy. Such ideologies claim to grasp the fundamental patterns that connect past, present, and future in often reconciliatory and optimistic ways. Even though these ideological accounts are ultimately mythic, when the imagined futures conjured by such paradigms congeal into settled expectations, habits, and affective states, a collapse in their plausibility and authority can nevertheless occasion despair and nihilism. Their collapse can unleash other crises in self-understanding, cultural interpretation, and political judgment.[65]

In the face of enduring oppression and defeated political movements, the modern ("time-conscious") nihilist may argue the past is too catastrophic to be redeemed, the present an enduring catastrophe too horrific to bear, and the future already foreclosed as anything other than the repetition of this traumatic present-past. Such nihilism gains currency in the wake of ideological collapse, weakening the attachment to life, tearing at social and political solidarities, and breeding cynicism. When tied to, or ostensibly justified by, appeal to a particular critical historical narrative, despair can seem like the only reasonable assessment of the historical "facts" at hand *and* the only rational stance toward the future.

The Afropessimist narration of history operates in this register. Their key problem is to somehow combine a non-foundationalist, semiotically-oriented, and historically contingent conception of blackness and antiblack racism *with* an argument that black subordination and domination are permanent. This is their most unique theoretical intervention and distinguishes them both from earlier deconstructionists who did not share their political and ontological despair or black nationalists who, while accepting much about the intractability of white racism, would refuse their deconstruction of blackness and skepticism concerning the life-affirming resources of black civil society and cultural vitality.

The juxtaposition *appears* contradictory at first glance, insofar as it tries to reconcile malleability and contingency in racial signification, with a social theory that posits the intractable, totalizing permanence of antiblack racism and the permanent association of blackness with abjection. Afropessimists, however, attempt to flesh out this contention and persuade their readers of their arguments through the mobilization of what I think can rightly be called *ironic* narratives of African American history.

Tropes and generic conventions associated with irony are critical to forging a narrative structure in historical discourse that conveys, as its overarching meaning, the *negation* of progress. As Joshua Dienstag writes, ironic conceptions of history insist that what "appears, on the surface, to be getting better" is, in fact, "getting worse (or, on the whole, no better)."[66] In Afro-American historiography, this usually means patterns of historical narration that show "the more things change, the more they say the same," and demonstrates deep anxiety about the asymmetries between "meaning" and language or linguistically mediated representation that give rise to the practice of irony.

Ironic history offers, against romantic optimism, a *qualified fatalism* skeptical that authentic emancipation, rationality, unity, consensus, etc., can be realized. Its vast *hermeneutics of suspicion* seeks to unmask ostensible moments of freedom as enduring domination or captivity, while finding fissures and subordination in every profession of unity or solidarity. Ironic narratives also subject claims about the efficacy of morality or good in the world to *unmasking*, claiming to reveal them as egoism and self-interest, duplicity and self-deception, or the unintended reconstitution of oppression. Lastly, ironist history can start to turn its powers of negation upon its own categories and self-conception, producing *radical doubts* about the vocabulary and practical identities thought to ground historical narration and social inquiry.[67]

Afropessimism's relentlessly "ironic" character is revealed within a narrative structure that eschews the chronological ordering of conventional historical discourse. Constantly juxtaposing and rearranging judgments about the past, present, and future, the accumulated weight of the story dramatizes the ironic phenomenon of unwavering continuity (antiblack domination) underneath apparent contingency (the changing significations of blackness). Once "unmasked" by ironist critique, this dynamic spills over, ever backward into the past. Appropriating (and ontologizing) more historically contextualized readings of nineteenth-century history by scholars like Hortense Spillers and Saidiya Hartman, Afropessimists regularly refer to emancipation as a "non-event" and all modern time as the time of slavery.[68] "Formally," they argue that the post-emancipation "Black subject was no longer a slave, but the same formative relation of structural violence that maintained slavery remained—hence preserving the equation that Black equals socially dead" into the present.[69]

For example, the idea that the civil rights movement represents "progress" is disingenuous on their account. The "reformist ideologies" of the movement and "their disastrous integration with bureaucratic machinery" fall into the impossible trap of trying to "affirm Blackness itself without at the same time affirming anti-Black violence."[70] Calvin Warren, for example, claims to unmask Martin Luther King's appeals to the redemptive power of the spectacle of voluntary and undeserved suffering in civil rights protest, as the cruelest ruse in American life: blood sacrifices for a multiracial democracy never to come.[71] Performances of antiblack violence, instead, serve to produce, regenerate, and stabilize the boundaries of society (by making the "socially dead," society's other) and the "psychic health" and coherent identity of non-Blacks (again, as their constitutive outside).[72]

The stability thesis is crucial. Unlike, for example, the tradition within Marxist social theory that posits that capitalism will collapse under contradictions and crises generated from its intrinsic dynamics, Afropessimists treat the antiblack world order they describe as totalizing, resilient, and so intractable as to be permanent and determinant.[73] Warren is, again, illustrative: "every emancipatory strategy that attempted to rescue blackness from antiblackness inevitably reconstituted and reconfigured the antiblackness it tried to eliminate." The persistent repetition of this pattern authorizes, for him, a judgment that, *even in the future and no matter the intentions behind our political strivings*, "anti-blackness will escape every emancipatory attempt to capture it."[74]

Therefore, in the Afropessimist formulation, an appeal to ironic history authorizes an opposition to practical faith in emancipatory political action, realistic utopias based on political and ethical ideals, and devotion to the idea of progress. In their place, Afropessimists argue for "a philosophy of personal conduct" and not "a scheme of ideal government structure or principles of justice."[75] For Warren, the appropriate stance toward politics is *apostasy*. Warren argues that the insistent proclamation of racial progress enables and authorizes a broader commitment to "political hope" that is not only illusory but ironically compels blacks to endure pointless suffering aimed at civic redemption through self-destructive libidinal attachments to "cruel optimism." Politics corrupts the very capacity for authentic hope via its attachment to a realm that can only produce antiblack domination.[76] Therefore, Warren's aim is not to "change political structures or offer a political program"—indeed, such investments would be worse than "pointless"—but instead achieve a kind of spiritual retrieval through turning inward. He calls for the recapture of hope from the grips of "the Political" and instead enacted within a "*spiritual* practice of denouncing metaphysical violence, black suffering, and the idol of anti-blackness" [emphasis added], as well as simply endure.[77]

Warren is undoubtedly correct to draw attention to the enduring persistence of antiblack racial ideology and various mutations of racial domination. A healthy suspicion toward the sweeping emancipatory descriptions of black politics are warranted, especially in light of criticisms concerning the "secondary marginalization" of different black subgroups (e.g., women, the poor, queer folk, etc.) from black radical traditions in the social sciences, philosophy, and history.[78] It is also essential to criticize the ways that romantic narratives can minimize the existential and ethical magnitude of suffering, either by treating past evils as the central evaluative standard by which to judge the present, or insulating their guiding ideals from critique by invoking a perpetually receding "not-yet" as the appropriate horizon of judgment. We should be especially skeptical of ideological uses of "sacrifice" that conscript the unredeemed sufferings of the past and present into romantic stories about social progress. Finally, Warren is to be applauded for insisting that what appears, in some interpretations, as black "pathology," actually contains philosophical content worth explicating as ethics, politics, and existential reflection.[79]

Despite these worthwhile aims, however, Warren's project reveals much that is politically retrograde, ethically objectionable, and epistemically incoherent in Afropessimist thought. Thankfully, West's longstanding interest in the problems of nihilism and hope, in *Race Matters* and elsewhere, remain especially powerful to draw upon for sketching a response, particularly concerning the problem of historical consciousness and the lurking metaphysics in Afropessimist thought.

Tragedy, History, Metaphysics

Part of what my emphasis on narrative modes and tropology in historical discourse means to unmask is a conceit that the relationship between historical reflection, contemporary judgment, and imagined future flows naturally and inevitably in that order. In reality, these hang together far more messily in ways to which the pragmatist tradition has been uniquely attuned. Social and political philosophy, Rorty rightly argues, has always relied upon and is often "parasitic on" historical narratives which purport to tether together a relevant past, an account of the present, and hopes or fears about the future.[80] Not only do what appear to be debates about our present or what futures remain possible turn on how we judge the past, but the happenings of our present often occasion us to see our traditions and pasts anew. Warren's remarks on the civil rights movement are, to put the point polemically, far more about Michael Brown than Martin Luther King.

What renders this problem challenging is not simply our persistent evasion of this reality but also that the contentions, claims, and concepts necessary to render political and normative arguments manifest are often left relatively *implicit* in historical discourse. More often, as the iconoclastic Hayden White has argued, they are most discernible at the level of *narrative form*. One significance of West's early insistence on taking the idea of "tragedy" and the "tragic" so seriously, therefore, is that it might name and clarify a particular *genre* of historical narration and "subversive memory." Might tragedy allow us to take full stock of the catastrophe of racial domination while avoiding both the cheap consolations of romantic optimism and the nihilistic cul-de-sac of Afropessimist philosophy? Where might we find such resources in the black tradition?

For West, the philosopher Josiah Royce is among the best at illuminating the connection between tragedy and catastrophe. "The worst tragedy of the world," Royce writes, "is the tragedy of brute chance to which everything spiritual seems to be subject amongst us—the tragedy of the diabolical irrationality of so many among the foes of whatever is significant." "These things do not make life merely painful to us," he continues, "they make it hideously petty."[81] On the other hand, West charges the black tradition's greatest intellectual, Du Bois, with being so beset by Victorian rationalism and elitism that he inevitably "falters in the face of death" and fails to grasp the "tragic plight and absurd predicament of Africans here and abroad."[82]

Yet, we might think with West against West and approach Du Bois's tragic sensibility with more charity. In "Black Strivings," West focuses primarily on Du Bois's mourning of his son and horror for the fate of the lynching victim Sam Hose. I have already expounded on the deeply pessimistic questions Du Bois entertains there, but I want to note that Du Bois's most melancholic and fully tragic laments lie not in stories of innocence destroyed (the theme of melodrama), but in his recollection of how heroic strivings on behalf of fairness and flourishing are defeated by cruelty and circumstance. Far from an unbridled "Victorian" faith in the powers of elite uplift and rational education, *Souls*' presentations of the race's "progress" are, at pointed interludes, confronted with the vast human wreckage that cannot be conscripted neatly into such paeans. Indeed, at times, Du Bois's mourning and trepidation for the future are so deep that they call into question the very category of progress and confront whether life is worth living.

"How shall we man measure Progress," Du Bois proclaims, lamenting the defeated strivings of his former student, "there where dark-faced Josie lies?" Among the "lowly," who nevertheless are "human and real," Du Bois recognizes their "life and love and strife and failure" and dwells in fear at not knowing whether their strivings portend "the twilight of nightfall or the flush of some faint-dawning day?"[83] Even more incisive is his eulogy for his mentor, Alexander Crummell, whose attempts at combating race prejudice and uplifting blacks in Africa and America would fall far short of his grand hopes. Crummell, Du Bois writes, "vainly sought his place in the world, ever haunted by the shadow of a death that is more than death,—the passing of a soul that has missed its duty."[84] In Du Bois's account, Crummell faces tests and temptations of hate, despair, and doubt, asking the life-negating question: "What, in God's name, am I on earth for?" The aspiration of the eulogy, a lament for a man who failed to achieve his strivings or aims, is to redeem his struggles nonetheless. As Du Bois writes: "He did his work,—he did it nobly and well; and yet I sorrow that here he worked alone, with so little human sympathy. His name to–day, in this broad land, means little, and comes to fifty million ears laden with no incense of memory or emulation. And herein lies the tragedy of the age: not that men are poor,—all men know something of poverty; not that men are wicked,—who is good? not that men are ignorant,—what is Truth? Nay, but that men know so little of men."[85]

Such passages anticipate Benjamin's and Hannah Arendt's critique of progress narratives. Du Bois worries that certain forms of progressive history will leave us with no vantage point to think from the standpoint of those actors or events that do not quite "fit" the storyline or whose appearance is in a subordinate role as the vanquished, the defeated, the failed. These persons are the "wreckage" of history, its "debris" in the storm of progress. When we let an ideal of historical progress sit in judgment over all of the happenings of history, the only criteria of significance, and the ultimate evaluative criteria of meaning, is an event or person's instrumental contribution to this direction. In Arendt's lectures on Kant's political philosophy, she puts this critique even more bluntly: "It is against human dignity to believe in progress."[86]

To combat this perspective of progress is the import of one of Arendt's favorite quotes, from Cato the Elder: "The victorious cause pleased the gods, but the defeated one pleases Cato." The "gods"—those who try (and fail) to survey the historical record from the Archimedean point of universal progress—are only interested in "victory." Yet in our capacity for human freedom, we can choose to honor the dignity of the defeated—that they shared, as human beings, the same capacity for action and beginning as the "victors"—and build anew upon the inspiration of their memory. We can do so, moreover, without the guarantee of "success."

My understanding of West's ideal of "keeping faith" is a part of this tradition. Keeping faith depends upon our ability to generate narratives capable of appreciating both the evil that provokes ironic retreat *and* the beauty or justice that the romantic optimist pretends is permanently in a state of becoming. In our re-description of the past, and invocations of historical exemplars, it requires that we tell stories that do not disparage nonsovereign, fragile, and finite strivings toward justice, and while keeping track of their failure, nevertheless does not use that failure to justify abstention from action.

So for West, like the Afropessimist, history is indeed catastrophic. Indeed, he explicitly invokes Benjamin's melancholy contention that, for the oppressed, the state of emergency is the norm, not the exception.[87] He argues that the "gravitas of the catastrophic" obligates us, in a spirit of mourning, to make "radical disappointment and profound disenchantment our constant companions" and be aware that we have an overwhelming chance of failure in our attempts to realize any utopian aspirations. However, we must persist "with a level of integrity and a quest for moral magnanimity" in the struggle for democratic justice. What allows us to keep faith with this demand is, in part, "a subversive memory in the folks that survived, and the texts that were written, and the stories that were passed on, and the narratives that were bequeathed to us." West is worth quoting at length on this point:

> Here I would fall back on Adorno when he says that any exhaustion has leftovers even in defeat. Even the memory of those lost doesn't fit within commemorations, because deep remembering is different than conventional commemoration. And so our task is to never lose sight of the leftovers, or what the great Arthur Miller would call "the misfits," the people who don't fit in, the experiences, and the doings and sufferings of fellow human beings who can't find a place in a moment of exhaustion, even though the exhaustion never goes all the way down. . . . You start with the leftovers, you start with the defeated, you start with the subjugated, and you start with the ways in which, even in the moment of exhaustion, they are not subsumed under the vocabulary of the exhausted.[88]

West's approach here calls for the cultivation and protection of a specific mode of historical consciousness, and resonates with the approach to history that Seyla Benhabib has characterized, building on Arendt and Benjamin, as "fragmentary historiography."[89]

The thinker who uses this fragmentary historiography breaks "the chain of narrative continuity . . . [inherent in] chronology as the natural structure of narrative, to stress fragmentariness, historical dead ends, failures, and ruptures."[90] The aim is one consonant with recognizing the dignity of past actors and the ideals and principles they championed, even though they will not benefit from it. Dignity could be said to enter into historical judgment through the hope "to do justice to the memory of the dead by telling the story of history in terms of their failed hopes and efforts."[91] More fundamentally, the incorporation of a duty to show reverence to dignity (thinking from the standpoint of others) into historical judgment, is above all, a rejection of those overarching approaches to history that refuse to place the *value* of "defeated causes" and their proponents at the center of historical judgment, or fails to take seriously the hermeneutic challenge of seeking out the "thought fragments" that might speak powerfully to a present changed by intervening developments.[92]

Tragedy, given its focus on human agency, even amid epistemological limitations, unintended consequences, and the fleeting opportunity structure for particular actions, can bear more easily accounts of history that emphasize the *interpenetration* and *semi-autonomous logics* of various political practices (e.g., antiblack racism, capitalism, sexism, and colonialism) rather than inflating one axis to a comprehensive, seamless totality and flattening out all human desire and action along its arc. Such a stance *trains* our judgment to see the seams for movement that emerge through the interpenetration of power systems and their emergent properties that no one can predict in total.

Contingency is crucial. The hopes embodied in struggles are only *possible* and not *guaranteed*—meaning that natality and tragedy go together in tandem. Thus, the recognition of the interrelation helps steel us against both the fetishism for spectacular eruptions that dominate romantic narrations and the paralyzing disappointment that governs ironic thought. Narrating the complex, long-term web of actions that coagulate into the statement of important ideals or, even, the achievement of partial victories helps orient political struggles toward the kinds of dispositions needed for what Du Bois, in one of his more prescient, if less lyrical moments, called "the long siege"—an appropriate description for emancipatory struggle without guarantees if there ever was one.[93]

This subversive, tragic imagination also helps inoculate us against a particular form of nihilism, one born from the *lack of epistemic humility* at the heart of the historical imagination promoted by Afropessimism. The insistence on, and demonstrated recovery of, contingency, unpredictability, and natality give reason to be critical of Afropessimism's unwarranted faith in the (metaphysical) ability to predict a *permanent future* of antiblack abjection. This epistemic arrogance is "sustained," as Theodor Adorno wrote of such doctrines, "by the false inference that because there has been no progress up until now, there will never be any."[94] While Warren excoriates "optimists" for shielding themselves from critique by appealing to an unknown and unknowable future, his futural gestures toward the "impossibility" of alternative political arrangements are even more insulated in a posture devoid of epistemic humility.

This is especially bewildering given that, for Warren, black abjection is not ordained by God, written into cosmology or biology, forged in a messianic transformation, or even the *necessary* outcome of human history. The antiblack order, insofar as one can discern from his account, is the artifact of a complex, interdependent web of human decisions, ideas, practices, desires, and other myriad strivings and sayings of human beings that fused to create the African slave trade, imperialism, and antiblack racial ideology. It is unclear how, without escaping these human dynamics into the realm of metaphysical speculation, the Afropessimist can presume, a priori, to predict the whole range of possible outcomes of interpenetrating complex systems of scientific research global governance, economic markets, cultural production, etc. It is impossible to avoid the sense in which the most extreme blend of ironic history and pessimistic prophecy is extraordinarily flattering to its proselytizers' supposed oracular, spiritual, and cognitive gifts.

Warren treats (black) suffering as the central evil of existence, and seeing no way to eliminate antiblackness in its totality or to impose a sovereign will upon the antiblack world, suggests, like Schopenhauer's ascetic, *withdrawal.* He counsels us to turn the will away from the world itself, and instead look inward, toward the worldly hopes, strivings, and desires that intensify our suffering instead. Such advice not only unjustly deepens our responsibility for our own suffering, as Nietzsche warned, but reflects, like Schopenhauer, the view that it would be best if the world did not exist.

Here, West's early attempts to develop a "tragic" pragmatism allows for a persuasive response, insofar as its overlap with Rorty and Ludwig Wittgenstein aims for a therapeutic approach to some philosophical problems. From this vantage, the arguments that Warren musters—from his sense of the irrelevancy of political organization to his broad dismissal of the enlargement of human flourishing occasioned by black political struggles to his paralysis in the face of the unintended consequences of political action—suggest a picture that lies behind his apostasy from political hope. This picture, which ennobles sovereign agency, the philosophy of the will, and an apolitical epistemology, may simply—like the view from nowhere or the fantasy of total consensus—be a picture that holds the pessimist captive. It may lead him to bludgeon the hard-won victories of the world as it is, with the image of a world that belongs more to God than the kind of beings we are. Insofar as Warren tells us that the ethical standard that authorizes his pessimism is the demand that recognition and flourishing, love and meaning, be placed "beyond extant structures of violence and destruction," and constructed upon foundations of self and society that are not "subject to shift, transform[ation], and decay," this is a standard of purity that is beyond any possible world, for blacks or anyone else.[95] This lurking ideal of purity and perfection authorizes the judgment of everything in history as profane and ironic and is, in the last instance, the most sweeping source of nihilism in Warren's account.

If, as West argues, nihilism demands a "politics of conversion," one essential and under-emphasized element of it must be about uprooting *these* fears, of ourselves and the world, that are reflected in such attachments to permanence and purity. Such a politics of conversion must aim, at bottom, to cultivate an ethos of care for the plurality, agency, and natality that makes life worth living, and the world worth our concern precisely because of our tragic fragility and finitude.[96] It does so, not simply through *critique* but through *critique and praxis*.[97] For West, even historical "evidence is dynamic, it is not static. It can be changed based on what we do."[98] The defense of political hope this mode of historical imagination engenders, *contra* Warren, is not rooted in optimism but the epistemic humility of tragedy. As West writes, "the decline and decay in American life *appears*, at the moment, to be irreversible; yet it may not be. This slight possibility—the historic chance that a window of opportunity can be opened by our prophetic thought and action—is, in part, what keeping faith is all about."[99] We do not lack for voices of those who claim to see nothing but darkness, in the past and on the horizon, but as West argues, "sometimes *you* have to create the light." The light—a metaphor that opens Arendt's *Men in Dark Times*—"is concretized, exemplified in your courageous thinking and courageous action," and the exemplarity that such thought and action might engender in the subversive memories that follow. The exhaustion of emancipatory ideals and struggles that would make nihilism victorious, and perhaps even true, can become "ubiquitous only when you reach the point in which everybody chooses to be cowardly, everybody chooses to be complacent, everybody chooses to be conformist."[100] The subversive memory of a past where such exhaustion did not come to pass stands as a perpetual rejoinder to this threat, making our historical imaginings and the genre of their articulation pressing questions of vice and virtue, hope and despair.

Notes

Epigraph: Friedrich Wilhelm Nietzsche, *Writings from the Late Notebooks*, trans. Kate Sturge, ed. Rüdiger Bittner (New York: Cambridge University Press, 2003), 83 (2:127).

1. Arthur Schopenhauer, "Additional Remarks on the Doctrine of the Suffering of the World," in *Philosophical Writings* (New York: Continuum, 1994), 35. While I focus on human life here, Schopenhauer also emphasizes the suffering of animals as well.

2. Schopenhauer, "Remarks," 35–36.

3. Friedrich Wilhelm Nietzsche, *On the Genealogy of Morality*, trans. Carol Diethe, ed. Keith Ansell-Pearson (Cambridge: Cambridge University Press, 2007), 44, 120.

4. Brian Leiter, "The Truth Is Terrible," *Journal of Nietzsche Studies* 49, no. 2 (2018).

5. Tamsin Shaw, "The 'Last Man' Problem: Nietzsche and Weber on Political Attitudes to Suffering," in *Nietzsche as Political Philosopher*, ed. Barry Stocker and Manuel Knoll (Boston: De Gruyter, 2014), 345–80.

6. Cornel West, "The Ignoble Paradox of Modernity," in *The Cornel West Reader* (New York: Basic Civitas, 1999), 51–54.

7. Bernard Reginster, *The Affirmation of Life: Nietzsche on Overcoming Nihilism* (Cambridge, MA: Harvard University Press, 2006), 28.

8. Friedrich Nietzsche, *The Will to Power*, trans. Walter Arnold Kaufmann and R. J. Hollingdale (New York: Random House, 1967), 318. [sec. 585 (Spring–Fall 1887; rev. Spring–Fall 1888)].

9. Reginster, *Affirmation*, 8. See Nietzsche, *Will to Power*, 9.

10. See, for example, Stephen Steinberg, *Turning Back: The Retreat from Racial Justice in American Thought and Policy* (Boston: Beacon Press, 1995), 130. Also, Michael Eric Dyson, "'We Were Never What We Used to Be': Black Youth, Pop Culture, and the Politics of Nostalgia," in *The Michael Eric Dyson Reader* (New York: Basic Civitas, 2004), 418–40.

11. See, for example, his indispensable social theoretic contributions in Cornel West, "Race and Social Theory," *Cornel West Reader*, 251–68; Cornel West, "The Paradox of the Afro-American Rebellion," *Social Text*, no. 9/10 (1984): 44–58; Cornel West, *Prophesy Deliverance!: An Afro-American Revolutionary Christianity* (Louisville, KY: Westminster John Knox Press, 2002), chap. 7.

12. For important critique of these failures in moral philosophy and social theory, see Bernard R. Boxill, *Blacks and Social Justice*, rev. ed. (Lanham, Md.: Rowman & Littlefield, 1992), 226–64. On why "troubling" cultural patterns would not preempt an ethical indictment of the basic structure of American society with regard to ghetto poverty, see Tommie Shelby, *Dark Ghettos: Injustice, Dissent, and Reform* (Cambridge, MA: Belknap Press of Harvard University Press, 2016).

13. Robert D. Putnam, "Bowling Alone: America's Declining Social Capital," *Journal of Democracy* 6, no. 1 (1995).

14. For a skeptical account of the use of nihilism that argues it is akin to "witchcraft," a term of abuse that tells us more about the political and cultural anxieties of the authors who deploy it, the classes they represent, and the disruptive forms of life caricatured by particular deployments than any profound social philosophical insight, see Meerten B. ter Borg, "The Problem of Nihilism: A Sociological Approach," *Sociology of Religion* 49, no. 1 (1988): 1–16, https://doi.org/10.2307/3711099, https://doi.org/10.2307/3711099.

15. James Weldon Johnson, *Black Manhattan* (New York: Knopf, 1930), 128.

16. Mary Church Terrell, *A Colored Woman in a White World* (Washington, DC: Ransdell, 1940), 395–96.

17. James Forman, *The Making of Black Revolutionaries* (Seattle: University of Washington Press, 1997), 224.

18. Kenneth B. Clark, "The Racial Prisons of America's Ghettos [June 1, 1970]," in *Unpublished Papers of Kenneth B. Clark* (Alexandria, VA: Alexander Street Press, 2004).

19. Malcolm X, "Malcolm X at UC Berkeley (October 11, 1963)," *Malcolm X: Collected Speeches, Debates and Interviews (1960–1965)*, ed. Sandeep S. Atwal, Online University of the Left, http://ouleft.org/wp-content/uploads/malcolm-collected.pdf. 164–65.

20. A persuasive charge that the contemporary opioid epidemic reflects a kind of nihilism, for example, is obligated to respond thoughtfully to defenses of narcotic use like Carl L. Hart, *Drug Use for Grown-Ups: Chasing Liberty in the Land of Fear* (New York: Penguin, 2021).

21. See, for example, Adolph L. Reed, "Tokens of the White Left," in *Class Notes: Posing as Politics and Other Thoughts on the American Scene* (New York: New Press, 2000), 71–76.

22. Mark David Wood, *Cornel West and the Politics of Prophetic Pragmatism* (Urbana: University of Illinois Press, 2000), 106–9.

23. This has been the subject of numerous recent books, including David Harvey, *A Brief History of Neoliberalism* (Oxford: Oxford University Press, 2005); Quinn Slobodian, *Globalists: The End of Empire and the Birth of Neoliberalism* (Cambridge, MA: Harvard University Press, 2018); Lester K. Spence, *Knocking the Hustle: Against the Neoliberal Turn in Black Politics* (Brooklyn, NY: Punctum, 2015); Wendy Brown, *Undoing the Demos: Neoliberalism's Stealth Revolution*, 1st ed. (Cambridge, MA: MIT Press, 2015); Angus Burgin, *The Great Persuasion: Reinventing Free Markets Since the Depression* (Cambridge, MA: Harvard University Press, 2012).

24. Nietzsche, *Will to Power*, sec. 2, 9.

25. *Will to Power*, sec. 12A, 12

26. West, *Prophesy Deliverance!*, 131.

27. West, "Paradox."

28. Friedrich Nietzsche, "The Case of Wagner: A Musician's Problem," in *The Anti Christ, Ecce Homo, Twilight of the Idols, and Other Writings*, ed. Aaron Ridley (New York: Cambridge University Press, 2005), 231–62.

29. Murray Forman, *The 'Hood Comes First: Race, Space, and Place in Rap and Hip-Hop* (Middletown, CT: Wesleyan University Press, 2002).

30. William J. Wilson, *The Declining Significance of Race: Blacks and Changing American Institutions*, 3rd. ed. (Chicago: University of Chicago Press, 2012).

31. Cornel West, *Keeping Faith: Philosophy and Race in America* (New York: Routledge, 1993), 282.

32. West, *Keeping Faith.*

33. Alexia Cooper and Erica L Smith, "Homicide Trends in the United States, 1980–2008," 1249573246 (Washington, DC: BiblioGov, November 2011).

34. Cornel West, "On Afro-American Music: From Bebop to Rap," in *Cornel West Reader*, 483.

35. Sylvia Ann Hewlett and Cornel West, *The War Against Parents: What We Can Do for America's Beleaguered Moms and Dads* (Boston: Houghton Mifflin, 1998).

36. In contrast to Caine, O-Dog's gangsterism is near-ontological. He is introduced in the film through Caine's narration as "America's nightmare: young, black, and didn't give a fuck." Little explication of his background or interior life is given beyond this (in)famous statement.

37. Crucially, the assault that Caine commits is against a man whose female cousin claims (likely correctly) that Caine is the biological father of her child. When the man confronts Caine to demand that he acknowledge and accept conventional duties of fatherhood, he is mercilessly beaten by Caine and his friends, underscoring, I think, for the Hughes brothers a fundamental and lamentable break in patterns of love and mutual concern. On the ethical questions raised by paternity and paternal support in the ghetto, see Shelby, *Dark Ghettos*, chap. 3.

38. Albert Camus, *The Myth of Sisyphus, and Other Essays*, 1st American ed. (New York: Knopf, 1955), 3.

39. Oppressed peoples, of course, resist their subjection in all manner of ways which are not appropriately described as collective or as aiming at an overthrow of the existing social order. For the classic treatment of this range of human action, see James C. Scott, *Domination and the Arts of Resistance: Hidden Transcripts* (New Haven, CT: Yale University Press,

1990). Also, see the penetrating normative treatment of "impure dissent" in Shelby, *Dark Ghettos*, 252–74.

40. Nietzsche, *Will to Power*, 10, 17 [sec. 5 and sec. 22].

41. *Will to Power*, 55 [sec. 90].

42. *Will to Power*, 55 [sec. 90].

43. West, "Introduction: To Be Human, Modern and American," xv.

44. Walter Benjamin, *Illuminations: Essays and Reflections*, trans. Harry Zohn, ed. Hannah Arendt (Boston: Mariner, 2019), 201.

45. Cornel West, *Democracy Matters: Winning the Fight Against Imperialism* (New York: Penguin Press, 2004), 218.

46. Reginster, *Affirmation*.

47. See, for example, the discussion of the blues in West, *Democracy Matters*, pp. 19–21.

48. Cornel West, "Brother Martin was a Blues Man," *Boston Review* (2018). http://bostonreview.net/race-podcast/cornel-west-brother-martin-was-blues-man; Tommie Shelby and Cornel West, "Fear and Courage," *Transition*, no. 123 (2017).

49. West, "Black Strivings in a Twilight Civilization," 87–118.

50. There are few descriptions of the degradations of childhood in a racist society more succinctly powerful than the one that begins Martin Luther King Jr.'s 1963 "Letter from Birmingham Jail" in King, *Why We Can't Wait*, 1964, The King Legacy (Boston: Beacon, 2010), 85–110.

51. W. E. B. Du Bois, *The Souls of Black Folk; Essays and Sketches* (Chicago: A. C. McClurg & Co., 1903), 213.

52. W. E. B. Du Bois, *Darkwater: Voices from Within the Veil* (New York: Harcourt, Brace and Howe, 1920), 202.

53. Du Bois, *Darkwater.*

54. Hannah Arendt, *The Human Condition*, 1958, 2nd ed. (Chicago: University of Chicago Press, 1998), 246.

55. Arendt, *Human Condition*, 176–177.

56. Nikolas Kompridis, *Critique and Disclosure: Critical Theory Between Past and Future* (Cambridge, MA: MIT Press, 2006), 14–15, 195–97.

57. Arendt, *Human Condition*, 246–47.

58. Richard Rorty, *Philosophy and Social Hope* (New York: Penguin, 1999), 120.

59. Du Bois, *Darkwater*, 204.

60. Illustrative texts include Frank Wilderson III, "Gramsci's Black Marx: Whither the Slave in Civil Society?," *Social Identities* 9, no. 2 (2003);" Frank B. Wilderson III, *Red, White & Black: Cinema and the Structure of US Antagonisms* (Durham, NC: Duke University Press, 2010); Jared Sexton, "The Social Life of Social Death: On Afro-Pessimism and Black Optimism," in *Time, Temporality and Violence in International Relations*, ed. Anna M. Agathangelou and Kyle D. Killian (New York: Routledge, 2016); Calvin L. Warren, *Ontological Terror: Blackness, Nihilism, and Emancipation* (Durham, NC: Duke University Press, 2018).

61. R. L., "Wanderings of the Slave: Black Life and Social Death," *Mute* (June 5, 2013). https://www.metamute.org/editorial/articles/wanderings-slave-black-life-and-social-death.

62. Calvin L Warren, "Black Nihilism and the Politics of Hope," *CR: The New Centennial Review* 15, no. 1 (2015): 226.

63. Jürgen Habermas, *The Philosophical Discourse of Modernity: Twelve Lectures*, trans. Frederick Lawrence (Cambridge, MA: MIT Press, 1987), 4–5.

64. Kompridis, *Critique and Disclosure*, 14.

65. Hannah Arendt, *Between Past and Future: Eight Exercises in Political Thought*, enlarged ed. (New York: Penguin, 1977).

66. Joshua Foa Dienstag, *Pessimism: Philosophy, Ethic, Spirit* (Princeton, NJ: Princeton University Press, 2006), 25, http://www.loc.gov/catdir/enhancements/fy0654/2005056513-d.html.

67. Hayden V. White, *Metahistory: The Historical Imagination in Nineteenth-Century Europe* (Baltimore: Johns Hopkins University Press, 1973), 37–38.

68. Hortense J. Spillers, "Mama's Baby, Papa's Maybe: An American Grammar Book," *diacritics* 17, no. 2 (1987); Saidiya V. Hartman, *Scenes of Subjection: Terror, Slavery, and Self-Making in Nineteenth-Century America* (New York: Oxford University Press, 1997).

69. Introduction to *Afro-Pessimism: An Introduction* (Minneapolis, MN: Racked & Dispatched, 2017), https://rackedanddispatched.noblogs.org/files/2017/01/Afro-Pessimism.pdf. 9.

70. Introduction to *Afro-Pessimism*.

71. Warren, "Black Nihilism," 216–17.

72. Frank Wilderson III, "Blacks and the Master/Slave Relation," interview by C. S. Soong, KPFA, Berkeley, CA, March 4, 2015," *Afro-Pessimism: An Introduction*, 19–24.

73. See, for example, David Harvey, *Seventeen Contradictions and the End of Capitalism* (London: Profile Books, 2014).

74. Warren, "Black Nihilism," 239.

75. Dienstag, *Pessimism: Philosophy*, 7. This element of Afro-Pessimism is, in my view, best excavated via sustained critical attention to the recurrent figures—the fugitive slave, the suicidal-matricidal slave, the rebel, the poet, and the apostate—that attain pride of place in Afro-Pessimist writing and the modes of action they perform.

76. Lauren Gail Berlant, *Cruel Optimism* (Durham, NC: Duke University Press, 2011).

77. Warren, "Black Nihilism," 244.

78. Cathy Cohen defines marginalization as the process through which the economic, political, and social resources used by dominant members of a society or group to guarantee the exercise of rights and privileges are denied to a group of persons based on the convergence of stigmatized identities, ostracizing social norms, ideological subordination and conflict, institutional exclusion, and discriminatory social networks. Secondary marginalization, therefore, is when the relatively privileged members of marginal groups *further marginalize* stigmatized members within the group. Cathy J. Cohen, *The Boundaries of Blackness: AIDS and the Breakdown of Black Politics* (Chicago: University of Chicago Press, 1999), 37–48, http://www.loc.gov/catdir/description/uchi052/98031088.html.

79. Although Warren seems to reduce this broad terrain of "pathology" to nihilism, this need not follow. There is a long tradition of black social thought, from Du Bois and King to Eldridge Cleaver, Huey Newton, and Angela Davis that suggests more robustly normative and even emancipatory content to such practices as refusal to work, drug abuse, crime, fraud, etc.

80. Rorty, *Philosophy and Social Hope*, 231.

81. Josiah Royce, quoted in West, *Keeping Faith*, 181.

82. West, "Black Strivings," 92–93.

83. Du Bois, *Souls of Black Folk*, 73.

84. *Souls of Black Folk*, 225.

85. *Souls of Black Folk*, 227.

86. Hannah Arendt, *Lectures on Kant's Political Philosophy*, ed. Ronald Beiner (Chicago: University of Chicago Press, 1982), 77.

87. Cornel West and David Kyuman Kim, "Democracy, the Catastrophic, and Courage: A Conversation with Cornel West and David Kyuman Kim," *Theory & Event* 12, no. 4 (2009). Unsurprisingly, West's humanist sensibilities make him far more attuned to non-black suffering than Afropessimist writers.

88. West and Kim, "Conversation."

89. Seyla Benhabib, *The Reluctant Modernism of Hannah Arendt*, new ed., Modernity and Political Thought (Lanham, MD: Rowman & Littlefield, 2003), 88.

90. Benhabib, *Reluctant Modernism*, 88.

91. *Reluctant Modernism*.

92. This sensibility, I think, is a *tragic* one, alive and well in the historiography of the "Long Civil Rights movement." These narratives begin in a critique of romance from a space of mourning, lingering over the wounds, defeats, and lost causes—especially economic justice—of the movement. Yet, the tone and tenor of Long Civil Rights historical writing emerges forcefully from its dogged attachment to the sense that things *could* have turned out differently—more just, more fair. Such a sentiment requires a commitment to the belief in the existence of genuine, significance choices that historical actors made and had to make, and part of the historian's task, on their account, is to locate those moments, and reconstruct the sense of possibility and structure of opportunity in ways that give credibility to the reality of an alternative direction and educate our judgment for action in the present amid the wreckage of antiblack racism, capitalism, sexism, and imperialism.

93. W. E. B. Du Bois, *Dusk of Dawn: An Essay Toward an Autobiography of a Race Concept*, The Oxford W. E. B. Du Bois (New York: Oxford University Press, 2007), 3, 148, http://www.loc.gov/catdir/toc/ecip0712/2007009255.html.

94. Theodor W. Adorno, "Progress," in *Can One Live After Auschwitz?: A Philosophical Reader*, ed. Rolf Tiedemann (Palo Alto, CA: Stanford University Press, 2003), 153.

95. Warren, "Black Nihilism," 221.

96. Martin Hägglund, *This Life: Secular Faith and Spiritual Freedom*, 1st ed. (New York: Pantheon, 2019).

97. Bernard E. Harcourt, *Critique and Praxis* (New York: Columbia University Press, 2020).

98. West and Kim, "Conversation."

99. West, *Keeping Faith*, xvi.

100. West and Kim, "Conversation."

CHAPTER 4

Not Nothing: A Mystical Theological Reading of "Nihilism in Black America"

Andrew Prevot

When I first read *Race Matters* more than ten years ago, I was especially struck by the first chapter, called "Nihilism in Black America," which still haunts me to this day. Although some critics accuse this chapter of "blaming the victim" (Steinberg 127–30; Hayes), this accusation seems unfounded to me. West does not blame nihilism on those it afflicts. The approach I take is more in line with sympathetic interpreters of this chapter, who appreciate West's analysis of the interlocking structural and existential factors contributing to such nihilism and who find encouragement in his love-oriented politics of conversion (Cowan 127–50; Gordon; C. Johnson 20–31; Brogdon). This chapter is still troubling to me, not because I disagree with it, which I do not, but because it exposes a problem so deeply buried in the fleshy hearts and sedimented histories of the United States and the larger world that I almost cannot bear to face it. This problem is ongoing. As I indicate in the first two sections of this paper, racialized nihilism partly explains—and takes on new forms in—the Movement for Black Lives and the recent rise of Afropessimist theory.

I agree with West that if there is an answer to the problem of nihilism in black America it will come from a politics of conversion rooted in love. What I want to add from the perspective of Christian mystical theology, especially as attested by the medieval mystical theologian Marguerite Porete, is an argument for the nihilism-defeating power of divine love. In particular, I argue that those treated as nothing by their societies, those whose identities are deemed illegitimate and whose murderous deaths are rationalized, are not nothing to God. Rather, God's tender embrace of the world's supposed "non-beings" both reveals and condemns the deadly lies of such social ontologies. The same divine love that vindicates Porete against the patriarchal, inquisitorial powers that burned her alive also vindicates poor, despised African Americans today, who are the "heretics" of an idolatrous American civil religion of whiteness. In the third and final section of this chapter, I retrieve Porete as a potentially illuminating spiritual source for the Christian-adjacent, spiritually plural, tragicomic politics of conversion that West proposes as a means of overcoming racialized nihilism. When integrated with West's practical analyses, Porete's argument that the annihilated are not only loved by God but can become, precisely in their annihilation, *nothing but* this very love, provides both a helpful mystical mirror for the Movement for Black Lives and a more liberative alternative to strict Afropessimism.

The "Nihilistic Threat" in the Context of #BlackLivesMatter

In the first chapter of *Race Matters*, West bemoans the fact that the persistent operations of antiblack racism and predatory capitalism in the post-civil rights era have left many impoverished black communities caught in structural and psychosomatic conditions of hopelessness and lovelessness that make black life feel like a living death or a hell on earth. The racially oppressive forces immanent in finance-dominated neoliberalism and increasingly virulent forms of xenophobic protectionism pressure black people and other dehumanized people of color to experience their existence as though it were nothing or worse than nothing. This is "*the nihilistic threat*" (12). West's argument echoes an insight from Martin Luther King Jr.'s 1963 "Letter from Birmingham City Jail," which holds that being black in America involves "a degenerating sense of 'nobodiness'" against which one must continually struggle (King 293). Although circumstances are not exactly the "same" as they were in the early 1960s when King wrote his letter or in the early 1990s when West wrote his essay (each historical moment requires its own analysis), black people are still fighting today for voting rights, equal protection under the law, access to the economic and cultural goods necessary for a life of dignity, a deep love for their embodied selves, and in some cases basic survival.

The nihilistic threat has taken on a particular character and become visible in a new way through public lamentations about Trayvon Martin's murder on February 26, 2012, and his killer George Zimmerman's acquittal on July 13, 2013, which sparked the Movement for Black Lives. Collective responses to subsequent murders of defenseless black men, women, and children, including Michael Brown, Tamir Rice, Sandra Bland, Eric Garner, Aiyana Jones, Philando Castille, Stephon Clark, Ahmaud Arbery, Breonna Taylor, and George Floyd (the list goes on and on) have galvanized and expanded this movement, to the point that it has become widely recognized as a significant site of social agitation in the contemporary moment. From its beginnings in the grassroots and social media activism of Alicia Garza, Opal Tometi, and Patrisse Cullors, this movement has fought back against the longstanding American practice of desecrating and discarding precious black lives. The problem addressed by this movement is not limited to this or that violent act and certainly not only to those committed by police officers (though such incidents are particularly revealing as examples of antiblack "state" violence). The problem is not even limited to unjust public policies in areas of law enforcement, health care, housing, education, and so on, which produce and fail to address excessive racial disparities. At a deeper philosophical, cultural, or existential level, the problem has to do with a racially specified nihilism that insinuates, in each particular case, that this was not even really a life to begin with, that this incident was not murder but the removal of an obstacle to society's flourishing, that the policies currently on offer work well enough for the lives that matter, that there was nothing real in this black body to protect, that this body was an incarnate nothing taking up space and causing a disturbance but nothing nonetheless. Trayvon, and countless others "like" him, have been treated as an evil without substance which must be exorcised for the safety of the (white or even multicultural) body politic.

Of course, any defensible ethics must somehow support the universalist claim that "all lives matter"—or, as West says in a 2017 interview, "everybody counts!" (West and Mendieta 146). But the question that the "all lives matter" retort, used precisely as a retort, deceptively masks is whether Trayvon's life was for the larger social imaginary even really a life. The most crucial part of the #BlackLivesMatter slogan is not the rather anodyne verb "to matter," but the subject, "black lives," which expresses the very presupposition that there is such a thing as a black life, that black flesh is home to what one means by a life, that a black body is not nothing but rather a living and sacred epiphany of being, which must be guarded and cherished.

To murder someone whom one recognizes as living is an evil act. But the particular evil of antiblack racism also operates at a more insidious level by symbolically annihilating the life in black persons prior to any corporeal deathblow. This happens through a white supremacist aesthetic, geographic, intellectual, commercial, and political culture, characteristic of Western modernity, which positions the black body as figurative adversary in the very drama of existence. In such a culture, the black body symbolizes the darkness of a primitive past, of unbridled sexuality, of social chaos, of the foreign invader, of demonic power, or of death itself, against which the living must strive in order to exist and to flourish. As a black person, you may be to others' trained eyes not a living human being but a physical apparition of the terrors of the night. Consider West's analysis of Carolus Linnaeus's 1735 *Natural System* in *Prophesy Deliverance!*, which shows an early European invention of a less than human, aesthetically and morally degenerate African race, against which white life would supposedly have to be safeguarded (56).

Many white Americans react defensively to the claim that black lives matter not out of a genuine concern for universal humanism, but rather because they have an unacknowledged discomfort with the very subject of the statement. Whether they admit it or not, many white Americans experience the very idea of black life as self-contradictory and hostile. Most of the white-dominant culture's models for what it means to live in the truest sense are not only not black but also caught symbolically in a struggle against all the antilife things (danger, chaos, death, and so on) that blackness has been made to represent. This deeply ingrained denial of black life as a coherent possibility and actually existing reality is the root of America's racialized nihilism, which shapes both the structures of this society and the psyches of those who live in it. Such nihilism is not confined to predominantly poor, black urban areas, which West problematically calls "asphalt jungles" (*Race Matters* 16) and others problematically call "ghettoes," though they are major targets. Its toxicity extends everywhere, even in "white spaces" (Anderson). This nihilism is the deadly background to the present era of renewed black consciousness and activism.

The Tragicomic: How West's Account of Nihilism Anticipates and Avoids Afropessimism

In response to such nihilism, West proposes a "*politics of conversion*" (*Race Matters* 18), which would be characterized by local, communal, grassroots practices of love and care, partly modeled on Baby Suggs' sermon in the clearing in Toni Morrison's *Beloved* (19)—a point that reveals the proximity of West's argument to those of many black feminist and womanist ethicists (hooks and West 55; Townes 47–67; Copeland 51–53). West emphasizes the need for agency and for "collective leadership" in the black community (*Race Matters* 19). He contends that this politics of conversion ought to recognize both the "liberal structuralist" insight that oppressive economic and political conditions are the material bases for such nihilism and, more controversially, the "conservative behaviorist" insight that black people are ethical subjects who, like all people, need to practice virtues in order to thrive (19). Moreover, he suggests that such a politics of conversion would benefit from the recovery of black cultural and religious traditions that used to serve as "powerful buffers to ward off the nihilistic threat" (15).

All of this seems right and reasonable to me. Not only that, this love-based politics of conversion seems crucially important given certain recent trends toward despair and pessimism in black studies and black popular culture. There is a rigorous logic behind this despondent mood. If one interprets antiblack racism as a powerful force that, despite being socially constructed, operates effectively as a social ontology, determining the meaning of black existence in this epoch, then one is only a small step away from an Afropessimist position in which to be black means to be a nothing or a negatively defined construct—as Frank Wilderson has it, "the Slave," the "anti-Human," whose life is a living death (11). Although Wilderson is perhaps the most explicit proponent of Afropessimism, there are other notable precursors and elaborators of this theory (Coates; Patterson; Sexton; Warren).

West, for his part, encourages us to attend to the tragic dimensions of reality: the evil and absurdity that are built into human history. In his early essay "Pragmatism and the Sense of the Tragic," he argues that Josiah Royce is more attuned to these tragic dimensions than his pragmatist peer John Dewey. Royce confronts the harsh and disappointing circumstances of quotidian life, as revealed for example by "one's own foolishness, one's ignorance, the cruel accidents of disease, the fatal misunderstandings that part friends and lovers, [and] the chance mistakes that wreck nations" (105). Drawing on Arthur Schopenhauer, Royce raises the stakes of these mishaps by noting that they have a certain absoluteness insofar as they are irreversible. No deed can be undone. Although this Roycean sense of the "absolute" tragedy of history comes close to Schopenhauerian pessimism, for theological reasons it does not finally succumb to it. Royce finds hope in "the suffering God . . . who actually and in our flesh bears the sins of the world" (106).

When one acknowledges that irreversible events include decisions that generate ontologically determinative structures of antiblack racism, one finds the logical grounds for Afropessimism. West's concern about such pessimism, and mine as well, is that it presents the threat of nihilism too much as a fait accompli. It not only seems to foreclose a future of alternative social and ontological possibilities; it also minimizes alternative meanings of black life that are already discernible in the past and present. West's more recent preference for speaking not merely of the tragic but of the "tragicomic" suggests a desire to explore creative possibilities within and beyond the irreversible facts of history. One sees this in his thoughts on Anton Chekhov and John Coltrane (Smith and West), as well as in his appreciation for Christian, Jewish, Buddhist, Sufi, and other spiritualities that "mitigate against the seemingly absurd character of our existence" (hooks and West 53). Without ignoring the nihilistic seriousness of antiblack racism, West refuses to absolutize it. The "comic" in his work is not equivalent to the silly, the escapist, or the deluded. Rather, it names a pluriform emergence of hope and love even in the midst of hopelessness and lovelessness. At a time when the nihilistic threat prompts both activist protests against the (state-sanctioned) murder of black people and the return of fatalistic ontology in some quarters of black studies, West's tragicomic, love-oriented politics offers a promising path forward.

The Anti-Nihilistic Significance of Marguerite Porete's Mysticism of the Annihilated Soul

Like Brother West, I am a Christian. Among other things, this means that I respond to the nihilistic threat theologically. I acknowledge that such a theological response may at first appear only to exacerbate the problems I have been discussing. In relation to the Creator's infinite being, one's comparative nothingness as a mere contingent product of dust, fashioned ex nihilo and enslaved to sinful desires, may seem all the more assured. The Christian life, moreover, is traditionally marked by the cross and governed by its apparent sanctification of suffering and death. A chorus of Christian mystics and saints teach by their cruciform lives that closeness with God demands a dying of the ego, a painful process of purgation and detachment so all-consuming as to be aptly named "annihilation." From this vantage point, Christian theology may seem more likely to reinforce nihilism than resist it. Even if Christianity promises a divine love preferentially oriented toward the poor and oppressed, as liberation theologians rightly insist (Cone; Gutiérrez), one cannot ignore the ways that a white, slaveholding, imperial Christianity has contributed to the current conditions of racialized nihilism (Douglas; Fletcher; Jennings).

Nonetheless, I contend that Christian theology—particularly a Christian mystical theology rooted in a life of prayerful union with God—offers those struggling with devastating experiences of existential nothingness, especially as occasioned by oppressive social ontologies, two powerful ways to know that they are not nothing. First, it shows such persons that they are loved with an infinite love, regardless of their standing in the world. Second, it teaches them that, through the power of this love, they have the potential to become nothing other than a vessel of love, which is the greatest and most exalted thing to be. This twofold theological insight appears in certain marginalized black Christian witnesses who suffer the lashes of a violent, white supremacist pseudo-Christianity; who struggle with their own internal fragilities such as fear, death, and sin; and yet who find solace and strength in the grace of a living God for whom such forces of existential nothingness are ultimately no match. Profound, life-sustaining wisdom appears in slave spirituals such as "Death Come to My House He Didn't Stay Long" (J. W. Johnson and J. R. Johnson 108), a hymn that confronts the ubiquity of death in slave existence while rejoicing in God's almighty power to resurrect, and in slave narratives such as that of Sojourner Truth, who after receiving a vision of God's greatness was first "seized by a dire dread of annihilation" and a desire to repent, only eventually to find her heart filled with joy through an experience of intimate union with Jesus (44–46). Truth's Christian spirituality is a key source of her feminist abolitionism.

In the history of Christian thought, one of the most striking witnesses to the nihilism-defeating power of divine love is Marguerite Porete, a vernacular Beguine mystical theologian of the annihilated soul who was burned at the stake in Paris on June 1, 1310, as a "relapsed heretic" (Babinsky; Field). Contemporary interpreters have drawn on Porete to address problems of trauma and abuse, especially related to gender-based oppression (Farley 85–114; Hollywood 173–206; Shooter 113–68). I suggest that Porete's example may also be valuable in the fight against racial oppression, insofar as her experiences of nothingness significantly parallel the externally imposed and internally endured features of nihilism in black America.

The precious human being Marguerite Porete was treated like a "nothing" by her society. She was marginalized and killed by the political, ecclesial, and epistemic structures of her day. Not part of an approved religious order; unprotected by monastic, scholastic, or clerical pedigrees; and perceived by male religious and aristocratic elites as a threat to the Catholic purity of the fledgling French nation-state, she was a persona non grata on multiple counts. Before she was condemned to die, attempts were made simply to silence her, but she refused to be silent. She continued to use her book, *The Mirror of Simple Souls*, to teach about the divine love that totally enveloped her. She would have been allowed to live had she consented to a life of non-expression, which is to say virtual absence, but she did not consent to be a nothing *in this sense*. Her execution was the violent imposition on her of the particular sort of nothingness which was attributed to her even as she lived. It was the public display of a doctrinal and ontological decision against her supposedly antilife way of being. To condemn her to die was to assert, by means of her burned corpse, that the spirituality that shaped her existence had no viable place, no recognizable standing, no legitimate status in this world. She reportedly remained silent during the court proceedings—a defiant act that spoke louder than words. One can ascertain all of this from the historical record of her trial and execution (Babinsky; Field).

Reading Porete's book reveals another dimension of nothingness, more internal than external. In this text, she explains various ways that she became a nothing to herself and in herself. More precisely, she writes about being a nothing in relation to the God whom she encounters within, who is the one and all. This interior nothingness, which she *does* embrace as descriptive of her existence—and which provoked the ire of the inquisitors because of its supposedly anti-institutional and antinomian implications—has several aspects that need to be distinguished. As a creature made by God out of nothing, she is not substantial in herself but utterly dependent on the Creator. Moreover, as a sinful person who has made decisions against God's will, turning against the very source of her being, she judges herself to be not merely nothing but "less than nothing" (ch. 107 and 109). Yet this recognition of her creaturely and sinful nothingness is just the beginning. It inaugurates a spiritual journey that culminates in a higher, purified form of mystical nothingness in which her soul is united with divine love. She associates the most advanced stages of grace with a radically annihilated condition of not-knowing and not-willing, in which she has died to her sin, to her nature, and even to her own spirit and lives only in and for God (ch. 59). This mystical annihilation has a very particular meaning. Porete understands herself to be nothing now in the theologically precise, and not primarily negative, sense that she is *nothing but* what God wants her to be. This nothingness is constituted as an absolute receptivity to divine love. It is a condition of oneness with the compassionate heart of being itself (ch. 118).

Reconceived in the context of twenty-first-century America, Porete's understanding of divine love may reveal a powerful counterforce against the nothingness that threatens black people from without and within. Assume, for the sake of argument, that black life is nugatory on the terms established by the antiblack social ontologies of the modern world, as Afropessimists contend. Assume too that, at an internal level, at the level of individual psyches, such a structural denial of black life leads some black people to despair, even one as strong as "Baby Suggs holy," from Morrison's *Beloved* (105). Assume that in some cases this despair even expresses itself violently, as it does in Sethe's killing of her child, also from Morrison's *Beloved* (193). Assume that, as a result of these interrelated external and internal factors, certain poor black neighborhoods find themselves mired in the destructive patterns of a hopeless, loveless, and therefore nihilistic condition. To be more concrete, consider the ways that the intergenerational effects of antiblack racism contribute to cases of drug and alcohol abuse, gang-related criminal activity, unhealthy sexual practices, and rising rates of suicide in some black communities (Hayden; Nutt; Poussaint and Alexander; Sutton, Valentine, and Jenkins; Thomas and Price). Consider all of these maladies suggested by West's analysis of nihilism in black America. Even under these worst imaginable circumstances, Porete would tell us that divine love knows and embraces black life, and promises it a sweeter future. She would argue that the murderous nothingness imposed upon and experienced by black people is not the whole story. There is a liberating divine love that paradoxically makes such an annihilated condition its preferred dwelling place.

Porete's love-centered mystical theology provides a rigorous counterpoint to modernity's punitive, pseudomeritocratic, market-driven "rationality," which is really a widespread mendacity: a lie about what makes a life valuable. Porete locates the value of life, not in social status as measured by wealth, achievement, or racial identity, but rather in one's inner condition of pliability to divine love. Porete's text preemptively denounces the impossible-to-satisfy politics of black respectability championed by conservative behaviorists, while challenging liberal structuralists to recognize that there are interior aspects to the nihilistic threat and its possible remedies. At this interior level, she resists the sort of sinful nothingness that distances one from God, which for black people would include any voluntary participations in the violence of the fallen world. At the same time, she affirms the sort of mystical nothingness that prepares one to receive and become God's love, a possibility that is discernible in certain Spirit-filled, black-led movements for amorous social transformation.

When drawing on mystical traditions in the Movement for Black Lives, I do not think it best to replace the idea of God with that of "blackness," construing blackness itself as a quasi-divine other, transcending being, which would offer the modern world a path of redemption. This is the rhetorical move recently employed by certain mystically informed "para-ontological" and "para-theological" black studies projects (Moten; Carter). Rather, I suggest that the more theologically compelling way to integrate mysticism with contemporary antiracist struggles is to argue that God—a real, living God, if one can believe it—loves black lives with an indomitable love even when they are afflicted by various kinds of nothingness from without and within. The mystical theological approach I advocate does not ask blackness to do the salvific work of a god but rather lets blackness remain the contingent feature of real human bodies and histories that it is. Although black theologians are right to assert that "God is black" (Cone 71), I do not believe it makes sense either theologically or practically to treat blackness as a substitute or successor for God, because to do so obscures the difference between created black lives that need to be affirmed and the infinite love of the Creator that forever holds and cherishes them.

The divine love revered by Christian mystical theology has the creative power to make something out of nothing. It has the saving power to restore a sense of being somebody to those who have been pressured to feel, time and again, like worthless nobodies. By embracing black lives even in their apparent forms of external and internal negation, this divine love demonstrates—as nothing else can—that these annihilated lives are in fact not nothing. They are beloved. And, if they are receptive to it, they may be gradually metamorphosed into love itself. These crucified ones may become temples of divine charity. Their actions, virtues, and powers, including their "black power," may ultimately be not simply of their own self-making but rather gifts emanating from a divine source within them. Porete suggests that, free of anxiety, such souls will "swim and flow in joy" (ch. 28). If ontology does its worst, as

Afropessimists believe it does (though their formulations remain debatable), theology still has a recourse.

The life of union with God exemplified by Porete is not easy. Porete, like King, like Trayvon, is murdered by a supposedly Christian nation. Many Christians do not know or practice the radical love that they profess. The suffering caused by such egregious Christian hypocrisy is only one of the many reasons why becoming one with love itself does not free one from the cross. But make no mistake, Porete's annihilated life is not the sort of quietist withdrawal from the world for which it might be confused but, rather, a continual struggle to be an aperture in the world for the sort of love which might yet transform it. It is the basis for a "politics of conversion," in West's sense. If I am a nothing according to every other logic, discourse, or structural analysis, and even in my own troubled self-estimation, this mystical-political theology of the annihilated soul still continues to whisper another possibility, addressed to me precisely in my nothingness, a possibility of being nothing but that love that God would like me to be, albeit in the limited ways that are possible for my finite, bodily existence. This love enacts a sublime affirmation of self and other, incarnated in my relationships and actions, which makes me fearless even on the front lines, even if I should be insulted, imprisoned, or killed. Like Brother West, I want to be nothing if not a lover of all my brothers and sisters, all my "siblings" in the human family that is struggling to become the beloved community of King's dreams. Such is my prayer and my Christianity.

The preceding argument should not be taken as suggesting that either West's project or the Movement for Black Lives *needs* an explicitly Christian mystical supplement, let alone the mystical doctrines of Porete in particular. If she deserves a hearing in the struggle against racialized nihilism, it is not because she offers something that its contemporary agents fundamentally lack. The love of which she speaks is already operative in this struggle. Rather, she offers something like a mirror—an instrument of reflection—that may be useful for black people today who are facing political and spiritual processes of annihilation that, in certain respects, resemble hers. By studying Porete and other similar mystical theologians, black scholars and activists may gain a deeper understanding of ourselves. Just as Porete's life was deemed heretical in her religious and social context, so too black life counts as heretical (or deviant, contradictory, criminal, impious) according to the antiblack standards of white American civil religion, which is itself a deadly Christian heresy, a demonic inversion of the gospel. The annihilation that she and we suffer because of such an unjust structural and historical positioning does not prevent either her or us from uniting with that world-transforming love that is the very essence of the divine. One who is regarded as nothing by any given patriarchal or white supremacist ontology may be, in various interiorly hidden or communally manifest ways, metamorphosed into *nothing but* that all-important love that demands that things change. And this is decidedly *not nothing.*

Works Cited

Anderson, Elijah. "The White Space." *Sociology of Race and Ethnicity*, vol. 1, no. 1, 2015, pp. 10–21.

Babinsky, Ellen L. Introduction. *The Mirror of Simple Souls*, by Marguerite Porete, translated by Ellen L. Babinsky, Paulist, 1993, pp. 5–61.

Brogdon, Lewis. *Hope on the Brink: Understanding the Emergence of Nihilism in Black America*. Cascade, 2013.

Carter, J. Kameron. "Paratheological Blackness." *South Atlantic Quarterly*, vol. 112, no. 4, fall 2013, pp. 589–611.

Coates, Ta-Nehisi. *Between the World and Me*. Spiegel and Grau, 2015.

Cone, James H. *A Black Theology of Liberation*. Orbis, 1990.

Copeland, M. Shawn. *Enfleshing Freedom: Body, Race, and Being*. Fortress, 2010.

Cowan, Rosemary. *Cornel West: The Politics of Redemption*. Polity, 2003.

Douglas, Kelly Brown. *Stand Your Ground: Black Bodies and the Justice of God*. Orbis, 2015.

Farley, Wendy. *The Thirst of God: Contemplating God's Love with Three Women Mystics*. Westminster John Knox, 2015.

Field, Sean L. *The Beguine, the Angel, and the Inquisitor: The Trials of Marguerite Porete and Guiard of Cressonessart*. Notre Dame UP, 2012.

Fletcher, Jeannine Hill. *The Sin of White Supremacy: Christianity, Racism, and Religious Diversity in America*. Orbis, 2017.

Gordon, Lewis R. "The Unacknowledged Fourth Tradition: An Essay on Nihilism, Decadence, and the Black Intellectual Tradition in the Existential Pragmatic Thought of Cornel West." *Cornel West: A Critical Reader*, edited by George Yancy, Blackwell, 2001, pp. 38–58.

Gutiérrez, Gustavo, O. P. *A Theology of Liberation: History, Politics, and Salvation*. Translated by Sister Caridad Inda and John Eagleson, Orbis, 1988.

Hayden, Tom. *Street Wars: Gangs and the Future of Violence*. New Press, 2004.

Hayes, Floyd W., III. "Cornel West and Afro-Nihilism: A Reconsideration." *Cornel West: A Critical Reader*, pp. 245–60.

Hollywood, Amy. *The Soul as Virgin Wife: Mechthild of Magdeburg, Marguerite Porete, and Meister Eckhart*. Notre Dame UP, 1995.

hooks, bell and Cornel West. *Breaking Bread: Insurgent Black Intellectual Life*. South End, 1991.

Jennings, Willie James. *The Christian Imagination: Theology and the Origins of Race*. Yale UP, 2010.

Johnson, Clarence Sholé. *Cornel West and Philosophy: The Quest for Social Justice*. Routledge, 2003.

Johnson, James Weldon and J. Rosamond Johnson. *The Books of American Negro Spirituals.* Da Capo, 1969.

King, Martin Luther, Jr. "Letter from Birmingham City Jail." *Testament of Hope: The Essential Writings and Speeches of Martin Luther King, Jr.*, edited by James M. Washington, HarperCollins, 1986, pp. 289–302.

Morrison, Toni. *Beloved.* 1987. Vintage, 2004.

Moten, Fred. "Blackness and Nothingness (Mysticism in the Flesh)." *South Atlantic Quarterly*, vol. 112, no. 4, fall 2013, pp. 737–80.

Nutt, Amy Ellis. "Suicide Rates for Black Children Twice That for White Children, New Data Show." *Washington Post*, 21 May 2018.

Patterson, Orlando. *Slavery and Social Death.* Harvard UP, 1985.

Porete, Marguerite. *The Mirror of Simple Souls.* Translated by Ellen L. Babinsky, Paulist, 1993.

Poussaint, Alvin F., and Amy Alexander. *Lay My Burden Down: Suicide and the Mental Health Crisis among African-Americans.* Beacon, 2000.

Sexton, Jared. *Amalgamation Schemes: Antiblackness and the Critique of Multiracialism.* Minnesota UP, 2008.

Shooter, Susan. *How Survivors of Abuse Relate to God: The Authentic Spirituality of the Annihilated Soul.* Routledge, 2012.

Smith, David Lionel, and Cornel West. "Chekhov, Coltrane, and Democracy." *The Cornel West Reader*, Basic Civitas, 1999, pp. 551–63.

Sutton, Madeline Y., Jo A. Valentine, and William C. Jenkins, eds. *Our Communities, Our Sexual Health: Awareness and Prevention for African Americans.* American Public Health Association, 2015.

Steinberg, Stephen. *Turning Back: The Retreat from Racial Justice in American Thought and Policy.* 3rd ed., Beacon, 2001.

Thomas, Yonette F., and LeShawndra N. Price. *Drug Use Trajectories among Minority Youth.* Springer, 2016.

Townes, Emilie. *In a Blaze of Glory: Womanist Spirituality as Social Witness.* Abingdon, 1995.

Truth, Sojourner, et al. *Narrative of Sojourner Truth*, edited by Neil Irvin Painter, Penguin, 1998.

Warren, Calvin. *Ontological Terror: Blackness, Nihilism, and Emancipation.* Duke UP, 2018.

West, Cornel. "Pragmatism and the Sense of the Tragic." *Keeping Faith: Philosophy and Race in America*, Routledge, 2009, pp. 96–106.

———. *Prophesy Deliverance! An Afro-American Revolutionary Christianity.* 20th anniversary ed., Westminster John Knox, 2002.

———. *Race Matters.* 25th anniversary, Beacon, 2017.

West, Cornel and Eduardo Mendieta. "What It Means to Be Human!" *Critical Philosophy of Race*, vol. 5, no. 2, 2017, pp. 137–70.

Wilderson, Frank B., III. *Red, White, and Black: Cinema and the Structure of U.S. Antagonisms.* Duke UP, 2010.

CHAPTER 5

What Manner of Man Is the Prophet? Cornel West, Abraham Heschel, and the Hebrew Prophets

Susannah Heschel

> The prophet is a man who feels fiercely. God has thrust a burden upon his soul, and he is bowed and stunned at man's fierce greed. Frightful is the agony of man; no human voice can convey its full terror. Prophecy is the voice that God has lent to the silent agony, a voice to the plundered poor, to the profaned riches of the world. It is a form of living, a crossing point of God and human beings. God is raging in the prophet's words.
>
> —Abraham Joshua Heschel, *The Prophets*

"Where in America do we hear a voice like the voice of the prophets of Israel?" asked Abraham Heschel when introducing Martin Luther King Jr. in 1968 to an audience of rabbis celebrating Heschel's birthday: "Martin Luther King is a sign that God has not forsaken the United States of America. God has sent him to us. His presence is the hope of America. His mission is sacred, his leadership of supreme importance to every one of us." King responded by declaring Heschel to be "a man that I consider one of the truly great men of our day and age. He is indeed a truly great prophet. . . . Rabbi Heschel is one of the persons who is relevant at all times, always standing with prophetic insights to guide us through these difficult days."

What makes someone a prophet? The term is used far more frequently in the United States than in most other countries, although it had a brief flourishing among German Jews in the nineteenth century. Attention to prophecy, and especially the classical Hebrew prophets of the Bible, is found in the religious texts and traditions of Black American Christians and, to a lesser extent, in white Protestant thought. American Jews inherited from German Jewish theologians an equation of Judaism with the prophetic tradition. German Jews called Judaism "ethical monotheism," claiming that only a monotheistic religion could be reliably ethical and assuming that prophecy is reducible to an ethical message that would win Jews political rights in a Europe at the height of its imperialist ethos. The great German Jewish philosopher Hermann Cohen argued in the years prior to World War I that "Deutschtum" and "Judentum" were essentially identical, or at least striving to realize the same ethical values of the Hebrew prophets. Equating Germany with Judaism was not well received. The German Protestant theologian Ernst Troeltsch did not simply demur, but attacked Cohen's claim with mockery: the prophets, Troeltsch claimed in a lecture in December 1915, were nothing more than country bumpkins whose naïveté about power and politics is revealed in their calls for turning swords into ploughshares.[1] The prophets never became a resource in Germany to demand social justice and peace and no one was called a prophetic voice until Hitler claimed the title.[2]

The prophetic tradition in America follows a very different trajectory, one that prefers to unite Jews and Christians, Black and white, in social, religious, and political critique as well as radical movements of liberation.[3] Prophecy has long been a particularly important mode of Black Christian and liberal Jewish political expression, in sharp contrast with European Christians. Among white American Christians, the prophetic tradition has played a mixed role, in both the jeremiads of the early Puritan preachers and the insistence on concern for injustice in the Social Gospel tradition; invocation of the words of Amos, Isaiah, Micah, and Jeremiah has been an American tool for religious leaders to voice a social critique. Among Black Christians and Jews, however, the prophetic tradition has been more an affirming voice of liberation from injustice and less a jeremiad.

Is Cornel West a prophet? In invoking the Hebrew prophets in his writings and speeches, Cornel West has come to exemplify the prophetic tradition in his person and in his teachings, continuing the heritage of King and Heschel. He comes to us with prophetic denunciation of injustice combined, I want to suggest, with the spirit of a Hasidic rebbe, an observation I offer from four decades of our friendship. Several elements strike me as acute in West's work, resonant with the prophetic tradition, and central to his intellectual contributions: his rejection of Afropessimism; his understanding of the Hebrew prophetic in the tradition of Heschel; his emphasis on the prophetic indictment of disavowal; the Hasidic spirit that West exudes; and his emphasis on the importance of the Blues both for Black religious aesthetics and for American democracy. Taken together, West's writings shine a strong spotlight on the whiteness of conventional Christian theology and demonstrate that the cohabitation of Christianity and Judaism in America can result not in the formalities of interreligious dialogues, but in shared religious expressions that bring vitality to both.

West's Critique of Afropessimism

"Black people in the United States differ from all other modern people owing to the unprecedented levels of unregulated and unrestrained violence directed at them." This is the opening sentence of the 2001 preface to West's best-selling book, *Race Matters*, originally published in 1993. In a 1996 essay he wrote, "To be a black human being under circumstances in which one's humanity is questioned is not only to face a difficult challenge but also to exercise a demanding discipline."[4] West echoes other theorists, such as Orlando Patterson, who describe Black American experience as a "social death." Shortly after publication of *Race Matters*, Lewis Gordon began a careful theorization and extension of "anti-Blackness" in his book, *Bad Faith and Antiblack Racism* (1995).[5] Afropessimism has by now become central to the discourse; Frank Wilderson's 2019 book dramatically shifted attention to the key claim: Black has been turned by whites into the antithesis of the human.[6] Slavery has not ended. Indeed, "Wilderson has written a slave narrative in the present, insofar as it is his contention that he actually is, under the terms of his philosophy, a slave right now."[7] Afropessimism is indebted to numerous intellectuals, including Patterson, Frantz Fanon, Saidiya Hartman, Hortense Spillers, among others. And it has international resonance; Tendayi Sithole's recent book, *The Black Register*, is a philosophical examination of Afropessimism in the South African context.[8]

Brilliant and devastating analyses of antiblackness have been developed by Afropessimists from Wilderson to Zakiyyah Iman Jackson. In Wilderson's definition, "Rather than celebrate Blackness as a cultural identity," he writes, "Afro-Pessimism theorizes it as a position of accumulation and fungibility; that is, as condition—or relation—of ontological death."[9] Racism is redefined as antiblackness, a condition of political ontology that defines, structures, and unifies the world on every level. As Ntozange Shange notes, "We are the unconscious of the entire Western world."[10]

Antiblackness constructs the "animal" and "the bestialization of blackness" and ultimately confounds the distinction between animal and human by questioning the humanity of Black people.[11] Sex, gender, and even species reproduction are defined for whites out of antiblackness. It is "black female flesh [that] persistently functions as the limit case of "the human" and is its matrix-figure."[12] Jackson writes, "racial slavery as well as early modern proto-racializing conceptions of "monstrous" races and births are integral to ideas of sex/gender, reproduction, and what it means to possess a body."[13] Life itself is denied to Blacks. Jared Sexton asks, "What would one hope for in a scenario where one's murder is required for others' peace of mind?"[14] Black life is nonlife, so that the 2012 Merikana massacre of striking miners by the police in South Africa, Sithole writes, was not viewed as murder: if Black people do not possess human life, there is no murder.[15] The analysis developed by Afropessimisim "is both an epistemological and an ethical project."[16] The insights and drama of Afropessimist scholarship bears some parallels with scholarship on antisemitism that similarly defines hatred of Jews as foundational to Western Christendom and all-encompassing in its modern, racialized form that led to the Nazi definition of Jews as vermin requiring extermination. Indeed, J. Kameron Carter has argued persuasively that "modernity's racial imagination has its genesis in the theological problem of Christianity's quest to sever itself from its Jewish roots."[17]

Yet West demurs from Afropessimism. Yes, like the Afropessimists he analyzes the production of racism by modernity and indicts the "forms of rationality, scientificity and objectivity as well as aesthetic and cultural ideals" that "require[d] the constitution of the idea of white supremacy."[18] He is strong in articulating the impact of racism: "The sheer absurdity of being a black human being whose black body is viewed as an abomination, whose black thoughts and ideas are perceived as debased, and whose black pain and grief are rendered invisible on the human and moral scale is the New World context in which black culture emerged."[19]

West's analyses of white supremacy, while severe, come with a crucial distinction from the Afropessimists. While West recognizes despair, he rejects pessimism as "a species of cowardice fearful of life and too spectatorial in its detached practice! It lacks the heightened vulnerability of deep love and the passionate uncertainty of genuine struggle for justice!"[20] Sorrow, suffering, mourning, and melancholy are essential elements of the religious life, but there is no room for holiness and transformation in pessimism. Pessimism does not inspire activism, nor does it encourage the empathy and relationships that heal; it is nihilistic and prophetic. West is joined in his critique by the philosopher Lewis Gordon, who writes of Afropessimism, "Do blacks, for instance, suffer social death in relation to each other?" and then asks, "Why must the social world be premised on the attitudes and perspectives of antiblack racists? Why don't blacks among each other and other communities of color count as social perspectives?"[21]

A key element of West's affirmation of Black suffering and culture focuses on sound. He writes that "the 'urtext' of Black culture is a guttural cry and a wrenching moan—a cry not so much for help as for home, a moan less out of complaint than for recognition."[22] Moreover, his Christian commitments, especially prophetic hope, do not allow him to abandon hope for this-world redemption. He writes that Christianity is an extension of prophetic Judaism.[23] Heschel's phrase that "some are guilty, but all are responsible" finds emphasis in West's work. The prophetic for West is not simply an extension of the pragmatic, nor does the prophet simply dream of a future; here West is misunderstood by the philosopher Richard Rorty, who imagines "the pragmatist as the dreamer who first glimpses the concrete outlines of a better future."[24]

The intellectual independence that has always marked West's career generates criticism in an era when the most radical and pessimistic voices are misperceived as the most interesting and significant. Yet what West offers is precisely what the Afropessimists ultimately wish to attain, what Kevin Quashie calls "Black Aliveness," the title of his recent book, and what Sithole calls the "Black register," a form of language that capacitates Black subjects to speak about their conditions, and what Elizabeth Alexander calls "The Black Interior."[25] Racism may indeed be the ultimate form of necropolitics, as Jackson asserts, but West keeps alive the souls of Black folks, the intellectual, cultural, religious, and musical vitality that is too precious, in his words, to be ignored or discarded as nothing more than a defensive response to white antiblackness. The nihilism of those theorists is far removed from

West's description of "the profoundly tragicomic character of black life,"[26] with its "individual and collective black resistance predicated on a deep and abiding black love."[27] Black souls, for West, are infused with the prophetic spirit, which articulates devastating critique of societal injustice yet also insists on the cultivation of the inner life of compassion for others. Prophecy brings together the exterior and the interior of human life, suffering with hope, devastating sorrow with redemptive love. As West puts it, for the Christian "a deep sense of the tragic is required, yet the world is not inherently tragic."[28] Too much tragic is also unacceptable. West writes: "My fundamental problem with Du Bois is his inadequate grasp of the tragicomic sense of life—a refusal candidly to confront the sheer absurdity of the human condition. This tragicomic sense—tragicomic rather than simply 'tragic,' because even ultimate purpose and objective order are called into question—propels us toward suicide or madness unless we are buffered by ritual, cushioned by community, or sustained by art."[29]

Addressing and ending America's economic, military, and political exploitation requires, for West, a combination of Socratic questioning, prophetic witnessing, and the power of democratic institutions. Here is where his critique of Afropessimism is sharpest: his emphasis on the prophetic as a source of compassion as well as critique, of vision and hope as well as demand for social change, an offer of optimism as well as rage at cruelty, an insistence on the spiritual dimension of our individual humanity as well as calling out the systemic racist structures that try to exert sovereignty over us. And, ultimately, West's insistence on cultivating the relationship between our interiority and the exteriority that define our lives: "My painful quest for wisdom is an endless journey that tries to delve into the darkness of my soul to create a more mature and compassionate person. My political project of deepening democracy in the world is a perennial process of highlighting the plight of the wretched of the earth and broadening the scope of human dignity."[30]

West insists that three pillars—the Socratic, the democratic, and the prophetic—are essential, with each a corrective of the other. Socratic critical thinking is essential and yet the dry, rational tradition of the Socratic requires the passion and compassion of the prophetic. He writes in his 2004 book, *Democracy Matters*: "We must out-Socratize Socrates by revealing the limits of the great Socratic tradition. My own philosophy of democracy that emerges from the nightside of American democracy is rooted in the guttural cries and silent tears of oppressed people. And it has always bothered me that Socrates never cries—he never sheds a tear. His profound yet insufficient rationalism refuses to connect noble self-mastery to a heartfelt solidarity with the agony and anguish of oppressed peoples."[31]

The limits of the Socratic—the absence of emotion, compassion, passion—lead West to define the crucial role of the prophetic. He draws from Heschel in understanding the prophet giving voice to suffering. The prophet, Heschel writes, is not a messenger of God, but "a person who stands in the presence of God (Jeremiah 15:19)."[32] That marks the difference, West would agree with Heschel, between philosophy with its proofs for the existence of God, and the crucial prophetic distinction: to be a witness to God.[33]

Socratic questioning, however clever, will not help people living in agony and the prophetic demand for justice becomes meaningless if it is only a dry, well-articulated argument. Here West shifts from prophecy as a message to prophetic subjectivity.

West and Heschel on Prophecy

For the foundation of his work, West is heir to both philosophical and theological traditions. He draws from Du Bois, Baldwin, the Blues, but also the work of Martin Luther King Jr., the Black church, prophetic liberal Christianity, Gandhian nonviolence, and what he calls "prophetic American civil religion," which "fuses secular and sacred history and combines Christian themes of deliverance and salvation with political ideals of democracy, freedom and equality."[34] "Prophesy Deliverance!" declares the title of one of West's early books, and while the Hebrew prophets are the biblical voices most important to his work, his understanding of prophecy stems from a particular theological tradition that differs in key ways from the liberal Protestant biblical scholarship and belongs instead to a counter-theological tradition.

West has frequently reiterated that he has been profoundly influenced in his understanding of the prophets by Heschel's book *The Prophets*, a groundbreaking study that was enormously influential among leaders of the civil rights movement, including King, James Lawson, Andrew Young, and C. T. Vivian, among others. Heschel's understanding of the prophets has not been well received by many white Jewish and Protestant Bible scholars, who criticize him for being overly critical of modern biblical scholarship and not engaging sufficiently with the theological implications posed by that scholarship.[35] By contrast, Heschel's approach bears remarkable affinities to theological traditions of the Black church, and his understanding of "prophetic consciousness" resonates today in both the writings and in the person of Cornel West. Indeed, Heschel may be better understood by Black theologians, Christian and Jewish, than by any other group, including Jews.

Often called a prophet of our time, West is indeed a voice today for the plundered poor, "raging against the profaned riches of the world," to borrow Heschel's language. Both West and Heschel write of prophecy and carry us with them in their prophetic journey to give voice to silent agony and bring hope for an ultimate redemption. Among contemporary thinkers, West stands out with his insistence that the prophetic tradition is essential for our society. He speaks of his work as "prophetic pragmatism," a far too modest depiction of the revolution his thought brings to the table of political thought as well as of Christian theology. The prophets stand at the very center of his corpus, bringing a crucial element—compassion: Socrates's "profound yet insufficient rationalism refuses to connect noble self-mastery to a heartfelt solidarity with the agony and anguish of oppressed peoples. Democracy needs Jerusalem."[36] And Jerusalem, for West, is the prophetic tradition, both its harsh critique of injustice and its dream of a new kind of world. It is therefore not surprising that West is sharply critical of the political Jerusalem of today for failing to act in the prophetic tradition he idealizes and admires; he wants the emergence of the "New Jerusalem" that James Baldwin had envisaged: "The day will come when you will trust you more than you do now, and you will trust me more than you do now. And we can trust each other. I do believe, I really do believe in the New Jerusalem, I really do believe that we can all become better than we are. I know we can. But the price is enormous—and people are not yet willing pay it."[37]

At a time when disdain for religion marks the political Left as well as philosophers and pragmatists, West's role has at times been viewed as discordant, marginal, and too religious. Even defining his role can be difficult: is he a scholar, a gadfly, a theologian, a philosopher, a cultural critic? Strikingly similar questions have long been asked about Heschel, who is similarly impossible to categorize. Both Heschel and West challenge disciplinary rubrics and violate intellectual boundaries, and both do so intentionally, as scholars who refuse to remain in their ivory towers and strive instead to make the words they write become instruments of dramatic social and cultural change. Most important, both speak out of the sources of their respective religious traditions in issuing dramatic critiques of society and culture, refusing to constrain their ideas to the disciplinary realms of politics and philosophy. In so doing, they do not merely cite the Bible, they give us new ways to understand the Bible; both Christianity and Judaism are recreated, born afresh.

To be a prophet is to live in anguish and voice the pain of those who suffer. Philosophy and politics are insufficient. Heschel writes, "The prophet's word is a scream in the night. While the world is at ease and asleep, the prophet feels the blast from heaven."[38] For some, the prophetic critique of society might be called "hysterical"—but if so, "what name should be given to the abysmal indifference to evil which the prophet bewails?"[39] For Heschel, prophecy does not redeem us, but calls upon us to redeem ourselves from the mendacity, corruption, and cruelty that plague society. To this West warns that passion, however well-intended, can also run the risk of turning into rage, intolerance, harsh dogmatism. Even the prophetic has the potential to turn dogmatic, West warns, requiring the structures and deliberations of the democratic. Democracy can give power to prophecy's critique and to its hope. Yet American democracy, both West and Heschel assert, is plagued by economic rapacity, militarism, and authoritarianism, an "anti-intellectual, market-driven civilization preoccupied with comfort, convenience and contentment."[40]

If Antonio Gramsci recast Marxism as a 'philosophy of praxis,' West turns to prophecy as the site of resistance to capitalism—at the very least, to certain crucial institutions on which capitalism rests its foundations—its social hierarchy, racism, of course—but especially its mentality of exploitation and destruction of love. "Racism predates capitalism," West writes.[41] James Lawson's pledge of nonviolence written for the demonstrators in the Birmingham campaign of 1963 is one of the powerful tools of praxis. If capitalism is a "many-headed hydra," then what is going on inside those many heads? How can we reach them, change those minds? We have Walter Benjamin's critique of the aesthetics of capitalist society; West gives us a prophetic critique of the religious practices of democratic capitalism.

West's concern, in other words, is not to try to understand the text of the Bible, its era of composition or its comparison with other religious communities, but rather to pose to the Bible the key questions: "What does it mean to be human? What does it mean to be modern? What does it mean to be American?"[42]

In contrast to the Afropessimists, West offers hope for redemption: redeeming America from the imperialism that led to its primal sins of genocide of Native peoples, enslavement of Black people, commodification of human life, war, and destruction: "spiritually empty, morally vacuous" was West's characterization of contemporary America in a lecture to the University of Oregon in May 2020.[43] His goal is that of the prophets, "to move the soul, to engage the attention by bold and striking images, and therefore it is to the imagination and the passions that the prophets speak, rather than aiming at the cold approbation of the mind."[44]

The redemption of America will not come simply through calls for justice. West instead draws on a more subtle aspect of prophetic tradition: the prophets' exposure and denunciation of disavowal.

West's Prophetic Critique of Disavowal

Whereas Heschel, like his Protestant counterpart Reinhold Niebuhr, frequently employed a trope of prophetic irony in his critique of the mendacity of state and religious power, West, in the tradition of James Baldwin, emphasizes the prophetic condemnation of disavowal. In so doing, he has also reconfigured our understanding of the prophetic imperative.

For West, American disavowal of its own crimes against humanity, and the denial by individuals of their own capacity for critical thinking, compassion for others, and acceptance of responsibility stands at the heart of prophetic condemnation. Jeremiah speaks directly to disavowal when he says, "On your shirt is found the life-blood of the guiltless poor. Yet in spite of all these things, you say: 'I am innocent.' Behold I will bring you to judgment for saying, 'I have not sinned.'" (2:14–15). America, too, disavows its crimes and claims innocence. West brings new urgency to the prophetic hermeneutics of disavowal: the prophet's condemnation of those who refuse to acknowledge that which is in full view and assume responsibility. For West, disavowal is the driving sin of America, the refusal to admit the reality of its war crimes, economic exploitation, and its racism.

In a 1914 article, "Remembering, Repeating, and Working Through," Freud writes that people enact what they strive to disavow. Disavowal is not the same as denial, which ends up in repression. Rather, disavowal knows what is present but refuses acknowledgement and rejects responsibility because it may be too painful, traumatic, or costly. When knowledge cannot be eradicated, it enters an enactment: racist murders continue because racism is disavowed: America claims, "I am innocent," disavowing its racism, then enacts murders of Black people. The psychoanalysts Jean Laplanche and Jean-Bertrand Pontalis have defined disavowal as the "refusal to recognize the reality of a traumatic perception."[45] False innocence is easier to claim than profoundly immoral, deeply rooted hatred, and cruelty. Disavowal has proved a helpful term for historians analyzing, for example, Europe's "disavowed modernity"[46] and the "implicated subject"[47] who denies responsibility in the crimes committed in an effort to maintain, at least in their own eyes, a sense of innocence and respectability.

In America, efforts to expose and expunge disavowal and face the history of the genocide of Native people and enslavement of Black people, and ongoing systemic racism, results in enactments that gratify and protect, producing resentment, rage, and often additional crimes defending a false innocence based on untruth. To disavow is not simply to turn away; West's critique of Obama's presidency lies precisely on the disavowal enacted through deeds: disavowing his own vote against the war in Iraq, Obama sent drones to kill people in Afghanistan; disavowing his responsibility for the poor, Obama made compromises on affordable health insurance; disavowing the crimes of Wall Street, he rescued their wealth in order, he claimed, to preserve the economic status quo.

The prophets go beyond condemning sin to condemning the disavowal of pretense and false innocence. Consider financial exploitation. All our religions warn us against economic corruption: Islam has strict laws regarding banking and investment; to violate them is to violate God's own will. For the prophets, those who plunder and exploit, cheat and imprison have not only sinned, but corrupted themselves: "Their heart is false," says Hosea (10:2). Those who engage in financial exploitation disavow their wickedness in the name of generating wealth (for themselves). Sometimes, West points out, it is called "capitalism" or "trickle-down economics." Those not caught by the law think they are home free. Their success is based on their ability to hide, to live a life of pretense, a life without conscience; this is life as a lie. But wealth cannot mask corruption for the prophets. As Baldwin recognized, Americans are "innocent" in that they destroy uncounted lives "and do not know it and do not want to know it."[48]

White racial politics are a politics of disavowal. In America, Blackness is the figure of disavowal—that which must be made unseen—and whiteness is the trope of disavowal as fantasized innocence, rejection of responsibility, sin, or the need for redemption. The language of Baldwin is blunt in addressing American racist disavowal in a 1979 interview: "White people go around with a very carefully suppressed terror of black people, a tremendous uneasiness, they don't know what the black face hides and they're sure it's hiding something. What it's hiding is American history, what white people know they have done and are doing. White people know very well one thing and it's the only thing they have to know. They know this, everything that's said is a lie. They know they would not like to be black here. They know that. Now they know that, and they are telling me lies."[49]

False innocence prevails: "they have destroyed and are destroying hundreds of thousands of lives and do not know it and do not want to know it. . . . It is the innocence which constitutes the crime."[50] Disavowal is a life without conscience and stands at the heart of the corruption denounced by the biblical prophets. The critique of America from Baldwin and West resonates with the prophetic spirit: "You felt secure in your wickedness; you said, No one sees me; your wisdom and your knowledge led you astray, and you said in your heart, I am and there is no one beside me" (Isaiah 47:10).

Sin is more than an action, and its afterlife is more than feelings of guilt. It is precisely the disavowal of having sinned that exemplifies what Michael Ignatieff describes as *The Lesser Evil*, pragmatic compromise, a "tolerated sin." "Liberal states establish mechanisms to regulate the breach of some human rights and legal norms and allow their security services to engage in forms of extrajuridical violence . . . in order to fend off or minimize potential greater evils, such as terror attacks on civilians of western states."[51] Drones kill people designated as enemies without due process. Eyal Weizman has described disavowal at work in certain forms of humanitarianism as *The Least of All Possible Evils*, writing, "The lesser evil is the argument of the humanitarian agent that seeks military permission to provide medicines and aid in places where it is in fact the duty of the occupying military power to do so, thus saving the military limited resources."[52] The Voting Rights Act of 1965 might be seen in similar terms: Congress enacted a law at the height of the civil rights era without addressing the underlying, pervasive racism that denied Black Americans the right to vote, so that the act, over time, came to be eviscerated by state legislatures, and even the chief justice of the United States disavowed the ongoing and foundational antiblackness of Americans.

Racism is the heart of American disavowal, and West carries, like a prophet, the mantle of exposing that disavowal. He writes, "We are exceptional because of our denial of the antidemocratic foundation stones of American democracy. No other democratic nation revels so blatantly in such self-deceptive innocence, such self-paralyzing reluctance to confront the nightside of its own history."[53] Yet for West, America is always in process of becoming, never completed, much like Soren Kierkegaard's understanding of a Christian: one is always only becoming one, so that "West understands his intellectual task as inherently a moral and prophetic one, as calling America back to its founding words and the job of enacting them."[54]

Disavowal is what structures America today; to "protect election fraud" Republican-controlled state legislatures work to disenfranchise Black voters. Claiming that America is not racist, politicians seek to ban critical race theory from schools and universities. As Grace Kyungwon Hong writes, "I define neoliberalism foremost as an epistemological structure of disavowal, a means of claiming that racial and gendered violences are things of the past."[55] Such disavowal is successful by rendering itself invisible: "Neoliberalism is a structure of disavowal, an epistemological framing, a way of seeing and not seeing,"[56] and it quickly becomes a matter of necropolitics: "It claims that protected life is available to all and that premature death comes only to those whose criminal actions and poor choices make them deserve it." This neoliberal disavowal legitimates the proliferation and exacerbation of what Ruth Wilson Gilmore has described as "the state-sanctioned and/or extra-legal production and exploitation of group-differentiated vulnerabilities to premature death, in distinct yet densely interconnected political geographies."[57]

The enactments of disavowal include racial capitalism, enslavement, and Jim Crow segregation; heteropatriarchal homophobic sexuality, misogyny that protects wealthy women and abandons poor women to sexual assault, harassment, and discrimination; and depoliticized intellectual jousts over intersectionality. Herein lies the root of West's critique of Ta-Nehisi Coates: Coates's pessimism is produced by focusing on racial identity rather than the deeper economic forces that construct American society. Participating in the disavowal, Coates allows white Americans to adore him because he takes the pessimism onto himself, as a Black condition, and avoids the call to revolution that would challenge more than their guilty emotions. White supremacy, to West, does not exist without capitalist economic structures, and pessimism over race becomes a tool to ignore those structures and disavow the need for radical economic overhaul. Racism keeps capitalism functioning, much as antisemitism was crucial in the political functioning of pre-1945 Europe; Hitler needed antisemitism to come to power and German antisemitism prevented their repudiation of fascism. West writes, "A race-transcending prophet is someone who never forgets about the significance of race but refuses to be confined to race."[58]

As George Shulman writes, the problem is "not quite ignorance, but the 'innocence' of whites who do not want to know, or who disavow what they already know, about racial injustice, the conduct of the state acting in their name, the humanity of the other."[59] As a "fantastic system of evasions," innocence itself is the crime.[60] Prophecy, for Baldwin, "does not decree a fate but demands a decision."[61]

The disavowal of racism is also an element in Baldwin's critique of America: "What is most terrible is that American white men are not prepared to believe my version of the story, to believe that it happened. In order to avoid believing that, they have set up in themselves a fantastic system of evasions, denials, and justifications, which system is about to destroy their grasp of reality, which is another way of saying their moral sense. What I am trying to say is that the crime is not the most important thing here. What makes our situation serious is that we have spent so many generations pretending that it did not happen."[62] And: "I know what the world has done to my brother and how narrowly he has survived it. And I know, which is much worse, and this is the crime of which I accuse my country and my countrymen, and for which neither I nor time nor history will ever forgive them, that they have destroyed and are destroying hundreds of thousands of lives and do not know it and do not want to know it."[63]

West as Hasidic Rebbe

As much as West calls himself a Christian pragmatist, his understanding of prophecy is deeply influenced by Heschel, and he has revived the bond that King enjoyed with the next Heschel generation. Not just West's relationships with Jewish thinkers and his constant emphasis on the dangers of both antisemitism and racism but the affinities between his work and theirs make him a staunch Black intellectual ally with Jewish intellectuals.[64] His friendship with Michael Lerner, editor of *Tikkun* magazine, led to the publication of their important joint book, *Jews and Blacks: Let the Healing Begin*, in 1995, in which they addressed antagonisms but also wrote that "Jews and Blacks have been linked in a symbiotic relation with each other" (4).

Moreover, there is something of the Hasidic rebbe about Cornel West. Walk with him down Broadway in New York City and watch him not simply smile but forge connection with everyone who greets him. Walking with Cornel, like walking with a rebbe, is inspiring, a religious act.[65] No wonder Heschel returned from Selma and said, "I was reminded of walking with Hasidic rebbes in Europe. I felt my legs were praying." There, on Upper West Side Broadway, Cornel walks to bring social change not by politicking but with the loving he gives to everyone he meets. He walks not as the famous professor but as the spirit overflowing with human generosity. I'm reminded of the Ba'al Shem Tov, the founder of Hasidism in eighteenth-century Ukraine, who famously brought wood to bring warmth to the hut of a blind, elderly widow instead of going to the synagogue on Yom Kippur, and of Rabbi Shlomo Carlebach, who was friends with every homeless person on the Upper West Side. Like a Hasidic rebbe, West stops to talk to everyone he encounters—a short greeting, smile, eye contact, or conversation. He hears their pain and takes it inside himself, offering not just words of comfort but the act of witnessing, one soul to another. He lifts sad hearts and brings smiles with words of humor, a brief exchange about politics, an expression of solidarity. The young students who come to shake his hand are thrilled and will remember this brief conversation with him as he asks about their studies, plans, and hopes. Like Abraham Heschel, my father, whom I watched as he greeted people and made it an experience of transformation: from strangers to friends. Heschel saw each encounter with a new person as an opportunity; each person is a unique reflection of the divine and a chance to know God in a new way.

Just as there is something Jewish and even Hasidic about Cornel West, there was something not quite white about Heschel. Indeed, many white Jews viewed Heschel as not white; he didn't fit into their model of scholarship, he criticized the powerful, dissented from the political mainstream, and he cannot be comfortably situated within the same theological traditions as white thinkers, Jewish or Christian—he never fit in with whiteness, Jewish or Christian. As West writes, "Jews are only white because there are black people in America."[66] And not all Jews are white. Heschel remains beloved to this day among his Black colleagues and friends who are still grateful, sixty years later, for his involvement in the civil rights movement. Yet among many white Jews he remains an enigma or a discomfort or a puzzle, certainly not beloved. As Heschel wrote, no doubt with himself in mind, "those [Jews] who are authentic speak in a small still voice which the Establishment is unable to hear."[67] A Hasidic Jew, Heschel was a brand plucked from the fires of Nazi Europe, a poor refugee whose mother and three sisters were murdered, a theologian who adamantly criticized Euro-American philosophical traditions as well as social theory. Judaism, he wrote, is a religion of dissent, precisely why he unleashed a massive critique of American religion, Jewish and Christian, writing that most synagogues are where prayer goes to die.

Rejected by the German Jewish establishment during his years in Germany, by many American rabbis during his lifetime, especially the Orthodox, and by the academic establishment in the state of Israel, Heschel wasn't acceptable to them because he didn't fit their agenda. He didn't present elaborate logical arguments but preferred persuasion; he failed to address the challenges to Judaism posed by Baruch Spinoza, Immanuel Kant, Georg Wilhelm Friedrich Hegel, and Martin Heidegger because he thought they failed to understand Judaism, making their claims irrelevant or even responsible for the rise of National Socialism; he was not interested in the social science scholars of religion because he thought they were spiritually tone deaf; nor did he care for philological methods of analyzing the Bible that missed the poetry, beauty, and inspiration that gave life and meaning to its readers. As he wrote, the Bible "is a sublime answer, but we do not know the question anymore. Unless we recover the question, there is no hope of understanding the Bible."[68]

In remarkably similar ways, West, too, does not fit the defined academic categories nor the disciplines that have become fixed with boundaries. He is a philosopher who takes religion seriously; a theologian who, like Heschel, believes that churches and synagogues have failed and must repent; an academic who speaks radical truth to the powers in government; a scholar of African American experience who cannot be limited to sociology, history, and literature alone, but insists that religion, too, must be brought into the African American studies. West doesn't answer the questions of the disciplines; like Heschel, he formulates the questions, and his questions are infused with the human condition of the here and now.

Perhaps we should not be surprised to find a Hasidic spirit about Cornel West. Heschel used to say that if there is any hope for the future of Judaism in America, it lies with the Black church, where he found the Hasidic spirit that he remembered from pre-Nazi Eastern Europe. In classical Hasidic thought, every deed can be infused with a spirit of holiness and can ascend to heaven to help bring redemption on earth. Worship can occur with the body, whether walking, eating, dancing, singing, making love, or praying, and does not require a negation of the body or an ascetic lifestyle—on the contrary, Hasidism insisted on worship with joy. Moreover, the Hasidic rebbe takes upon himself the sins and the suffering of his followers, offering consolation and inspiration; his purpose is to repair broken souls. Here is how West describes his rebbe-like encounters:

> I remember meeting one of these disconnected, tortured youngsters at a talk I gave at a community center in Newark, New Jersey. . . . The young man listened closely and then, in obvious pain, said, "Here's the score—I'm in this world by myself. My mother's strung out and tuned out. I have brothers, but I don't know them, and as for my father, where he is nobody knows. I sure have never seen him." I remember feeling totally helpless. I had no recipe to heal these open wounds. The only thing I could think of doing was to bow before the enormity of his misery, kiss the young brother's hand and mumble some words of empathy. "My God, I can't imagine—it's beyond my experience. You've got things you can teach me—you've been somewhere I've never been. I've read a ton of books on alienation, but I cannot grasp what you are living. . . . I cannot understand what it must be like to have never been loved." I then simply told him to stay strong and don't forget to pray. . . . This young man is not alone. In modern America, across race, gender and class, millions of children are in terrible trouble.[69]

Blues: The Unique and Crucial Contribution of Black Americans to Democracy

Disavowal is challenged by the Blues: "the blues are all those who are willing to look unflinchingly at catastrophic conditions," West told an interviewer, combining catastrophe with hope. "The blues is an autobiographical chronicle of a personal catastrophe expressed lyrically and endured with grace and dignity."[70] West describes himself: "I come from a blues people whose anthem is, "Lift Ev'ry Voice and Sing." And "I'm a bluesman in the life of the mind, and a jazzman in the world of ideas."[71] What is a "bluesman"? The "bluesman descends from both the griot tradition and the prophetic tradition."[72] He continues, "I must fuel the fire of my soul so my intellectual blues can set others on fire."[73]

The Blues is an expression of both catastrophe and hope, essential to preserving our humanity as well as American democracy. There is a prophetic quality to the voice of the Blues for West: it is the voice of Black America's agony and yet, he argues, also gives voice to hope within tragedy. Eduardo Mendieta calls attention to the contrast between Richard Rorty's understanding of irony as the expression of democratic maturity and West's emphasis on the hope that stems from Blues, aligning West's stress on hope with the hope that is central to the writings of the German Jewish philosopher Ernst Bloch and the German Catholic theologian Johannes Baptist Metz. In prophetic and messianic traditions, Mendieta argues, hope is not an erasure of memory. West does not suggest that hope requires forgetting or forgiving; rather, hope is sustainable because it glimmers in the Blues as an expression of Black experience and the memory of devastating human cruelty to body and soul. In writing about West, Mendieta emphasizes that "hope without memory is empty, and memory without hope is blind. And both without a democratic ethos are powerless."[74] That hope, Mendieta points out, is of body and soul since democracy's members are embodied: raced and sexed, so that we require "a somatics of democratic trust, vulnerability and reciprocity."[75] The Blues sensibility, West said in an interview with George Yancy, is a "profound sense of the tragic and the comic rooted in heroic efforts to preserve human dignity on the night side, the underside of modernity."[76]

Where is the hope? Jacob Goodson points out that West concludes one of his essays on race with the words, "hope against hope," an echo of a central idea in Hasidism, that despair is forbidden because we are never abandoned by God, only hindered when we fail to perceive God's presence all around us.[77] Heschel writes that "evil is never the climax of history." West wrote that for Heschel the prophets combine "a very deep love, a very powerful dissent, a painful rebuke, with unwavering hope."[78] Precisely because Heschel was not white and can never be made white he was vilified or condescendingly dismissed by so many in the Jewish establishment in his day, including for his antiracism work. West joins Heschel in rejecting despair and pessimism, "Daily we should take account and ask: What have I done today to alleviate the anguish, to mitigate the evil, to prevent humiliation?"[79]

Unique among public intellectuals, West challenges all sides of each community. As a bluesman he articulates suffering and offers hope: "Despair and hope are inseparable. One can never understand what hope is really about unless one wrestles with despair."[80] To the religious, he demands, "How does a present-day Christian think about and act on enhancing the plight of the poor, the predicament of the powerless and the quality of life for all in a prophetic manner?"[81] To the political theorists, especially those on the Left who often view religion as irrelevant or even damaging to society, he writes, "Notwithstanding the secular sensibilities of most leftist intellectuals and activists, religion permeates and pervades the lives of the majority of people in the capitalist world."[82] Without recognizing the religious dimension of political struggle, the Left cannot succeed, just as political struggles must recognize "the poisonous mixture of race and class."[83] A simplistic analysis that ignores the absurd, tragic, and evil nature of human beings is doomed, but so is an analysis that abandons the need for somatic survival and the spiritual sustenance of hope.

Redemption Comes from Prophetic Expression

Are there dreams left to us in an era when racism is so relentless that it seems unconquerable, and authoritarianism seems, to too many people, preferable to democracy? Is there an answer to Afropessimism? Has racism made real the warning on Dante's entry to hell, "Abandon hope all ye who enter here"? Political theorist Susan Buck-Morss has written of the collapse of modernity's dream of utopia, a dream that had driven both capitalism and socialism. Neither succeeded and the end of the twentieth century has left not only political and economic systems in chaos but crushed our hopes as well. Buck-Morss speaks of "a utopian desire for social arrangements that transcend existing forms," betrayed by "global systems that exploit both human labor and natural environments . . . [with] a panoply of phantasmagoric effects that aestheticize the violence of modernity and anaesthetize its victims." She is not nihilistic, however; drawing from Walter Benjamin's notion of "dreamworld," she calls on us to "salvage modernity's universal intent" in the face of the exclusivity of nationalism: "political collectives proclaim themselves champions of human rights and the rule of law and then deny these to a whole list of enemy exceptions, as if humanity itself were the monopoly of their own privileged members."[84]

To some commentators, the present day has lost the capacity for the radicalism of the prophetic tradition. James Darsey writes, "[Todd] Gitlin and [Billy] Graham may be worlds apart in their evaluations of what has been lost, but there is a high degree of consensus that it is gone, and that we have found nothing yet to replace it. Radical discourse understood in terms of biblical prophecy has no potency in such a world."[85]

Here is where Cornel West's contribution intervenes. He points to the "rich prophetic legacies of Sojourner Truth, Walter Rauschenbusch, Dorothy Day, Abraham Heschel, and Martin Luther King Jr., [that] now lay nearly dormant—often forgotten—and the possession of a marginal few."[86] Yet, like Darsey, West agrees that "American religious life is losing its prophetic fervor."[87] He calls instead for a "principled prophetism."[88] Hope is not the domain of political promises, nor of Christian missions to unite all humanity in the baptismal font, nor is it the avant la lettre effort of a universalist "Marrano strategy," as Agata Bielik-Robson argues.[89] For West, it is the prophets who give us the dream and the voice: "Prophetic pragmatism, with its roots in the American heritage and its hopes for the wretched of the earth, constitutes the best chance of promoting an Emersonian culture of creative democracy by means of critical intelligence and social action."[90]

What is that principled, prophetic pragmatism? Is it not, as Richard Rorty has argued, a contradiction in terms, that pragmatism needs prophecy like fish need bicycles.[91] Here Rorty fails to understand what West means by the prophetic, namely, Heschel's understanding of prophetic passion. In responding to Rorty, West presents an elucidation of Heschel's importance as well as that of prophecy. He explains that philosophy without prophecy is like bodies without souls, and that without the prophetic dimension, philosophy cannot understand the passions that motivate, inspire, and console human beings and will ultimately fail to be meaningful. Black musical traditions, especially Blues, West emphasizes, convey an aesthetic appreciation of the prophetic by giving voice to intense suffering and yet offering hope as a redemption from suffering. Here he echoes a comment by Toni Morrison, "For a long time, the art form that was healing for black people was music."[92] Just as the prophet hears and gives voice to the silent agony of the oppressed, so too the Blues give voice to precisely those within the "democracy" who have been enslaved, brutalized, and at times denied the right to live. Yet hope arises: the civil rights movement offered the United States the possibility of becoming a democracy by granting the right to vote to all of its citizens. Black Americans rescued American democracy, and by redeeming America became the messianic figures of prophetic hope. Today, of course, it is not clear that the United States wants to be a democracy, as the courts and state legislatures eviscerate voting rights legislation.

Still, there is an important caveat to be raised here. West, like King and many other Black theologians and intellectuals, is cautious about claims that Blacks can "redeem and transform the modern world through the truth and clarity of perception that emerge from their pain."[93] As Craig Evans argues in his book *The Burden of Black Religion*, there is a long tradition of white assumption that Blacks are innately religious, a claim used by abolitionists to counter beliefs in Black savagery. After the Civil War, the rhetoric shifted, and Black religion was blamed for the alleged inability of Black Americans to modernize. During the Harlem Renaissance of the 1920s and '30s, Black intellectuals like Langston Hughes and Zora Neale Hurston valorized the "primitive" spirit and emotional expression of Black religion as antidotes to stultifying bourgeois society, paralleling the European Orientalism of the same era that turned to Eastern religions. Yet during the same period, there were white intellectuals, such as Gunnar Myrdal, who depicted Black religion as dysfunctional. By the civil rights era, Black religiosity became a reassurance to whites that Blacks demanding an end to segregation were pastors and churchgoers; religion was thought to mitigate the danger of Black rage. At the same time, Black piety was invoked as inspiration for civil rights with a promise to "save the soul of America." In each era, the formula suggested that slavery, racism, and oppression generated intense emotional piety in Black men and women, and the very intensity of their piety would in turn redeem their white oppressors. That is the "burden of Black religion" whose logic Evans outlines in his book.

Where does Cornel West's analysis fit into this schema? The Socratic and prophetic are shared with whites, as is the democratic. The fault line is exemplified by the Blues: can white people understand and be inspired and transformed by Black aesthetics, able to sense the hope that can nonetheless be embedded in the pain and suffering that are resonant in the Blues? The literary critic Stanley Crouch polemicized against presentations of Black suffering as a martyrdom that would then convey a kind of "moral magic."[94] If that is the message of the redemptive nature of Christ's crucifixion, the Christian cross as a promise of hope after death, does the Blues, in West's terms, function as its substitute, as the expression of suffering—and even death—as the necessary martyrdom for a hope that redeems?

Thanks to West's decades-long engagement with the prophets, his answer is no. Without repudiating the redemptive death of Christ, West nonetheless shifts attention from the Jesus as the Son of God to Blacks as God's prophetic witnesses. Here we see a different sensibility, and West's understanding of the redemptive nature of Blues stands in that context. The promise of the prophet lies not in a text nor in a death, but in a voice, and it is a voice carrying the compassion of God. Sound is the medium, whether prophetic words or Blues music.

The prophet is not simply a mouthpiece for God, but a person imbued, as Heschel writes, with sympathy, attuned to God's own pathos that is shaped by God's emotional response to the suffering of human beings. Heschel draws on an ancient Jewish understanding, expressed in biblical and rabbinic texts, that there is a *zorech gavoha*, a divine need: God is in need of human beings, receiving strength from our good deeds and in pain when we harm one another. Anguish for the silent agony of the oppressed is expressed by the prophet because it is the suffering of God. The prophet's expression of anguish is itself a balm for those who suffer, and the Blues offer a similar balm, in West's presentation. Not the suffering, but the expression of it creates the hope that emerges from the Blues; redemption does not come from death or pain, but from suffering's prophetic resonance and empathic expression. West writes, "Black bonds of affection, black networks of support, black ties of empathy, and black harmonies of spiritual camaraderie provide the grounds for the fragile existential weaponry with which to combat black invisibility and namelessness."[95]

West's theology is not in quest of prophetic states of ecstasy, convulsions, or irrational states, nor has he any inclination to belittle the Bible or Judaism or paganism. His is the rare Christian theology that does not ride a seesaw of self-elevation by denigrating another faith. Nor does West look for voices of calm reason, rationality, and self-importance as a source of religious inspiration. His spirit, like the prophets, turns to the artists who give voice to the silent agony; he writes of Anton Chekhov, for example, "Like the best blues and jazz artists, he enacts melancholic yet melioristic indictments of misery without concealing the wounds inflicted or promising permanent victory."[96]

The prophetic spirit for West is not only an expression of the horrors of the world, it is also a rousing call to justice. "To prophesy," he writes, "is not to predict an outcome but rather to identify concrete evils."[97] It is in this role that West reminds us that we hold up crucial principles of social justice in the United States yet fail to live up to them. Perfection is not possible; West knows from Reinhold Niebuhr that man may be moral, but society is inevitably immoral. Yet in that immoral society there must be a prophetic voice to chastise us—indeed, to condemn us—and never permit our immoral society the excuse of original sin. The prophets' condemnation of their societies seems to us extravagant; were things really that bad or did they have unrealistically high standards, as Kenneth Seeskin has asked.[98] For Heschel—and West, in this respect, is his disciple—the exaggerated prophetic response is a sign of the passion that the prophet brings by viewing human beings from

God's perspective. Heschel writes, "The prophet's words are outbursts of violent emotions. His rebuke is harsh and relentless. But if such deep sensitivity to evil is to be called hysterical, what name should be given to the abysmal indifference to evil which the prophet bewails?"[99]

West reminds his readers that "The black church tried to hold together both the dignity and depravity of persons in such a way that God—like Yahweh with the children of Israel—identifies with the disinherited and downtrodden, yet even the disinherited and downtrodden are sinners in need of conversion and sanctification."[100]

Conclusion

In a recent interview with *The Times of Israel*, West said, "Part of my mission is to make the world safe for the legacy of Martin Luther King Jr., and Heschel is one of the major figures who enables King. Heschel puts the stress on deeds, courage, sacrifice, service to others. He is a bearer of that great spiritual moral revolution all the way back to Hebrew Scripture."[101] The significance of prophecy to West begins with the ability to perceive the silent sigh of human anguish. While most were thrilled with the election of a Black president, West heard the anguish of those rendered penniless by corruption in the economic markets and he was outraged that "not one Wall Street criminal executive went to jail." United States drones killed civilians overseas, while police killed civilians on the streets of our cities. Twenty-five million Americans received health-care insurance, but twenty million remained without. Ultimately, the "top 1% got nearly two-thirds of the income growth in eight years even as child poverty, especially black child poverty, remained astronomical."[102]

The problem, as West defines it, is not political policy, but a moral challenge. He told CNN on June 22, 2015, "I would say the first black president has become the first niggerized black president." By that he meant, "A niggerized black person is a black person who is afraid and scared and intimidated when it comes to putting a spotlight on white supremacy and fighting against white supremacy. . . . White supremacy has nothing to do with just skin pigmentation, it has to be what kind of person you want to be, what kind of nation we want to be. Democrats and Republicans play on both of those parties in terms of running away from the vicious legacy of white supremacy until it hits us hard."[103]

"Where in America do we hear a voice like the voice of the prophets of Israel?" Like West, the biblical prophets were often lonely figures, alienating the pious as well as the wicked, priests and princes as well as false prophets.[104] Yet their legacy as some of the most disquieting people in history continues in their heirs, including the great figures of the civil rights movement, King, Baldwin, Heschel, and West. Standing in the prophetic tradition, Cornel West is not simply a leader or public intellectual, but a prophetic figure who condemns disavowal, denounces indifference, and proclaims that God is never unmoved but suffers with us. Like the prophets, both West and Heschel understand that the ultimate expression of God is not wisdom, magnificence, land, glory, nor even love, but rather justice: justice is the tool of God, the manifestation of God, the means of our redemption, and the redemption of God from human mendacity.

Notes

Cornel West has been a friend of mine since the 1990s and I have enjoyed our conversations and the many public dialogues we have presented on Black-Jewish relations. We have never agreed on everything, which has made our dialogues interesting; as Bernice Johnson Reagon pointed out in her 1995 essay, "Coalition Politics," it's not a coalition if everyone is in agreement. I do not agree with Cornel's support for BDS, but I also don't walk away from a disagreement and instead pursue the argument. My chapter was written prior to his resignation from Harvard Divinity School, and I strongly disagree with his claim that Harvard rejected his request for tenure because of his pro-Palestinian politics. Cornel was my colleague briefly at Dartmouth College and I am grateful for his warmth, for his remarkable gifts as a teacher and for the generous attention he gave to our students and faculty. I am very glad he is returning to teach at Union Theological Seminary, which was a very welcoming faculty home for my father many years ago and which offered me use of its an incomparable library collection for my own research. I would also like to thank my colleague J. Kameron Carter for very helpful conversations as I was writing this chapter.

Epigraph: Abraham Joshua Heschel, *The Prophets* (New York: Harper and Row, 1962), 5.

1. On Troeltsch's attack on Cohen, see Torsten Lattki, *Benzion Kellermann: Prophetisches Judentum und Vernunftreligion* (Göttingen: Vandenhoeck & Ruprecht, 2016), 281–316.

2. In his speech to the Reichstag on January 30, 1939, Hitler declared, "In the course of my life I have very often been a prophet and have usually been ridiculed for it." Jeremy Noakes and Geoffrey Pridham, *Nazism 1919–1945: A Documentary Reader*, vol. 3 (Exeter, UK: Exeter University Press, 1998), 1049.

3. James Darsey, *The Prophetic Tradition and Radical Rhetoric in America* (New York: NYU Press, 1997).

4. Cornel West, "Black Strivings in a Twilight Civilization," in *The Future of the Race*, ed. Henry Louis Gates, Jr., and Cornel West (New York: Knopf, 1996), 80.

5. Lewis Gordon, *Bad Faith and Antiblack Racism* (Amherst, NY: Humanities Press, 1995).

6. Frank Wilderson, *Afropessimism* (New York: Liveright, 2020).

7. Jesse McCarthy, "On Afropessimism," *Los Angeles Review of Books*, July 20, 2020.

8. Tendayi Sithole, *The Black Register* (Medford, MA: Polity, 2020).

9. Wilderson, *Afropessimism*, 58.

10. Elizabeth Alexander, *The Black Interior: Essays* (St. Paul, MN: Graywolf, 2004), 4.

11. Zakiyyah Iman Jackson, *Becoming Human: Matter and Meaning in an Antiblack World* (New York: NYU Press, 2020), 17.

12. Jackson, *Becoming Human*, 4.

13. Jackson, *Becoming Human*, 11.

14. Jared Sexton, "Afro-Pessimism: The Unclear Word," *Rhizomes: Cultural Studies in Emerging Knowledge* 29 (2006), 16, https://doi.org/10.20415/rhiz/029.e02.

15. Sithole, *Black Register*.

16. Sexton, 16.

17. J. Kameron Carter, *Race: A Theological Account* (New York: Oxford University Press, 2008), 4.

18. Cornel West, *Prophesy Deliverance! An Afro-American Revolutionary Christianity* (Philadelphia: Westminster, 1982), 47.

19. Cornel West, "Black Strivings," 80.

20. Cornel West, communication with author, June 21, 2021.

21. Lewis R. Gordon, "Thoughts on Two Recent Decades of Studying Race and Racism," *Social Identities* 24, no. 2 (2018): 29–38; 32.

22. Cornel West, "Black Strivings," 81.

23. Cornel West, *Brother West: Living and Loving Out Loud, A Memoir* (Smiley Books, 2009), 186.

24. Richard Rorty, "The Philosopher and the Prophet," review of *The American Evasion of Philosophy*, by Cornel West, *Transition* 52 (1991): 70–78; 75.

25. Kevin Quashie, *The Sovereignty of Quiet* (New Brunswick, NJ: Rutgers University Press, 2012); Sithole, *Black Register*; Alexander, *Black Interior*.

26. West, "Black Strivings," 82.

27. West, "Black Strivings," 90.

28. *Cornel West Reader* (Civitas Books, 2009), 389.

29. Cornel West, "Black Strivings in a Twilight Civilization," in *The Future of the Race*, ed. Henry Louis Gates, Jr., and Cornel West (New York: Knopf, 1996), 57.

30. *Cornel West Reader*, 165

31. Cornel West, *Democracy Matters: Winning the Battle against Imperialism* (New York: Penguin Press, 2004), 213.

32. Heschel, *The Prophets*, 21.

33. Heschel, *The Prophets*, 22.

34. West, *Democracy Matters*, 426.

35. See, for example, Jon D. Levenson, "Religious Affirmation and Historical Criticism in Heschel's Biblical Interpretation," *AJS Review* 25, no. 1 (2000–2001): 25–44. By contrast, see the very positive reception of Heschel by the Jewish scholar Benjamin Sommer, *Revelation and Authority: Sinai in Jewish Scripture and Tradition* (New Haven, CT: Yale University Press, 2015).

36. West, *Democracy Matters*, 213. Note the critique of West by James Conlon: West credits the Jews with "the invention of the prophetic commitment to justice (*Democracy Matters*, 17) and does not explore the African religious tradition in this regard. Despite his intellectual commitment to moving 'beyond Eurocentrism' (West, 1993, p. 3), he himself makes relatively

few references to intellectual sources outside the European tradition." James Conlon, "Cornel West's Pragmatic Understanding of America," *Journal of Black Studies* 48, no. 1 (2017): 41.

37. *James Baldwin: The Price of the Ticket*, PBS American Masters, https://www.pbs.org/wnet/americanmasters/database/baldwin_j_interview.html.

38. Heschel, *The Prophets*, 16.

39. Heschel, *The Prophets*, 5.

40. https://news.stanford.edu/news/2004/october6/west-106.html.

41. *Cornel West Reader*, 258.

42. *Cornel West Reader*, Preface.

43. https://www.youtube.com/watch?v=Aekb3ppKm5w.

44. Heschel, *Prophets*, vol. 2, 38.

45. Jean Laplanche and Jean-Bertrand Pontalis, *The Language of Psychoanalysis*, trans. Donald Nicholson (New York: Norton, 1974), 118.

46. Sibylle Fischer, *Modernity Disavowed: Haiti and the Cultures of Slavery in the Age of Revolution* (Durham, NC: Duke University Press, 2004), 37; Jeanne Morefield, *Empires Without Imperialism: Anglo-American Decline and the Politics of Deflection* (New York: Oxford University Press, 2014).

47. Michael Rothberg, *The Implicated Subject* (Palo Alto, CA: Stanford University Press, 2019).

48. James Baldwin, *The Fire Next Time* (New York: Dial, 1963), 5–6; cited by Christopher Z. Hobson, *James Baldwin and the Heavenly City*, 117.

49. James Baldwin, interview by Joseph Lovett (1979), *Esquire*, June 15, 2021, https://www.esquire.com/entertainment/books/a36727428/james-baldwin-1979-abc-interview-buried-surfaced/?fbclid=IwAR0SMDpTMKUGcCkH3Lf8cqN9juUryO7OWWI4v2O3KsTG7-SnW_i4BxIUiIw.

50. Baldwin, *Fire Next Time*, 6.

51. Michael Ignatieff, *The Lesser Evil*; cited by Eyal Weizman, *The Least of All Possible Evils: Humanitarian Violence from Arendt to Gaza* (London: Verso, 2011), 8.

52. Weizman, *Least*, 9.

53. Cornel West, *Democracy Matters*, 41.

54. James Conlon, "Cornel West's Pragmatic Understanding of America," *Journal of Black Studies* 48, no. 1 (2017): 34–5.

55. Grace Kyungwon Hong, *Death Beyond Disavowal* (Minneapolis: University of Minnesota Press, 2015), 7.

56. Hong, *Death Beyond Disavowal*, 17.

57. Ruth Wilson Gilmore, "Race and Globalization," in *Geographies of Global Change*, ed. R. J. Johnston, Peter J. Taylor, and Michael J. Watts (London: Blackwell, 2002), 261. Cited by Hong, 17.

58. bell hooks and Cornel West, *Breaking Bread: Insurgent Black Intellectual Life* (Boston: South End Press, 1991), 49.

59. George Shulman, "Acknowledgment and Disavowal as an Idiom for Theorizing Politics," *Theory & Event* 14, no. 1 (2011): 11.

60. James Baldwin, *The Cross of Redemption: Uncollected Writings*, ed. Randall Kenan (New York: Pantheon, 2010), 95.

61. George Shulman, *American Prophecy: Race and Redemption in American Political Culture* (Minneapolis, University of Minnesota Press, 2008), 167.

62. James Baldwin, "The White Problem," in *Cross of Redemption*, 95.

63. James Baldwin, *Fire Next Time*, 5.

64. At the same time, West has been subjected to two major public attacks on his academic integrity by Jewish men, Leon Wieseltier, then literary editor of *The New Republic*, and Lawrence Summers, then president of Harvard University, signaling that their failure to understand West matches Wieseltier's denigration of Heschel. Perhaps it is the Jewish quality of West's prophetic ethos that made him a target, like Heschel, of those who have eyes but do not see, with minds but do not understand. After all, the prophet "employs notes one octave too high for our ears. . . . Often his words begin to burn where conscience ends." Heschel, *The Prophets*, 10.

65. Elliot R. Wolfson, "Walking as a Sacred Duty: Theological Transformation of Social Reality in Early Hasidism," in *Hasidism Reappraised*, ed. Ada Rapoport-Albert (London: Valentine Mitchell, 1996), 180–207.

66. Cornel West, *Race Matters*, 108–9.

67. Heschel, "Dissent," in *Essential Writings of Abraham Joshua Heschel*, ed. Susannah Heschel (Maryknoll, NY: Orbis, 2016), 106–7.

68. Heschel, *God in Search of Man*, 168–69.

69. *Cornel West Reader*, 339.

70. James Baldwin, "Strength in the Blues: An Interview with Cornel West," interview by Jake Uitti, *Monarch Review* (September 2012), http://www.themonarchreview.org/cornel-west-strength-in-the-blues/.

71. The epigraph of his memoir, Cornel West, *Living and Loving Out Loud*, also cited in an interview by Neil Conan, *Talk of the Nation*, NPR, October 29, 2009, https://www.npr.org/templates/story/story.php?storyId=114287606.

72. Cornel West, *Brother West*, 180.

73. *Brother West*, 5.

74. Eduardo Mendieta, "Translating Democracy or Democratic Acts of Translation," *Contemporary Pragmatism* 4, no. 1 (June 2007): 25–37; 29.

75. Mendieta, 31.

76. *Cornel West Reader*, 25.

77. Jacob Goodson interprets this in line with Stanley Cavell and the Transcendentalist tradition of American thought; Jacob L. Goodson, *Strength of Mind: Courage, Hope, Freedom, Knowledge* (Cascade, Open Library, 2018), chap. 1, Kindle Location 4786.

78. Cornel West, "The Radical Heschel," *Jewish Currents* (December 23, 2020), https://jewishcurrents.org/the-radical-heschel/.

79. Heschel, "Religion and Race," in *The Insecurity of Freedom* (New York: Farrar, Straus and Giroux, 1966).

80. *Cornel West Reader*, 554.

81. West, *Reader*, 359.

82. West, *Reader*, 372.

83. Cornel West and Roberto Mangabeira Unger, *The Future of American Progressivism: An Initiative for Political and Economic Reform by Cornel West* (Boston: Beacon, 1998), 18.

84. Susan Buck-Morss, *Hegel, Haiti, and Universal History* (Pittsburgh: University of Pittsburgh Press, 2009), ix, 149.

85. Darsey, 11.

86. *Cornel West Reader*, 357.

87. *Cornel West Reader*, 357.

88. West, *Reader*, 358.

89. Agata Bielik-Robson, "Marrano Universalism: Benjamin, Derrida and Buck-Morss on the Condition of Universal Exile" (paper presented at the 2015 Telos Conference, New York, NY February 13–15, 2015).

90. West, *Reader*, 150.

91. Richard Rorty, "Feminism and Pragmatism," in *Truth and Progress: Philosophical Papers*, vol. 3 (Cambridge: Cambridge University Press, 1998), 202–27.

92. Mari Evans, ed., *Black Women Writers: Arguments and Interviews* (London: Pluto, 1983), 340; cited by Paul Gilroy, *The Black Atlantic: Modernity and Double Consciousness* (Cambridge, MA: Harvard University Press, 1993), 219.

93. The phrase is from Gilroy, *Black Atlantic*, 216.

94. Stanley Crouch, "Aunt Medea," in *Notes of a Hanging Judge* (New York: Oxford University Press, 1990), 205; cited by Gilroy, 217.

95. Cornel West, *Prophetic Fragments: Illuminations of the Crisis in American Religion & Culture* (Grand Rapids, MI: Wm. B. Eerdmans Publishing, 1993), 95; West, "Black Strivings in a Twilight Civilization," in: *Cornel West Reader*, 108.

96. West, Reader, 23.

97. Jeff Sharlet, "The Supreme Love and Revolutionary Funk of Dr. Cornel West, Philosopher of the Blues," *Rolling Stone*, May 28, 2009.

98. Kenneth Seeskin, "The Prophets as Moral Idealists" (paper presented at the Association for Jewish Studies, Boston, MA, December 2018).

99. Heschel, *Prophets*, 4–5.

100. West, *Reader*, 429.

101. Cornel West, interview by Diane Cole, *The Times of Israel*, January 23, 2013.

102. Cornel West, "Pity the Sad Legacy of Barack Obama," *Guardian*, January 9, 2017, https://www.theguardian.com/commentisfree/2017/jan/09/barack-obama-legacy-presidency.

103. Cornel West, "The First Black President has Become the First Niggerized President," RealClearPolitics, posted June 22, 2015, https://www.realclearpolitics.com/video/2015/06/22/cornel_west_on_obama_the_first_black_president_has_become_the_first_niggerized_black_president.html.

104. Heschel, *Prophets*, 18.

CHAPTER 6

Prophetic Fightback: Cornel West, *Race Matters*, and the Black Church

Nkosi Du Bois Anderson

In his new introduction for the twenty-fifth anniversary edition of *Race Matters*, Cornel West grimly asserts that "we live in one of the darkest moments in American history—a bleak time of spiritual blackout and imperial meltdown" (xv). The signs of spiritual blackout are threefold. First, it pertains to the normalization of dishonesty and criminal behavior present throughout the halls of financial and political power. Evidence of our spiritual blackout is also seen in the extolment of cruelty, indifference, and avarice. Third, predatory capitalism is hegemonic, commodifying more and more aspects of society and even our own psyches. For instance, the value of serving others and living lives of deep moral conviction are overshadowed by lure and attraction to the superficial spectacle of our rampant and vapid celebrity culture (*Race Matters* xv–xvi).

This spiritual blackout is inextricably linked to the imperial meltdown facilitating so many of the key crises of our time—economic, ecological, nuclear, political, civic, and cultural. West explains that America's imperial meltdown finds its roots in the country's very foundation. The nation remains both haunted and cursed by its refusal to truly face and address its history of settler colonialism, slavery, and other forms of domination. "Like all empires, the American Empire has been unaccountable to its victims," he writes (*Race Matters* xvii). Here we see the deep connection for instance, between race and empire. Lastly, the way of military might (i.e., violence, conquest, toxic masculinity, etc.) is both promoted and reflected within our domestic cultural sphere, further highlighting the linkages between America's spiritual blackout and imperial meltdown (*Race Matters* xv–xx).

In a last-ditch effort to counter this joint onslaught, West declares that "our last and only hope is prophetic fightback—a moral and spiritual awakening that puts a premium on courageous truth telling and exemplary action by individuals and communities" (*Race Matters* xv). Contemporary examples of this prophetic fightback include the Movement for Black Lives; the March 8, 2017, "Day Without A Woman" protest; the struggle in Standing Rock against the Dakota Access Pipeline; and the ongoing work of other activists, clergy, and intellectuals. In this "moral and spiritual war over resources, power, souls, and sensibilities," West writes, those who choose to rise up against dishonesty, greed, superficiality, and the crimes of empire, place themselves within "a long tradition of love warriors" (*Race Matters* xxiv, xxv).

The black freedom movement stands as one of the greatest love warrior traditions in the history of the American empire.[1] Inseparable from this legacy has been the role of black religious leaders committed to activist politics and the fight against injustice. This essay takes up West's call for the "remembrance, reverence, and resurrection" (*Race Matters* xxv) of our grand traditions of prophetic fightback by looking at the social justice heritage of the black church in America. Though not addressed at length in *Race Matters*, the black church is still very pertinent for a discussion on the text. This is for three reasons. The first is due to the historical role and continued relevance of the Christian church in black American life. The second reason concerns the significant place of the black church in West's own personal background and formation. Third, prophetic criticism and the aims of racial uplift and liberation that sit at the center of *Race Matters* reflect the best of the black prophetic Christian tradition. Therefore, this chapter sets out to examine this black Christian mode of prophetic fightback, its place in West's life and work, as well as the challenge that *Race Matters* presents for the black church today.

The Black Church and Social Justice

It must be stated up front that the black church is not a monolithic entity. In many ways, *black church* is an all-encompassing term used to describe a multitude of religious practices, theological beliefs, denominational polity, social doings, political actions, history, etc. of black Christians and their predominantly black congregations within the United States. Such diversity keeps the black church from being reducible to any singular vision or definition. It stands as but a component and an aspect of black life in America. Yet, as Henry Louis Gates Jr. writes, "No pillar of the African American community has been more central to its history, identity, and social justice vision than the 'Black Church'" (1).

That social justice vision is the concern of this section. Here I turn to the work of Peter J. Paris, Gayraud S. Wilmore, and Gary Dorrien, to help illustrate how scholars of religion have both theorized the justice-seeking impulse that has animated so much of the black church's mission and how they have chronicled black Christianity's rich history of social activism.

In *The Social Teaching of the Black Churches*, Paris analyzes the official records of black Baptist and Methodist denominations to present a constructive interpretation of their religious ethics.[2] The African American experience has been significantly shaped by the struggle against white supremacy in its various forms (slavery, segregation, discrimination, etc.). The black church has always responded to the reality of black suffering in the here and now while also holding out hope for a future free from injustice. For instance, during slavery, for most blacks, the question of *how to cope* under such oppressive conditions was paramount. An early form of resistance was the spirituals.[3] Ultimately, seeking a place of refuge became a central focus. This led to the existence of the "invisible institution" in the South,[4] and later, the independent church movement in the north.[5] As Paris writes: "While the larger society sought to victimize blacks, the black churches aimed at socializing their members into creative forms of coping along with the development of imaginative styles of social and political protest, both grounded in a religious hope for an eschatological victory" (6).

What Paris calls *the black Christian tradition* refers to the commonly held values that represent the particular world view that has shaped the thought and actions of the black church in America. It is a response to white supremacy as it pertains to mitigating the harmful effects of racism, caring for the black community, and ensuring their survival. In this way, the black Christian tradition functions in a priestly capacity (11).

It also functions in a prophetic role, working to transform society through critique, moral reform, and political action. This was the impetus for the rise of the independent churches in the North—the first black freedom movement in America. The black Christian church emerged out of the contradictions of the white Christian church. That is to say, the incompatibility between racism and a biblical anthropology that "affirms the equality of all persons under God regardless of race or any other natural quality," Paris writes (11). The belief in "the parenthood of God and the kinship of all peoples" presents a theological view of human equality (10). Eradicating racial inequality thus becomes a moral aim brought about through moral action (religious or political forms of prophetic protest). The black church gives this morality institutional backing. Furthermore, the black church functions as a moral institution in so far as it remains committed to this justice seeking mandate (Paris 14).

Paris further emphasizes the centrality of the prophetic principle to the black Christian tradition. Since it is "both cause and norm of the independent black churches," it stands as a unifier and "the basis for an associational theory" (20). Moreover, "for the black churches every aspect of history must be related to this tradition" (13). It is therefore a normative principle for the black church and by extension, the larger black community.

Paris's study provides an insightful look at the justice imperative that sits at the center of the black church's social ethic. He summarizes and concludes his argument as follows: "The black churches represent in their thought and disposition the universality of Christianity manifested in the midst of racial particularity. Their primary mission has always been that of calling the nation to effect racial equality and justice (that is, the kinship of all peoples) within its borders" (134).

In *Black Religion and Black Radicalism*, Gayraud S. Wilmore offers a historical interpretation of black religion. He maintains that black society is intricate, particular, and reflects great diversity across a range of social indicators. Yet, "religion has been and continues to be an essential thread interweaving the fabric of black culture" (Wilmore 253). Its place throughout the African diaspora is therefore significant.

Wilmore marks three traditions/stages within the development of black religion in the United States. The first is *the survival tradition*. Wilmore asserts that the will to live and maintain one's sanity "best explains the tenacity and functionality of black religion in the plantation South" (255). Eventually, the idea of securing something greater than mere survival entered the imagination and freedom dreams of an enslaved people. Throughout slave narratives, letters, church sermons, and other documents, Wilmore notes the frequent mention of the words "elevation" and "uplift." The advancement of black civil society, under the auspices of the independent churches in the North, placed a growing emphasis on self-development and promotion. The second movement and phase of advancement, Wilmore calls *the elevation tradi-*

tion. Moral uplift and the pursuit of material growth are its hallmarks. The third stage is *the liberation tradition*. Around the start of the nineteenth century, emancipation became the imperative of black clergy, black laity, and their white abolitionist allies. Wilmore writes that "this extraordinary emphasis on the Christian religion as the foundation for a liberation movement and liberation itself as the primary message of the gospel is reflected in every African American institution of the nineteenth century" (268). For Wilmore, the liberation tradition "stands out as the single most important and characteristic perspective of black faith from 1800 to the Civil Rights movement" (267).

Wilmore rejects the notion that enslaved black people accepted Christianity uncritically. He explains that "the religious beliefs and rituals of a people are inevitably and inseparably bound up with the material and psychological realities of their daily existence" (22). Therefore, for many blacks, a blanket acceptance of Christianity as it was articulated by racist white society did not occur. Rather, "its truth was authenticated to them in the experience of suffering and struggle, to reinforce an enculturated religious orientation and to produce an indigenous faith that emphasized dignity, freedom, and human welfare" (25). The principle of liberation that sits at the core of Christian teaching, yet is overlooked by the white church, offered great appeal to oppressed blacks. Furthermore, Wilmore suggests that this justice imperative "opened up the possibility of an African American radicalism that broke out first in independent churches and religious movements, and gradually worked its way into the most permeable institutions of the black secular community" (198).

Wilmore argues that black radicalism is different from other forms of radical thought due to the emphasis that it places on the problem and task of overcoming white supremacy in the Western world. In Wilmore's view, black radicalism focuses less on politics and theory and instead, "has been a homegrown, race-conscious, unsystematic attack on the roots of black misery in American life—racism" (197). In addition, he writes that it is "a form of protest specific to the black community in its struggle for freedom and a more humane existence" (198).

With respect to the political nature of black religion, Wilmore contends that historically, it has swung back and forth between conservative and radical perspectives. He champions the latter heritage. Wilmore attempts to locate and trace what he identifies as the "radical tradition that has ebbed and flowed in black religion" (ix). His survey studies the resistance literature of

Robert Alexander Young and David Walker to glean insight into the religious beliefs of rebellious blacks seeking freedom. Wilmore examines the role of biblical narratives and spiritual conversion in inspiring Gabriel Prosser, Denmark Vesey, and Nat Turner to lead slave insurrections in 1800, 1822, and 1831, respectively. He emphasizes the threat to the white power structure that the independent black churches of the North represented. Wilmore illuminates the religious underpinnings of black nationalism, highlights the religious/political leadership of Henry McNeal Turner, Marcus Garvey, Martin Luther King Jr., and Malcolm X, notes the significance of black theology, and recognizes the varied contributions of black women like Fannie Barrier Williams, Nannie H. Burroughs, and Delores Williams to the elevation of the race. All in all, Wilmore's study deduces three defining features of the radical tradition found within black religion: the pursuit of freedom from white control, the upliftment of Africa's esteem in the world, and the use of protest and agitation in the struggle for freedom of all oppressed people (ix).

The third perspective on black Christianity's social justice tradition that I want to highlight is that of Gary Dorrien. His project is a recovery of *the black social gospel.* The black social gospel, a movement similar to its white counterpart, emerged out of a belief that the Christian church has a social mission to advance the cause of justice in the world. Salvation was not just seen as something personal, but rather, society itself was also the subject of redemption. Both traditions embraced modern science and recognized the place and function of social structures in ordering the world. Yet black social Christianity also prioritized fighting racism through political activism and uplifting black dignity. And while the public influence of the white social gospel began to rapidly fade in the 1930s, its black counterpart saw its impact reach an apex during the racial justice movements of the 1950s and 1960s (Dorrien, *New Abolition* and *Breaking White Supremacy*).

The black social gospel started to emerge over the last three decades of the nineteenth century. It dealt with the defeat of Reconstruction and began to bloom in the Progressive Era. Dorrien identifies four traditions of black social Christianity that along with a small Marxian socialist stream encapsulate the breath of African American Christian thought and activism in the early twentieth century. These variants, especially the third, laid the groundwork for what would eventually blossom into a mature black social gospel (Dorrien, *New Abolition* and *Breaking White Supremacy*).

The first group Dorrien labels are those within the camp of Booker T. Washington. Washington's philosophy of accommodation, industrialism, self-help, and vocational education appealed to black denominational leaders, not to mention white financial and political elites.

Individuals belonging to the second stream placed an emphasis on black nationalism. Figures like Alexander Crummell, James Theodore Holly, and Henry McNeal Turner advocated African emigration (Haitian, in the case of Holly). They believed that black separation was the only recourse to the problem of white supremacy.

The third tradition is represented by W. E. B. Du Bois, Reverdy Ransom, Ida B. Wells, Richard R. Wright Jr., and others committed to activist politics and social justice. They founded organizations like the Niagara Movement (a precursor to the National Association for the Advancement of Colored People—NAACP), operated in both religious and secular spaces, and stood against the power and influence of Washington's "Tuskegee Machine."

The fourth vision sought middle ground between the pragmatism of the first group and the outspoken activism of the third. Leaders belonging to this tendency included Nannie H. Burroughs, Adam Clayton Powell, Sr., Alexander Walters, and others.

Lastly, Dorrien identifies a fifth stream of individuals for whom the critique of capitalism and the advancement of Socialist politics were essential to any future vision of racial and economic justice. George Washington Woodbey and George W. Slater Jr. were two ministers favoring this perspective. It should be noted that there is overlap across these four traditions. For example, Du Bois, Ransom, and many others belonging to the third group also embraced socialism and radical critiques of the prevailing economic order.

Dorrien is making a continuity argument in his advocacy of the black social gospel. Part of the legacy of these early pioneers is that they inspired subsequent generations of black church leaders to carry on in the work of social activism. Racial justice, socialism, black internationalism, Gandhian nonviolence, and feminism were some of the causes championed by black social gospelers like Mordecai Johnson, Benjamin E. Mays, Howard Thurman, Adam Clayton Powell Jr., and Pauli Murray. Furthermore, this tradition helped produce Martin Luther King Jr. and undergirded the theology and social philosophy of the civil rights movement. Lastly, its influence continued to be seen in the emergence of both black and womanist theologies to follow. To summarize, Dorrien offers a working definition of the black social gospel that I quote here at length: "The full-fledged black social gospel stood for social justice religion and modern critical consciousness. It combined an emphasis on black dignity and personhood with protest activism for racial justice, a comprehensive social justice agenda, an insistence that authentic Christian faith is incompatible with racial prejudice, an emphasis on the social ethical teaching of Jesus, and an acceptance of modern scholarship and social consciousness" (*Breaking White Supremacy* 3).

This section surveyed three landmark studies on black Christianity and social justice. Across these interpretations there exist both overlap and disagreement. Each provides insight into the justice-seeking vision of the black church. Paris illuminates the prophetic impulse found within the black Christian tradition. Wilmore provides a historical reading of what he isolates as the radical steam of black religion. He contends that it has developed in response to black people's needs for survival, elevation, and liberation. Dorrien draws attention to the black social gospel movement and its rich legacy of social activism. Now we turn to exploring Cornel West's connection to the black church and how he's conceived of its prophetic tradition.

Cornel West and the Black Prophetic Christian Tradition

Cornel West describes himself as "a Shiloh Baptist kind of brother" (West and Ritz 8). Here, he is paying homage to the black church that he and his family attended during his youth in the Glen Elder neighborhood of Sacramento, California. Growing up in this working-class and segregated black neighborhood afforded him the chance to "revel in black humanity" ("Intellectual Vocation" 19) as he was shaped and formed by family, the church, and the surrounding community. He explains: "I view myself as an extension of where I came from. The West family, Shiloh Baptist Church, the chocolate side of Sacramento, Glen Elder. That's who I grew up with. That's who loved me" (Kazembe 10).

For generations, Christian faith and the religious life of the black church played a central role in West's family. His paternal grandfather, Clifton L. West Sr., was a Christian minister. For over four decades, he pastored at the Metropolitan Baptist Church in Tulsa, Oklahoma. West's father, Clifton L. West Jr., ran the social outreach initiative for Shiloh Baptist Church and helped create a Little League program for local kids—even building the ballpark from scratch! On his maternal side, West's grandfather, affectionately referred to as "Big Daddy," was a deacon at the Mount Zion Missionary Baptist Church. West's mother, Irene B. West, was a pioneering educator, who held the love of Jesus in her heart, humbly devoting herself to charitable work. As West asserts: "Following Jesus was no small matter in the West household" (West and Ritz 10).

West is commonly mistaken for a Christian minister, in the formal sense. This is largely due to his oratorical style and frequent use of the words "brother" and "sister" when addressing others. Yet he is neither licensed nor ordained. But undoubtedly three Christian ministers in particular had a profound impact in shaping West's understanding of the Christian religion and his eventual vocational path. They served as models of virtue, leadership, and faith. The first was his aforementioned paternal grandfather, the Reverend Clifton L. West Sr. West describes him as "a tower of strength and a paragon of Christian compassion. His life was all about self-sacrifice and spiritual growth" (West and Ritz 14). The second figure was Reverend Willie P. Cooke, who served as pastor of Shiloh Baptist Church from 1957 to 1983, and again as interim pastor from 1990 to 1991 (Barrow). West remembers him as being sincere, given to deep discernment, charitable, and humble (West and Ritz 40). The third example was the Reverend Dr. Martin Luther King Jr. In 1963, West's parents took him, at the tender age of ten, and his older brother, Cliff, to hear King speak at the Memorial Auditorium. King's humility, love of others, and sense of urgency resonated with West. His parents recall that West was later moved to tears when describing to his sisters, Cynthia and Cheryl, the experience of witnessing King in person (West, "Introduction"; West and West viii).

If religion held great significance within the West home, so did education and intellectual inquiry. West sees as his foundation, family, the quest for the truth, and the Christian call to bear witness to love and justice. In his memoir he writes, "I cannot overstate the importance of my relationship to Jesus Christ and my relationship to books in the developing of my character" (West and Ritz 22). The value of connecting the life of the mind to one's own personal development, faith, and the call to lovingly serve others was impressed upon West at an early age. His parents supported and nurtured his intellectual interests while always reminding him about the central importance of love and compassion when trying to change the world. From them he received the gift of unconditional love. He also saw that same love embodied by them in their interactions with others ("Intellectual Vocation" 21; West and Ritz 22).

Through his experiences growing up in the black church and being surrounded by exemplars of this tradition, West began to develop an understanding of the Christian faith, rooted in principles of love and justice. His parents write, that during his teenage years, "as a member of the church . . . he voiced very strong convictions of what a Christian and community layperson ought to be about in eliminating or at least addressing, in some meaningful manner, the social ills of our society" (West and West viii). As he matured and throughout the course of his vocational life, West has continued to fashion, articulate, and champion his perspectives on what it means to be a Christian. For instance, he explains that "to be a Christian is fundamentally to live a certain kind of life, to live a sacrificial life, a love-informed life, a life of care and a life of giving" ("Prophetic Theology" 230). Elsewhere he writes that "to be a Christian—a follower of Jesus Christ—is to love wisdom, love justice, and love freedom. This is the radical love in Christian freedom and the radical freedom in Christian love that embraces Socratic questioning, prophetic witness, and tragicomic hope" (*Democracy Matters* 172).

West identifies as "a prophetic Christian freedom fighter principally because of distinctive Christian conceptions of what it is to be human, how we should act toward one another, and what we should hope for," he explains ("Introduction" xxviii). Prophetic Christianity places an emphasis on critical consciousness, the inherent belief in the equality and value of all persons, especially the downtrodden, and the hope in a future beyond human suffering, that is to say, the coming of the kingdom of God. It affords wisdom to address and face life's existential dilemmas, such as fear, despair, cynicism, nihilism, and death ("Introduction" xxvii–xxviii). As West confesses, "it is the love ethic of Christian faith—the most absurd and alluring mode of being in the world—that enables me to live a life of hope against hope without succumbing to a warranted yet paralyzing pessimism or to an understandable yet miserable misanthropy" ("Preface: The Difficulty of" xi).

With this brief biographical and religious sketch of West, I am not attempting to present a definitive account of his Christian faith. He's defined himself in a variety of different ways, from being a Chekhovian Christian to a revolutionary Christian, both for example.[6] Rather, my aim is to highlight the impact of family, community, and specifically, the role of the black church in both his personal formation and in his conception of what it means to be a particular kind of Christian. Ultimately, West describes himself as "just a brother who comes out of the black church on the block, trying to make sense of the world, and making a blow for freedom in the short time that I'm here, and having fun in the meantime" ("Intellectual Vocation" 33).

West has devoted considerable attention to analyzing the black church's legacy of social justice activism to which he refers to as *the black prophetic Christian tradition*. At its core sits a preoccupation with freedom and liberation from the tragic predicaments that have shaped black life since slavery. In this way, the black interpretation of Christianity in the United States has its own particularity. Israel's exodus out of bondage, Job's persecution, the anguish found in Ecclesiastes, and the image of both the suffering and risen Christ, all for example, resonated with a people subjected to their own forms of horrific social agony ("Subversive Joy").

Concerning this idea of freedom, West argues that it contains three dimensions. The first is the existential. This is the refusal to succumb to feelings of dread and despair caused by prevailing social conditions. The tools used in this struggle for survival are the "rhythmic singing, swaying, dancing, preaching, talking, and walking" of black life ("Subversive Joy" 162). Modes of joyful celebration that both show an appreciation for one's very existence and that shape one's disposition towards life's difficulties. West cites the spirituals as an example and manifestation of this existential freedom. ("Subversive Joy" 162).

The second aspect of freedom that we see within black Christianity is social and pertains to the cultural solidarity that it engenders. The bonds of family, friends, and church community work as buffers against the antagonisms of a hostile society ("Subversive Joy" 163).

The third dimension is eschatological but not in the sense of escapist thinking. Rather, this vision of liberation recognizes the ever-present reality of black suffering and in turn, calls for direct opposition to it by individuals themselves and the community at large. West explains that, "black Christian eschatology focuses on praxis against suffering, not reflection upon it; personal and collective resistance to suffering, not a distancing from it. And ultimately, with the aid of divine intervention, suffering is overcome" ("Subversive Joy" 165).

To be clear, this vision of freedom does not equate to an eradication of tribulation. Suffering is a condition of black life and because of that, a sense of tragedy is attached to it. Nevertheless, black people have still been able to find happiness, all the while patiently waiting and fighting for a brighter day. West describes this as having an "*engaged gaiety*, *subversive joy*, and *revolutionary patience* which works for and looks to the kingdom to come" ("Subversive Joy" 165). Freedom is a constant struggle, indeed.

West periodizes the black prophetic Christian tradition—which here he refers to as *black theology*—into four distinct phases. The first stage he calls "Black Theology of Liberation as Critique of Slavery." This occurred from the middle of the seventeenth century to 1863. Black people's experience under slavery fueled their prophetic theological critiques of it. The prophetic Christian faith of Gabriel Prosser, Denmark Vesey, and Nat Turner actually compelled these men to lead slave insurrections in 1800, 1822, and 1831, respectively (*Prophesy Deliverance!* 101–2).

The second historical phase of the black prophetic Christian tradition can be seen as "Black Theology of Liberation as Critique of Institutional Racism." This age lasted from 1864–1969. It is marked by the black prophetic response to institutional racism, segregation, and lynching terror. The adverse conditions affecting blacks during this period popularized the idea of leaving America for Africa, championed by many black prophetic Christians including Henry McNeal Turner and Marcus Garvey. This stage of the black prophetic Christian tradition ends with the culmination of the civil rights movement, including the leadership and ultimate assassination of Martin Luther King Jr. in 1969 (*Prophesy Deliverance!* 102–3).

West calls the third stage, "Black Theology of Liberation as Critique of White North American Theology." This phase of the black prophetic Christian tradition arose out of the Black Power movement and lasted from 1969–1977. It witnessed black theologians in the academy affirming both their Christian identity as well as their blackness—quite a radical move at the time. They also drew attention to the failure of white Christianity to address racism and the injustices levied upon blacks in society. The ground of contestation for black prophetic Christian intellectuals during this stage was mainly theological. They called into question white Christian understandings of the faith and argued that the language of liberation for the oppressed, found throughout the Bible, spoke to the current condition of blacks fighting against racism in America. Theological reflection cannot exist independent of social context. Black theologians argued that the failure to both recognize and subsequently confront white supremacy was not simply wrong, but antithetical to the Christian faith (*Prophesy Deliverance!* 103–4). Bruce L. Fields explains the significance of these theological efforts as they pertain to black strivings: "As liberation relates to the African American community, it involves not only social, political, and economic empowerment. It also demands the right of self-definition, self-affirmation, and self-determination for the African American community. Black theology provides the theological legitimacy for such a process" (15).

The fourth stage of the black prophetic Christian tradition West defines as "Black Theology of Liberation as Critique of U.S. Capitalism." This period saw black theologians begin to give greater attention to the role of capitalism in the oppression of black people. In 1980, West called for the development of a fifth stage, "Black Theology of Liberation as Critique of Capitalist Civilization." This would encompass a deeper interaction with progressive Marxist thought and result in an increased analysis and critique of hegemonic structures within society (*Prophesy Deliverance!* 104–6 and "Black Theology"). To date, such an advancement has yet to occur.

This section looked at West's personal and longstanding connection to the black church and how he has theorized its prophetic tradition. For West, the black prophetic Christian tradition remains fixated on liberating black people from the damaging effects of white supremacy. This conception of freedom manifests in existential, social, and eschatological dimensions. The black prophetic Christian tradition has been shaped by its response to various forms of black suffering. Through this lens, West offers a four-part framing of the tradition's historical and thematic development. Ultimately, West sees the legacy of the black prophetic Christian tradition as threefold: its bold challenge to white supremacy, its commitment to bearing witness to love and justice, and the sustaining hope that it provides in the prolonged struggle for freedom (*Democracy Matters* 158).

Some additional points need to be made. First, West is clear that the black prophetic Christian tradition is but a part of the larger *black prophetic tradition* (itself but a component of an even grander *prophetic tradition*). The black prophetic tradition reflects a variety of different perspectives that cut across religion (prophetic Muslim practices), gender (prophetic womanist practices), political ideology (prophetic black socialist practices), etc. West writes that modes of black prophetic thought and action "consist of protracted and principled struggles against forms of personal despair, intellectual dogmatism, and socioeconomic oppression that foster communities of hope" ("Prophetic Tradition" 38). Of the black prophetic tradition, it is also important to note, as West writes, that it "has never been confined to the interests and situations of Black people . . . its message is for the country and world" (West and Buschendorf 165).

Lastly, West laments what he sees as a decline in the black prophetic tradition. He identifies three causes. The first is the shift that has occurred in black leadership. It has transitioned from largely consisting of social movement leaders to mainstream elected officials, more concerned with defending and serving political power than critiquing it. Second, West points to the seductive power of success and its ability to undercut prophetic energies. The third contributing factor to the decline of the black prophetic tradition is a state repressive apparatus that slanders, incarcerates, and assassinates prophetic figures. For these reasons, the black prophetic tradition has waned (West and Buschendorf 161–62). This has negatively affected the black prophetic Christian tradition as well. The next section takes a look at the state of the black church today and how *Race Matters* pushes for a rejuvenation of its prophetic spirit.

The Challenge of *Race Matters* for the Black Church Today

In February 2021, the Pew Research Center released its most comprehensive study to date on black religion in the United States. The report is based on a national survey of 8,660 black adults along with supplementary small group discussions and interviews with black clergy. The findings glean insight into topics such as black religious affiliation, belief, and practices. Pew's research also examines the connections black people discern between religion and a variety of social issues including race, gender, sexuality, and politics (Pew Research Center).

One major takeaway from this report is the declining yet continued relevance of the black church in the lives of black Americans today. For instance, younger blacks attend black churches less than older generations. 49 percent of black Americans from either the Greatest Generation or Silent Generation say that they frequent a black church. This is compared to 36 percent from Generation X, 27 percent of Millennials, and 29 percent of Generation Z. Forty-seven percent of black adults believe that black churches in their community hold less influence today than they did fifty years ago. However, 30 percent argue that black churches are actually more influential today while about 20 percent feel that things have more or less remained the same. The staying power of black religious institutions is seen by the fact that 60 percent of black Americans who go to religious services attend black congregations (Pew Research Center).

Another key insight from this report is what it reveals about the attitudes held about the black church and its connection to racial justice. Approximately 75 percent of those surveyed believe that the black church has played "some" role in the struggle for racial equality, with 30 percent saying that it has actually done "a great deal" in this regard. Opposing racism is seen as essential to faith or "being a moral person" by 75 percent of respondents. Finally, 44 percent of black Protestant churchgoers said that within the last twelve months they heard a sermon or lecture on race relations and/or racial inequality. In that same one-year period, 32 percent heard criminal justice reform discussed (Pew Research Center).

The black church continues to matter in the lives of black Americans and can still exist as a site of social consciousness building, political struggle, and possibility. Yet this can only happen if its prophetic disposition is kept alive. This applies to both its public witness to love and justice in the world *and* in its own self-inventory and ethical critique. It is this latter point that drives the focus of this section.

Race Matters addresses a wide range of issues concerning black people in America and race in general during the early 1990s. Its topics include affirmative action, black conservatism, black sexuality, black-Jewish relations, Malcolm X and black rage. A deep love for black people sits at the center of the text. This plays out in the book's commitment to racial uplift and liberation by analyzing many of the destructive forces operating not just outside of the black community but also from within. This is why a discussion of *Race Matters* within the context of elevating the prophetic leanings of the black church is apropos. The constraints of this essay keep me from analyzing, for instance, the cultural catastrophe visited upon women and LGBTQ+ folk, so often by the very church that claims to love them.[7] Or the essential role of coalition-building across lines of difference—be they racial, religious, or ideological. The black musical tradition, especially its connection to the black prophetic Christian tradition, was not given adequate attention here. These and other vitally important matters concerning the freedom and well-being of the black community are touched upon in *Race Matters* and their import for the black church and vice versa deserve further consideration.

Here I shall focus on what West identifies as "ever-expanding market culture" (*Race Matters* ix) and its connection to economic catastrophe—signs of spiritual blackout and imperial meltdown, respectively. As West explains, widespread commercialization and commodification—hallmarks of market culture—"weaken nonmarket activities of caring and sharing, nurturing and connecting. Short-term stimulation and instant titillation edge out quality relations and substantive community" (*Race Matters* ix). Furthermore, capitalism's emphasis on individualism and private success curtail democratic accountability, leaving workers and the poor most vulnerable.

This is evident in the black community as "the impact of the market culture on black life has been devastating" (*Race Matters* ix). Black people in America have always had to deal with what West calls the nihilistic threat—"*the lived experience of coping with a life of horrifying meaninglessness, hopelessness, and (most important) lovelessness*" (*Race Matters* 14). It is the hope born of love that has allowed black people to survive the various forms of persecution that they have faced through the ages—slavery, lynching, segregation, economic exploitation, police brutality, and so on. As West asserts: "For as long as hope remains and meaning is preserved, the possibility of overcoming oppression stays alive" (*Race Matters* 15). It has largely been black religious and civic institutions that have undergirded families and communities with the support needed to survive. They have acted as buffers against the nihilistic threat and preserved meaning, hope, and love within black America. West writes that they have "constituted ways of life and struggle that embodied values of service and sacrifice, love and care, discipline and excellence" (*Race Matters* 15). Yet, as West explains, the nihilistic threat remains strong because of "the saturation of market forces and market moralities in black life and the present crisis in black leadership" (*Race Matters* 16). In many ways, it is the pursuit of *pleasure*[8] promoted by corporate market forces that pushes aside "nonmarket values—love, care, service to others—handed down by preceding generations" (*Race Matters* 17). Simply put, the proliferation of market values and their infiltration into the black church pose a great threat to its prophetic orientation and its ability to help stave off nihilism and other forms of black suffering.

Nowhere is this more evident than in the rise of the prosperity gospel movement. The prosperity gospel, or prosperity theology, is an offshoot of Pentecostalism. It has a number of variants around the world and has enjoyed tremendous success since the 1990s. Prosperity theology is a Christian doctrine that finds its roots in the New Thought Movement and positive thinking tradition dating back to the nineteenth century. It holds that wealth, physical healing, and other forms of worldly success can be attained through faith in God. Indeed, it argues for a direct correlation between a person's belief and their material prosperity. In other words, prosperity theology states that if someone is rich it is because they have found favor in the eyes of God. Conversely, if someone is poor and/or suffers in any other way it is considered their fault because they did not have enough faith. For someone to become wealthy, it reasons, they must increase their faith in God. It is important to note that unlocking the power of this faith comes through seed giving or, in other words, making monetary donations to the church. Prosperity gospel ministers enjoy wealthy lifestyles befitting Hollywood entertainers, professional athletes, and the one percent. They stand as the emblem of the faith and must therefore embody the hallmarks of affluence and success. A cult of personality develops around them. Lastly, it is important to note that the prosperity gospel offers no analysis of structural inequality. It insists on individual attitudinal solutions to poverty, racism, and other social ills.

In her article "Capitalism, Immigration, and the Prosperity Gospel," Daisy L. Machado argues that the prosperity gospel represents a deadly nexus between Christianity and capitalism. She writes that "it is the mixing of evangelical faith with an uncritical embrace of capitalism that makes these believers a new kind of neoliberal twenty-first-century Christian. And the number of these Christians is on the rise" (Machado 729). Absent from this theology is any concern for social justice. Responding to society's ills and the role of economic policy in creating them are ignored. Rather, as Machado explains, with the prosperity gospel, "the emphasis is on personal individualistic economic gain as a result of a very clear-cut relation with God where negotiation for blessing is a core element" (728). She continues: "one's religion is meant to enlarge and expand one's vision of what can be in the here and now" (729).

Keri Day examines the prosperity gospel in her text, *Unfinished Business: Black Women, the Black Church, and the Struggle to Thrive in America*. Day's analysis of the prosperity gospel explicates its historical roots and trajectory within black American Christianity. She argues that the rise of the prosperity gospel occurred during economic shifts in the 1980s and 1990s that created a growing black middle class. Day explains that "prosperity gospel teachings were able to reinterpret the quest of the American dream as central to Christian experience" (109). At the same time, it provided a rationale for poor people's deprivation—lack of faith. The prosperity gospel enabled affluence on one hand and, on the other, held poor people responsible for their own poverty, refusing to consider or critique structural forces like capitalism, imperialism, and the economic exploitation of labor. As Day writes: "The prosperity gospel message often fails to acknowledge that socioeconomic status is less an issue of faith and more an indication of structures that reproduce the unequal distributions of income, resources, and wealth" (112).

For Fredrick C. Harris, the prosperity gospel not only "represents a clash with core political values in the black church tradition" (77) but its rise also holds significant ramifications for the future of black politics. He explores this in his book *The Price of the Ticket: Barack Obama and the Rise and Decline of Black Politics*. Harris argues that the prosperity gospel's focus on individualism threatens to undermine black solidarity and values of communal uplift, collective efforts to dismantle institutional racism, and the civic traditions found within black churches. At its core, the conflict between the prophetic black church tradition and the prosperity gospel is both "a theological *and* ideological debate" (Harris 80).

The prosperity gospel's incessant focus on individualism, financial gain and excess, along with its denigration of the poor and lack of concern for social justice places it in direct opposition to the black prophetic Christian tradition. It is a theology completely consumed by market culture and is a sign of deep spiritual blackout. The connection to imperial meltdown is that the prosperity gospel must be viewed in light of the economic catastrophe that has befallen our society. According to the Supplemental Poverty Measure of the US Census, 43 percent of people in the United States are poor or low-income. This amounts to 140 million individuals. Within black America, 59.7 percent fall into this category, equating to 23.7 million (Barnes). A theology that refuses to address this reality and the need for economic justice fails in its duty to serve the needs of the people and further fuels the nihilistic threat to black America.

The challenge that *Race Matters* presents for the black church today is that it pushes for a rejuvenation of its prophetic spirit. The text shines a light on black suffering and critiques the structures of oppression that black people face from both outside the community and from within. It calls black people to live up to the best of its freedom tradition and opt for the values of love, service, sacrifice, community, hope, and justice over market virtues and those tied to empire.

In *Race Matters*, West also highlights the crisis of black leadership and its role in enhancing the nihilistic threat. As a solution, he forwards the idea of what he calls *the race-transcending prophet*. This model of leadership works to hold power accountable and advance the moral and political change needed to alleviate forms of social suffering. West writes: "To be a serious black leader is to be a race-transcending prophet who critiques the powers that be (including the black component of the Establishment) and who puts forward a vision of moral regeneration and political insurgency for the purpose of fundamental social change for all who suffer from socially induced misery" (*Race Matters* 46).

To conclude this section, I return to West's call for the "remembrance, reverence, and resurrection" (*Race Matters* xxv) of our great exemplars of prophetic fightback by lifting up the leadership example of George Washington Woodbey.

With some notable exceptions, Woodbey has been criminally neglected by research in the academy. He was born enslaved, on October 5, 1854, in Johnson County, Tennessee. He was largely self-educated, learning to read after Emancipation. Woodbey was ordained as a Baptist minister when he was twenty years old. He was very active in politics, serving in leadership for both the Republican and Prohibition Parties. Under the latter, Woodbey even ran for lieutenant governor and for Congress in Nebraska. In 1890 he joined the Populist Party. He ultimately found himself in the camp of the great Socialist politician Eugene V. Debs.

In 1902 Woodbey moved to California and quickly began to develop his fame within the Socialist ranks. He became known for his dynamic lecture-hall orations and soapbox speeches. He was widely referred to as "The Great Negro Socialist Orator." He was even elected a member on the state executive board of the Socialist Party.

This is not to say that he did not experience racism from comrades within the party. Woodbey was the sole black representative at the 1904 and 1908 Socialist Party conventions. He was even nominated as a potential running mate for Debs in 1908 but received only one (nominating) vote. The Negro Question went largely ignored by the Socialist Party of America and the larger Second International. Racism was seen as a direct effect of capitalism. The party line was that the overthrow of capitalism would lead to the end of racism. As a result, talk of racial justice was widely subordinated.

Woodbey was a prolific writer, authoring numerous articles and pamphlets. His three major pamphlets were *What to Do and How to Do It: or, Socialism vs. Capitalism* (1903); *The Bible and Socialism: A Conversation Between Two Preachers* (1904); and *The Distribution of Wealth* (1910). The brilliance of Woodbey's writings is that he attempted to articulate the Socialist cause in the simplest ways possible. His works were noted for their high readability. For example, in *What to Do and How to Do It*, the narrative is a basic conversation between Woodbey and his mother in which he attempts to and is ultimately successful in convincing her to join the Socialist effort. The text critiques the ills of capitalism and explains how society would function more justly under socialism.

It is vital to note that Woodbey remained a preacher and never lost his desire to spread the gospel. His understanding of his Christian faith led him to embrace Socialist politics. This was an underlying theme in almost all of his work. He was constantly trying to articulate the congruence between principles of Christian faith and socialism. But beyond his theological convictions, Woodbey understood the importance of winning Christians to the Socialist cause from a strategic point of view. If the Socialist Party ever hoped to become a viable player in American politics, it had to reach the masses of American Christians. Woodbey was a sojourner, stuck in a dialectical tension between two worlds. In the mostly secular world of Socialist politics, Woodbey stressed the necessity of outreach to the religious community. Among Christians, Woodbey strove to connect biblical ethics to socialist action.

Woodbey addressed issues beyond economics and religion. He persistently argued that socialism would serve to liberate women from the sexism inherent in capitalist civilization. On the issue of race, he advocated a similar position—that African Americans had the most to gain from a socialist society. Despite the Socialist Party's general avoidance of race, at the 1908 convention for example, Woodbey angered some of his Socialist comrades when he spoke out against opposition to Asian immigration. In his speech he even accurately predicted that American corporations would eventually find ways to exploit cheap labor overseas.

Woodbey's beliefs often placed him at odds with various constituencies. He was therefore in many respects a marginalized figure. Woodbey was the frequent victim of police harassment and brutality. He was arrested on numerous occasions and even hospitalized once. Still, he persisted in his lifelong crusade for justice.[9]

Woodbey was a race-transcending prophet who fought against racism, sexism, and xenophobia. His crusade for socialism was in direct opposition to the forces of capitalist exploitation and the market moralities of his day. He stands in the best of the black prophetic Christian tradition.

Conclusion

On May 25, 2020, George Perry Floyd Jr. was murdered by Minneapolis police officer Derek Chauvin. The brutal scene of Floyd pinned down by officers as he lay face first on the street, gasping for breath and begging for his life while Chauvin mercilessly kneeled on his neck for nine minutes and twenty-nine seconds while onlookers pleaded for Chauvin to stop, was all captured on cell-phone video by teenager Darnella Frazier. The footage went viral, sparking both national and international outrage. In the weeks to follow, in the United States alone, thousands of protests involving estimates of up to twenty-six million people took place as supporters of the Black Lives Matter movement demanded justice for Floyd, Ahmaud Arbery, Breonna Taylor and other victims of unjust police violence and murder (Buchanan et al.).

Floyd's funeral occurred on June 9, 2020, at The Fountain of Praise Church in Houston, Texas. The service was broadcast and livestreamed for people around the globe to see. The ceremony could have easily *and perhaps understandably* been a vehicle through which Floyd's family and other mourners at the church expressed feelings of hatred and a desire for violent retribution. Yet the world witnessed a very different response. Later that evening, Cornel West was a guest on CNN's *Anderson Cooper 360*, where he was asked to reflect on what he observed while watching the funeral. West stated: "I saw in the hearts and minds and souls not just of the Floyd family, but of the church, of the music, the preaching, a love. Not one reference to hatred or revenge. It was all about love and justice. It's in the great tradition of the best of black people" (*Anderson Cooper 360*).

The incredible public witness of the Floyd family and those who gathered at the funeral is proof that the black church still possesses tremendous power to heal and sustain community in the face of injustice, suffering, and despair. Commitment to its prophetic tradition of speaking truth to power in the name of love and justice is the black church at its best. As it remains connected to social movements, builds lines of solidarity across difference, is self-critical, and keeps its focus on fighting for liberation against all forms of oppression—white supremacy, sexism, poverty and economic injustice, homophobia, transphobia, militarism and other manifestations of violence, ecological catastrophe, etc.—the church honors the richness of its social justice heritage and stands as a bulwark against the forces of spiritual blackout and imperial meltdown. But if the black church continues to fall victim to the seductive temptations of market moralities and superficial measures of success, subserviently bows down to the imperial ambitions of both neoliberal and neofascist modes of government, and is given to callousness and indifference toward those outside of the church and some even within, then it will represent a betrayal of its own social mission and prophetic tradition.

Fortunately, the social justice heritage of the black church is rich and a perpetual wellspring from which to draw strength and inspiration for the prophetic fightback ahead. The black prophetic Christian tradition is filled with countless examples of people who led by their faith in a God of liberation, bore witness to love and justice in the world. West both inherits and stands as a paragon of this tradition. His lifelong dedication to living and loving out loud not only places him as "the leading religious public intellectual of his generation" (Dorrien, *Social Ethics* 563), but more important, his commitment and example inspire others to march on through the darkness with a subversive joy, keeping faith, until the battle for freedom for all is won.

Notes

1. West calls the black freedom struggle "*the greatest* tradition of prophetic fightback in the American Empire" (*Race Matters*, xx; my emphasis). He links it directly to the black musical tradition he refers to as "the greatest tradition of moral and spiritual fortitude in the American Empire" (*Race Matters*, xx).

2. Specifically, Paris studies the African Methodist Episcopal Church and the National Black Baptist Convention, USA. These are two of the seven major black Christian denominations in the country. They are also the two oldest and most prominent. Paris's study found no significant variance in their social thought.

3. For further reading on the spirituals see Howard Thurman's "The Negro Spirituals Speaks of Life and Death" and James H. Cone's *The Spirituals and the Blues: An Interpretation*.

4. For information on the black church in the South during the time of slavery, also known as the "invisible institution," see Albert J. Raboteau's *Slave Religion: The "Invisible Institution" in the Antebellum South*.

5. For information on the independent black church movement in the North see Gayraud S. Wilmore's *Black Religion and Black Radicalism: An Interpretation of the Religious History of African Americans*, 99–124.

6. West talks about being a Chekhovian Christian in "Introduction: To Be Human, Modern and American"; "Chekhov, Coltrane and Democracy"; and "Afterword: Philosophy and the Funk of Life." West addresses what it means to be a revolutionary Christian in David Zeiger and Andy Zee's *Revolution and Religion: The Fight for Emancipation and the Role of Religion—A Dialogue Between Cornel West and Bob Avakian* and in his interview with Michael Brooks.

7. For perspective on how this is also driving younger generations away from the black church, see Christina Turner's "Where does the Black church fit in today's Black Lives Matter movement?"

8. West describes *pleasure* in the American sense as having to do with "comfort, convenience, and sexual stimulation" (*Race Matters* 17).

9. This cursory history of George Washington Woodbey is adapted directly from the work of Philip S. Foner. See his introduction in George W. Woodbey's *Black Socialist Preacher*.

Works Cited

Anderson Cooper 360 [@AC360°]. "In today's funeral for George Floyd there was 'not one reference to hatred or revenge. It was all about love and justice,' says Dr. @Cornel West." *Twitter*, 9 June 2020, 8:26 p.m., http://twitter.com/AC360/status/1270512602175676417?s=20.

Barnes, Shailly G. "Explaining the 140 Million: Breaking Down the Numbers Behind the Moral Budget." *Kairos Center*, 26 June 2019, https://kairoscenter.org/explaining-the-140-million/.

Barrow, Genoa. "Shiloh Mourns the Loss of Willie P. Cooke." *The Sacramento Observer*, 25 Sept. 2012, https://sacobserver.com/2012/09/shiloh-mourns-the-loss-of-rev-willie-p-cooke.

Buchanan, Larry, et al. "Black Lives Matter May Be the Largest Movement in U.S. History." *New York Times*, 3 July 2020, https://www.nytimes.com/interactive/2020/07/03/us/george-floyd-protests-crowd-size.html.

Cone, James H. *The Spirituals and the Blues: An Interpretation*. 1972. Orbis, 1991.

Day, Keri. *Unfinished Business: Black Women, the Black Church, and the Struggle to Thrive in America*. Orbis Books, 2012.

Dorrien, Gary. *Breaking White Supremacy: Martin Luther King Jr. and the Black Social Gospel*. Yale UP, 2018.

———. *The New Abolition: W.E.B. Du Bois and the Black Social Gospel*. Yale UP, 2015.

———. *Social Ethics in the Making: Interpreting an American Tradition*. Wiley Blackwell, 2009.

Fields, Bruce L. *Introducing Black Theology: Three Crucial Questions for the Evangelical Church*. Baker Academic, 2001.

Gates, Henry L., Jr. *The Black Church: This Is Our Story, This Is Our Song*. Penguin Press, 2021.

Harris, Fredrick C. *The Price of the Ticket: Barack Obama and the Rise and Decline of Black Politics*. Oxford UP, 2012.

Kazembe, Lasana, editor. *Keeping Peace: Reflections on Life, Legacy, Commitment and Struggle*. Foreword by Michael Simanga. Third World Press, 2018.

Machado, Daisy L. "Capitalism, Immigration, and the Prosperity Gospel." *Anglican Theological Review*, vol. 92, no. 4, 2010, pp. 723–730.

Pew Research Center. "Faith Among Black Americans." 16 Feb. 2021, https://www.pewforum.org/wp-content/uploads/sites/7/2021/02/PF_02.16.21_Black.religion.report.pdf.

Raboteau, Albert J. *Slave Religion: The "Invisible Institution" in the Antebellum South*, updated ed., Oxford UP, 2004.

Revolution and Religion: The Fight for Emancipation and the Role of Religion—A Dialogue Between Cornel West and Bob Avakian. Directed by David Zeiger and Andy Zee, The Bob Avakian Institute / Revolution Books NY, 2015. https://revcom.us/film/index.html.

Thurman, Howard. "The Negro Spiritual Speaks of Life and Death." *African American Religious Thought: An Anthology*, edited by Cornel West and Eddie S. Glaude, Jr., Westminster John Knox Press, 2003.

Turner, Christina. "Where Does the Black Church Fit in Today's Black Lives Matter movement?" *PBS News Hour*, 30 Mar. 2021, https://www.pbs.org/newshour/nation/where-does-the-black-church-fit-in-todays-black-lives-matter-movement.

West, Cornel. "Afterword: Philosophy and the Funk of Life." *Cornel West: A Critical Reader*. edited by George Yancy. Blackwell Publishers, 2001.

———. "Black Theology of Liberation as Critique of Capitalist Civilization." *Black Theology: A Documentary History*. Vol. 2, edited by James H. Cone and Gayraud S. Wilmore, Orbis Books, 1993.

———. "Chekhov, Coltrane and Democracy." *The Cornel West Reader*. Basic Civitas Books, 1999.

———. *Democracy Matters: Winning the Fight Against Imperialism*. Penguin Press, 2004.

———. Interview by Michael Brooks. *The Michael Brooks Show*. *YouTube*, 23 Apr. 2020, https://youtu.be/Mw3bzHTllLM.

———. "Introduction: The Making of an American Democratic Socialist of African Descent." *The Ethical Dimensions of Marxist Thought*. Monthly Review Press, 1991.

———. "Introduction: To Be Human, Modern and American." *The Cornel West Reader*. Basic Civitas Books, 1999.

———. "On My Intellectual Vocation." Interview by George Yancy. *The Cornel West Reader*. Basic Civitas Books, 1999.

———. "Preface: The Difficulty of Keeping Faith." *Keeping Faith: Philosophy and Race in America*. Routledge, 1993.

———. *Prophesy Deliverance!: An Afro-American Revolutionary Christianity*. Anniversary ed. Westminster John Knox Press, 2002.

———. "Prophetic Theology." *Prophetic Reflections: Notes on Race and Power in America*. Common Courage Press, 1993. Vol. 2 of *Beyond Eurocentrism and Multiculturalism*.

———. "The Prophetic Tradition in Afro-America." *Prophetic Fragments: Illuminations of the Crisis in American Religion & Culture*. Wm. B. Eerdmans Publishing, 1993.

———. *Race Matters*. 25th anniversary ed., Beacon Press, 2017.

———. "Subversive Joy and Revolutionary Patience in Black Christianity." *Prophetic Fragments: Illuminations of the Crisis in American Religion & Culture*. Wm. B. Eerdmans Publishing Co., 1993.

West, Cornel and Christa Buschendorf. *Black Prophetic Fire*. Beacon Press, 2014.

West, Cornel and David Ritz. *Brother West: Living and Loving Out Loud*. SmileyBooks, 2009.

West, Irene and Clifton West. Foreword. *Prophetic Thought in Postmodern Times*, by Cornel West. Common Courage Press, 1993. Vol. 1 of *Beyond Eurocentrism and Multiculturalism*.

Wilmore, Gayraud S. *Black Religion and Black Radicalism: An Interpretation of the Religious History of African Americans*. 1973. 3d ed., Orbis Books, 1998.

Woodbey, George W. *Black Socialist Preacher: The Teachings of Reverend George Washington Woodbey and His Disciple Reverend George W. Slater, Jr.* Edited and with an introduction by Philip S. Foner. Synthesis Publications, 1983.

PART III

Social Justice and Historical Witnessing

CHAPTER 7

Race (and Love) Matter More Than Ever Now: Affirmative Action, Alliances, and Anti-Asian Hate

Matthew M. Briones

I remember sitting in a small seminar room, next to the departmental office, on the second floor of the Barker Center in Cambridge: room 226, I think it was. It's actually a fairly tiny space that seats eight people, at best, and houses all the bound dissertations of American Civilization graduates, luminaries ranging from Henry Nash Smith, Daniel Aaron, Edmund Morgan, and David Brion Davis to Cheryl Wall, Rafia Zafar, Imani Perry, and Jeff Ferguson. The room cloyingly hems in its occupants, not-so-subtly reinforcing the expectations and high stakes for students hoping to pass their comprehensive exams to reach ABD status. My own oral exam was nearing the three-quarters mark as ninety minutes had elapsed and I had completed three of my four fields of study. But I was starting to fatigue and most of the adrenaline that had carried me through to that point in the exam had sweated out. I was relieved to pivot toward my final examiner, a warmly receptive and reassuring face, but my brain was starting to short-circuit. He leaned in over the seminar table, rested his right elbow on its surface, and started stroking his neatly groomed goatee.

"Let's talk about Du Bois," he said.

I exhaled slowly. "OK," I replied.

"When we grapple with *The Souls of Black Folk*, we've talked about the contradictory impulses of Du Bois: his affinity and call for a Talented Tenth yet his supposed appreciation for the souls of the Black Belt; his distant scholarly approach yet his lyrical rendering of the passing of his son. . . ." Thankfully my examiner continued in this manner: he was purposely vamping, kindly giving me a breather to catch up and gather my thoughts. He knew I was flagging. After noting that I had finally reconnected to the room's proceedings, he asked: "Do you recall what Du Bois uses as a framing device in *Souls*, and can you discuss the implications of his choosing such a device?"

I was fried. So many different ideas were running through my mind: "Was it the veil and double consciousness? Was he talking about the color line? Sam Hose? 'Of the Coming of John?"' I made no reply, but my expression must have given away how dumbfounded I was because my examiner kept dropping clues, in a gradual but exceedingly generous and obvious manner.

"He writes of our spiritual strivings and even spends the final chapter on it?"

I hesitated. "The Afterthought?" I meekly answered. Most professors would probably have dismissed me in exasperation at that point, but not this one. Like a shepherd gently coaxing his wounded lamb to water, he indulged me on my intellectual walkabout and then brought me back to center: "Remember how Baraka, Ellison, and Murray talked about being a bluespeople?"

And I blurted out like a game show contestant: "The Sorrow Songs!" Backing up, nervously unsure, I queried in a falsetto: "The Sorrow Songs?" And then, trying to remain cool, I mercifully at last declared: "I mean, yes, *of course*, the Sorrow Songs." The room breathed a collective sigh, and I stopped sweating like Nixon during the 1960 presidential debate.

I'm hoping this anecdote will serve as a worthy frame of its own, given that it best captures the legacies of what I feel Cornel has passed on to me as one of his students: first, an engaging, highly rigorous yet compassionate pedagogical approach; and, second, the sheer power, both intellectual and emotional, in understanding the tragicomic sensibility of the sorrow songs and Cornel himself. I used to think that scholarly work required the discipline of using the intellect alone, of striving for what Peter Novick knowingly termed "that noble dream" of social scientific objectivity.[1] I was confused in graduate school when classmates and professors would declare with such certainty that the political wasn't necessarily personal. As an undergraduate, I had been an English major focusing on Zora Neale Hurston and Richard Wright, so my orientation as a humanist was challenged when I got to graduate school to study history. Initially taking classes with the likes of Alan Heimert, I wasn't dissuaded from that notion—that the study of history, the marking of change over time—was near-scientific, never emotional, and never personal. Thank heavens for Evelyn Brooks Higginbotham, however, as she introduced me to the work of Lawrence Levine, Tera Hunter, Joe Trotter, Mia Bay, and Nathan Huggins, scholars who helped me rediscover the personal and the emotional in the historical record, just as Werner Sollors had introduced me to Janie and Tea Cake in the Everglades and Bigger Thomas on the South Side the decade before. I was learning that history was as much art as it was science, as much humanities as it was social science.

Famously, of course, if not also fleetingly, Du Bois himself came to this realization very soon after earning his doctorate at Harvard in 1895. In the span of a few weeks in the spring of 1899, he experienced both the mutilation and lynching of Sam Hose and the tragic death of his two-year-old son, Burghardt. In *Dusk of Dawn*, Du Bois characterized Hose's murder as "a red ray . . . [that] . . . broke in upon my work and eventually disrupted it . . . one could not be a calm, cool, and detached scientist while Negroes were lynched, murdered, and starved" (67). In a 1961 interview with Folkway Records, he elaborated: "And then I made up my mind that knowledge wasn't enough, that even if people were ignorant of essential matters which they had to know, they wouldn't correct their actions without more realization of just what the difficulties were. They had not only to know, but they had to act. And so I changed from studying the Negro problem to propaganda, to letting people know just what the Negro problem meant in what the colored people were suffering and what they were kept from doing" (*Recorded Autobiography* 3).

Cornel opened up this world of interpretation for me. I had heretofore only read Du Bois in excerpts, selectively and partially, as an incredible elitist, a staid, late-Victorian man of respectability. I hadn't studied or evaluated his struggle with sadness and loss, or his attempt to understand his own humanity. But Cornel encouraged me to return again and again to the sorrow songs and to strive past Du Bois's own words. "Through all the sorrow of the Sorrow Songs there breathes a hope—a faith in the ultimate justice of things," Du Bois wrote. "The minor cadences of despair change often to triumph and calm confidence. Sometimes it is faith in life, sometimes a faith in death, sometimes assurance of boundless justice in some fair world beyond" (*Souls* 188). It was in this text, and in Cornel's teaching and searing critique of it that I began to understand the tragicomic in history and culture. Cornel wrote: "My fundamental problem with Du Bois is his inadequate grasp of the tragicomic sense of life—a refusal candidly to confront the absurdity of the human condition. This tragicomic sense—tragicomic rather than simply 'tragic,' because even ultimate purpose and objective order are called into question—propels us towards suicide or madness unless we are buffered by ritual, cushioned by community, or sustained by art." Despite his best intentions to close the scientific distance mentioned above, Du Bois nonetheless fell short of the mark. Cornel continued: "He certainly saw, analyzed, and empathized with black sadness, sorrow, and suffering. But he didn't feel it in his bones deeply enough, nor was he intellectually open enough to position himself alongside the sorrowful, suffering, yet striving ordinary black folk. Instead his own personal and intellectual distance lifted him above them even as he addressed their plight in his progressive writings" (*Future* 57–58). I was beginning to heed Cornel's warning, to view Du Bois as a type of intellectual cautionary tale: "As with any great figure, to grapple with Du Bois is to wrestle with who we are, why we are what we are, and what we are to do about it" (*Future* 57).

In *Souls of Black Folk*, I came to understand, the Sorrow Songs captured our tragicomic sensibility more than its author did. This was a useful lesson moving forward. How could I balance potentially divergent impulses, the personal and the intellectual? Or the emotional and the social scientific? To paraphrase Cornel, how was I to understand what it meant to be both an academic and a human?

In my own work after graduate school, I tried my best to follow the Westian approach of employing a critical scholarly lens while working hard never to lose sight of what made the historical actors I studied *American*, *democratic*, and *human*. My dissertation, which Cornel supervised alongside Werner, and the subsequent book, entitled *Jim and Jap Crow: A Cultural History of 1940s Interracial America*, attempted to tell the story of Charlie Kikuchi, a second-generation Japanese American incarcerated during the Second World War. Through his personal diaries (which spanned over four decades and nearly 100,000 pages), I tracked Kikuchi's journey from a child orphaned at eight in Northern California, to San Francisco State student and temporary migratory farm laborer during the Depression, to a social welfare master's student at Cal up to Pearl Harbor. Prior to and during his incarceration in Gila River, Arizona, Kikuchi made the awkward decision of reuniting with the parents and siblings who had abandoned him as a child, while he found surrogate family members and collaborators in progressive intellectuals, like Louis Adamic, Carey McWilliams, W. I. Thomas, and Dorothy Swaine Thomas. Although he would briefly work with the Chicago school of sociology during the war, Kikuchi self-consciously chose social work as his calling, working predominantly with the Veterans Administration (VA) Hospital in New York until 1973. Throughout all of his diaries and correspondence, one gains the sense of an earnest man, a true democrat, trying his hardest to understand the situation under which he and 120,000 other Japanese Americans were placed, while always contextualizing the incarceration within the longer history of oppressed, racialized peoples in the United States, especially African Americans. In fact, in the wake of his release from the camps, Kikuchi was far more interested in the possibility of multiracial alliances in America, especially in the gloam of the postwar, pre-cold-war era. He spent much of his post-camp life in Chicago living on the South Side, interacting with "everyday people," and then another twenty-eight years in New York, working mostly with African American veterans at the VA; he ultimately resigned in protest due to the poor treatment veterans of color were receiving at his hospital in the midst of the Vietnam War. He died while on a peace march in the Soviet Union in 1988.

I argued that the 1940s was a moment of great possibility for interracial relations and multiracial alliances. Although initially Du Bois and the Socialist Norman Thomas were the lone progressive voices of dissent, eventually other racialized groups and leaders protested the unconstitutional imprisonment of their fellow citizens, while Japanese Americans themselves—if they hadn't already—grew to understand and experience the bitter reality of what sociologist Gunnar Myrdal called "the American dilemma": the hypocrisy of American democracy that denied African Americans full rights and recognition as citizens. Along the West Coast, in former Japantowns and Little Tokyos, African Americans, Mexican Americans, and Filipinos competed and negotiated for housing and jobs. When some, though not all, of their Japanese neighbors returned in the later years of the war, conflict and compromise ensued, inevitably inducing debate and conversation across racial lines in neighborhood councils, Black and ethnic newspapers, labor unions, and more. Many Japanese American "resettlers," as the government euphemistically labeled them, began new chapters of their lives in Chicago, Detroit, New York, and other urban centers in the Midwest and Northeast. Some, like Kikuchi and many of his progressive-minded peers, immediately committed themselves to active civic participation in their new home cities. Interracial political coalitions were becoming more of a reality, especially between Japanese Americans and African Americans. Sociologists Horace Cayton and Setsuko Nishi, for example, joined forces to run race and housing commissions in Chicago, while a Black newspaper, the *L.A. Tribune*, hired Japanese American staff members and op-ed writers, including the famous short story writer Hisaye Yamamoto. The most famous collaborations would come two decades later, when more radical Asian American activists joined groups like the Black Panthers, and civil rights icon Yuri Kochiyama apprenticed with Malcolm X before tragically bearing witness to his assassination in the Audubon Ballroom in February 1965.

Not unlike what Cornel mentions in his introduction to *Race Matters*, my point of inspiration for researching and writing this history was the Los Angeles uprising. After watching the strain, tragedy, and violence between Korean Americans and African Americans in 1991 and 1992, I wanted to prove that we all *can* indeed just get along. History would demonstrate that, like C. Vann Woodward's Southern folkways in *The Strange Career of Jim Crow*, relations between Asian Americans and African Americans were not immutable. There was a history of both confluence and conflict, and the proof of such history seventy-five years ago could serve as a guide to renewed potential alliances, a hopeful (not naïvely optimistic) blueprint of promise and possibility in a challenging twenty-first-century racial climate.

Of course, much doubt and sheer cynicism exists about this formulation, thanks to a deeply engrained set of structural and systemic impediments established since at least the 1960s to triangulate and pit model minorities against so-called protest minorities. To signify on Michael Omi and Howard Winant's theory of racial formation, self-conscious and significant racial projects have served to drive wedges between many different racialized groups and have infected our "common sense" about interracial relations.[2] For example, in 1966, a year after the *Moynihan Report* assailed the African American family, and mere months after L.A. Police Chief William Parker labeled Watts residents "monkeys in a zoo" during the L.A. rebellion, sociologist William Petersen extolled the virtues of Japanese Americans in the *New York Times*, propagating the myth of the model minority at the expense of other "problem minorities," presumably African Americans, Latinxs, and Native Americans. He exclaimed: "Barely more than 20 years after the end of the wartime camps, this is a minority that has risen above even prejudiced criticism. By any criterion of good citizenship that we choose, the Japanese Americans are better than any other group in our society, including native-born whites. . . . Even in a country whose patron saint is the Horatio Alger hero, there is no parallel to this success story" (21).

Petersen, like many others, credited strong family structures, an emphasis on education, and respect for authority as keys to nascent Asian success in America. What the selective analysis obscured, of course, was that Asian families or individuals were not monolithic, and that in particular, Japanese Americans faced unremitting challenges in relation to unemployment, unfair housing, welfare, and simple community rebuilding in the wake of the traumatic incarceration era. Although the contemporaneous 1965 Immigration Act was heralded as a symbol of American exceptionalism during the cold war and an index of further commitment to "a nation of immigrants," the master narrative often glossed over the fact that all Asians had been excluded from the United States for four prior decades, and the Chinese for nearly a century. Nonetheless, *U.S. News and World Report* would shame African Americans with the putative "success story" of Chinese Americans in 1966, snidely proclaiming: "What you find, back of this remarkable group of Americans, is a story of adversity and prejudice that would shock those now complaining about the hardships endured by today's Negroes" (73).

This divisive, wedge-driving narrative would continue well into the 1970s and 1980s, as the Nixon-Reagan-Bush axis of evil rolled out alarmingly effective anti-Black propaganda of "law and order," welfare queens, and Willie Horton. Contemporaneously, *Newsweek* credited Asian Americans with "Outwhiting the Whites" in 1971, and with rising to "the top of the class" in 1984. Meanwhile, the *New Republic* celebrated "The Triumph of Asian-Americans" as "America's greatest success story" in 1985, and *Time* magazine featured "Those Asian-American Whiz Kids" on the cover of a 1987 issue. Once again, our "common sense" about race and the races was being falsely constructed. And nowhere has this tortured dynamic been more evident than in the red-herring debate over Asian Americans and affirmative action policies in general and specifically at Harvard and Yale since the 1980s.

Though the setup has taken the fair reader way too far on another intellectual walkabout of mine, this is the nexus at which all the relevant lines of my inquiry intersect, regarding *Race Matters* then and now, the relationship between African Americans and Asian Americans, the relationship between one particular African American teacher and his Asian American student, and the necessity of integrating the personal and the scholarly, the emotional and the intellectual.

As we know, the most recent cases against Harvard and Yale's admissions policies are nothing new, just another opportunity for the right to make overtures to what they believe is an unwitting Asian American electorate (and I do not wish to be naïve here: some of these attempts *will* gain purchase among a minority of aggrieved Asian Americans). Much like their campaign in the

1980s, conservative forces persuaded the Justice Department to investigate claims that Asian American students are unfairly evaluated in the admissions process, in an effort to curb overrepresentation of worthy Asian candidates and to prop up percentages of ostensibly less worthy applicants from historically underrepresented groups. In the Harvard case, a group called Students for Fair Admissions (SFFA) first brought the suit in 2014, claiming discrimination against Asian American applicants in favor of African American and Latinx students. In 2019, a Federal District Court in Boston found that Harvard's policy did not discriminate, and its use of race was in line with Supreme Court precedent. A year later, the US Court of Appeals for the First Circuit upheld the lower court's ruling. In June 2021, the Supreme Court effectively postponed hearing the case, asking the new Biden administration to weigh in on the complaint, a political punt if there ever was one.

In Yale's case, the Trump administration itself levied a discrimination lawsuit against the university and its admissions policy in October 2020. An SFFA ally, the Asian American Coalition for Education, complained in 2016 that Yale, Brown, and Dartmouth all employed policies disfavoring Asians and whites. On February 3, 2021, the Biden administration dropped the suit "in light of all available facts, circumstances, and legal developments" but did not elaborate. One of the coalition's cofounders, Swan Lee, decried the news, without a trace of irony, calling it "a racist decision because it preserves discrimination in education." (Counterpoint of fact: although we're only 6.5 percent of the population in the United States, Asian Americans represent nearly 25 percent of Harvard's undergraduate body. In other words, as affirmative action grew, so did the number of Asian American students on campus.) Anxiety remains, however, as the conservative-heavy Court agreed on January 24, 2022, to hear cases the following October brought against Harvard (a private institution) and the University of North Carolina (a public institution) for their consideration of race in admissions processes. In the wake of its overturning of *Roe v. Wade* on June 24, 2022, the Court may feel emboldened to similarly upend its own precedent rulings affirming the use of race in college admissions policies. Despite his ostensible attempts to insulate the Court from appearing too political, Chief Justice John Roberts has consistently voted against such admissions policies in the past, going so far as to state that "it's a sordid business, this divvying us up by race" (Gayle). Given that Roberts was the justice who likely saved Obamacare, it's cruel irony that affirmative action may indeed be on life support.

Critics of the Harvard policy point to court documents released at trial in 2018 that showed the admissions office consistently gave Asian Americans lower ratings on personality traits, such as likability, integrity, courage, and positivity. A familiar narrative of excellent grades and high test scores but poor personality ratings simply reinforces the stereotype that Asians are monolithic, technically proficient but socially awkward. Like the model minority myth itself, this script flattens all Asian Americans into a singular, undifferentiated mass, without individuation and diversity. It also obscures, even trivializes, the more rigorous, holistic evaluation process of Harvard admissions. This tale most glaringly ignores the success Asian Americans have enjoyed under affirmative action. As my dear friend and former graduate school classmate Hua Hsu states in the *New Yorker*: "While the Harvard admissions process sucks up the headlines, Asian-Americans have benefitted as much as anyone else from increased opportunities in education, employment, and government service. And the current terms of debate don't capture the full complexity of the Asian-American community. Researchers believe that efforts toward 'data disaggregation,' or the breaking down of large categories, like Asian-American, into smaller, more descriptive subgroups, could bring increased focus to poor, underserved populations, like Southeast Asians" (Hsu). In the absence of such a nuanced approach, however, Asians remain a "yellow peril," an aggregation of bucktoothed, slant-eyed half-men and dragon ladies waiting to infect the American body politic. Does this type of discrimination need to be addressed? Yes, it does. Is the eradication or radical reform of affirmative action policies in university admissions the answer? Not by a long shot.

Unfortunately, like many debates in the culture wars, we lack adequate context. First, taking the view from 30,000 feet, the majority of Asian Americans and Pacific Islanders (or AAPIs) support affirmative action policies in higher education, employment, civil rights enforcement, and beyond. The National Asian American Survey in 2016 found that nearly three-quarters (or 72 percent) of Asian Americans supported the government's doing more to give African Americans equal rights with whites (Ramakrishnan *NAAS*). Asian Americans see the proverbial forest through the trees: while affirmative action in higher education is important, the "bamboo ceiling" after college is a reality. As Jennifer Lee, a sociologist at Columbia, has argued: "Research shows that Asian American men earn 8 percent less than white men, even with the same years of education, school type, major, and region of residence.[3] Asian American women are likely to earn as much as white women, but are less likely to hold supervisory positions.[4] So even when Asian Americans attend the right schools and get the right jobs, they do not do as well as whites in the labor market" (Lee, "Ending Affirmative Action").

Another study found that white job applicants enjoyed a callback rate 28 percent higher than applicants with obvious "ethnically Asian" names (Banerjee et al.). And despite the fear-mongering claims by Steve Bannon, executive positions in Silicon Valley are not being overrun by Asian or South Asian CEOs. As a hopeful sign of Asian America's investment in interracial solidarity, during the 2015 Supreme Court case, *Fisher v. University of Texas*, more than 160 Asian American/Pacific Islander advocacy groups filed amicus curiae briefs in support of affirmative action. At the time, Laboni Hoq, litigation director at Asian Americans Advancing Justice asserted: "Such broad support for race conscious admissions policies sends a clear message that AAPIs overwhelmingly support these policies and will not be used as a racial wedge to disenfranchise other communities of color" (AALDEF "Over 160"). Millions of Asian American students and college graduates across the country recognize the value of diverse student bodies, viewpoints, and classrooms. Many, like me, appreciate that they themselves undoubtedly benefited from affirmative action, or adjacent-affirmative action policies. And they realize that the latest campaign is a bald-faced attempt to preserve the status quo and prevent race-conscious policies from hurting *white* America; few believe that this is actually about advancing justice for Asian Americans.[5]

Second, when we're talking about Asian Americans, whom are we talking about? Let's disaggregate. While Chinese, Japanese, and Indian Americans have met with relative success, many other immigrants of Southeast Asian and South Asian descent, Native Hawaiians and Pacific Islanders can hardly claim the benefits of being a model minority. For example, the poverty rates for Mongolian and Burmese in the United States are 15 percent higher than the official national rate; Bangladeshi and Nepalese are nearly 10 percent higher. Hmong, Laotian, Burmese, Samoan, Tongan, and Bhutanese Americans are 20 to 25 percent less likely than the average American to earn a bachelor's degree (Pew). And lest we think that immigration is only a brown issue, 1.7 million Asians are undocumented, or one in every seven Asian immigrants. The three largest groups in this category are Chinese, Indians, and Filipinos (Ramakrishnan, "One"). Only 20 percent of eligible Asian recipients applied for DACA status, leaving 70,000 or so of our own students in limbo (MPI).

Third, as Lee has trenchantly observed in a 2018 *L.A. Times* op-ed, the lack of proper context shifts our attention from the more troubling admissions policy, one that makes any concerns over affirmative action pale by comparison (pun intended), and that is the long-standing policy and practice of legacy admissions at Harvard. To quote at length, Lee writes:

> The personal rating incorporates numerous factors . . . [and] . . . the assessment of various personality traits is only part of this broader category. The personal score is one of four overarching categories of ratings—the other three being academic, athletic and extracurricular.
>
> Across these four categories, there are a number of observable trends. For instance, on average, Asian American women received higher personal ratings and extracurricular ratings than Asian American men. . . . In fact, analyses of the data show that Asian American women had a small advantage over white women, although the difference was not statistically significant.
>
> But the clearest trend concerned legacy applicants, or candidates with at least one parent who attended Harvard. . . . From 2010 to 2015, Harvard's admission rate for legacies was 34%, while its admission rate for non-legacies was 6%. . . . Not surprisingly, legacy applicants are likely to be white. More than one-fifth of white applicants admitted to Harvard between 2010 and 2015 were legacies. . . . The number of white legacy students admitted to Harvard exceeded the number of African American, Hispanic and Asian American legacy students combined . . .
>
> . . . But rather than pointing to the glaring evidence of the school's preference for legacies, the plaintiffs have focused on the weaker argument about alleged bias against Asian Americans. (Lee "Harvard")

At a moment when the spurious research claims by Charles Murray, of *Bell Curve* infamy, are being revived, having literally influenced actionable policy in the Trump administration, we must recognize that this false hand-wringing about Asians and affirmative action is merely a red herring to distract from the continued preservation of whiteness and white privilege at the highest levels. An equal aim of this movement, this project, is to dehumanize and denigrate Black, brown, and red people while hiding behind yellow ones. When Cornel wrote about affirmative action in *Race Matters*, he presciently warned: "Although many of my liberal and progressive citizens view affirmative action as a redistributive measure whose time is over or whose life is no longer worth preserving, I question their view because of the persistence of discriminatory practices that increase black social misery, and the warranted suspicion that good will and fair judgment among the powerful does not loom as large toward women and people of color" (65). Especially with the imminent dismantling of affirmative action by this newly reborn Taney's zombie of a Supreme Court, I think it's fair to say that Asian Americans have heeded his call. As my esteemed colleague Michael Dawson might say, our fates are linked with that of our African American brothers and sisters.

Our fate is also linked with that of our Latinx brothers and sisters. While the affirmative action debate is an attempt to distract, we have kept our eye on the ICE detention centers and the immoral separation of parents and children. The Japanese American Service Committee (JASC), an organization founded in 1946 in Chicago to aid the relocating incarcerated after the war, has spoken out in protest over the zero tolerance policy of the Trump administration. Its CEO, Michael Takada, stated: "The civil and human rights which are the bedrock of this country and of international law are most meaningful under times of strain. For the Japanese American community, xenophobia, racism, and the failure of political leadership resulted in one of the most egregious violations of civil and human rights in 20th century America. Today similar factors are at play in 21st century America in the scapegoating and targeting of the most vulnerable members of society" (JASC).

Our fate is also linked with that of our Muslim brothers and sisters. In her dissent to the Supreme Court's upholding of the Muslim travel ban in *Trump v. Hawaii*, Justice Sonia Sotomayor pointed to the pyrrhic victory in the court's (effective, not literal) overturning of the wartime *Korematsu* case, stating: "The formal repudiation of a shameful precedent is laudable and long overdue. But it does not make the majority's decision here acceptable or right . . . and the court redeploys the same dangerous logic underlying *Korematsu* and merely replaces one 'gravely wrong' decision with another" (28). The Asian American Legal Defense and Education Fund officially "deplored" the court's majority opinion, and one of its staff attorneys averred, "As an Asian American civil rights organization, we are all too aware of the direct thread running from the Chinese exclusion laws of the 1880s and the internment of Japanese Americans during World War II to the president's travel ban" (AALDEF "Muslim Ban"). We must also not forget how the post-9/11 surveillance state, especially in New York City, has disproportionately affected Muslim Americans, many from Asia, in a grotesque Orientalist twist on "Jim and Jap Crow" (Bridge Initiative Team "Fact Sheet").

We are living in a cruel historical moment. Only a few years removed from the murders of George Floyd, Breonna Taylor, Ahmaud Arbery, among too many others, and in the clutches of a worldwide pandemic that has disproportionately affected communities of color, the Asian American and Pacific Islander family is facing historic levels of violence. Stop AAPI Hate, a national coalition aimed at addressing anti-Asian discrimination during the pandemic, recorded over 3,800 hate incidents between March 2020 and February 2021, up 150 percent over the previous year (the NYPD reported such crimes jumped 1,900 percent in New York City alone). That number skyrocketed to 6,603 in March 2021. Many reports came in retroactively, likely motivated by the tragedy of the shooting and murder of eight people, six of whom were Asian women, in three Atlanta-area spas on March 16. The racially and sexually motivated rampage pointed up the fact that a significantly higher percentage of Asian American women had been targeted for such crimes (65 percent) during this period.[6] Only a month later, on April 15, 2021, a gunman killed another eight people, four of whom were Sikh American, in an Indianapolis FedEx facility. The conflagration of anti-Asian hate incidents was no doubt fueled in part by the racist accusations made by the 45th president about the "kung flu" and the "China virus." Other government officials and talking heads threw gasoline on the fire, falsely but directly scapegoating Asian bodies as the source, the diseased carrier of the coronavirus, a foreign element poisoning America's physical "constitution."

Let me be clear: these reactionary, nativist, plainly racist, and mean-spirited forces won't win. As challenging and, frankly, saddening, a present we face, a hopeful future may be informed by our past. As immigration historian Paul Kramer reminds us, "Our xenophobic impulses and loftiest ideals have been in conflict since the founding" (Kramer). And I don't mean at all to fall into the trap of idealizing American history as exceptional, and blindly believing in the potential of our American democracy: Americans and humans, by nature, are far too fallible. But we have been here before, or perhaps we've been here all along. And, as Cornel might say, we've always fought, we've always maintained our hope, and we've kept keeping on; this is nothing new to the long-distance runners in the fight for freedom. Race matters, full stop. And love matters more than ever now, to counter the rising tides of hate (be it anti-Asian, anti-Black, anti-woman, anti-queer, among many other grotesqueries).

These past few years, in the unhealthy orange glow of the Trump era, especially the January 6 insurrection, I have consistently redirected my students' attention to the period after the first World War a century ago: a moment of virulent scientific racism and eugenics (Charles Murray is merely Madison Grant and Lothrop Stoddard in sheep's clothing, for instance); an explosion of race riots from 1919 Chicago to 1921 Tulsa; numerous Supreme Court cases that specifically denied Asian Americans named Thind, Lum, and Ozawa citizenship and civil rights; a sitting president felled by scandal and corruption; a National Origins Act that assured exclusion of unwanted immigrants in 1924; a march on Washington by five million Ku Klux Klan members in 1925; the execution of two innocent anarchists from Italy in 1927 with the help of a Harvard president; and a nation that rejected membership in the League of Nations in favor of isolationism. The script sounds all too familiar. But we fought and we kept our hope alive. We embraced the tragicomic and, catching hell from all corners, we struggled, failed, and struggled again. A great people migrated, women fought for the right to vote, the Left built a Popular and cultural front, unions earned the right to collectively bargain, and despite being imprisoned behind barbed wire, Japanese American boys earned nearly 10,000 Purple Hearts in World War II while nearly the same number of No-No Boys—young men from the same camps who refused to take a loyalty oath during the war—proudly carried on the distinctly American tradition of dissent.

Again, I do not mean to idealize, smooth, and gild these strands of our historical narrative when so many twisted and rotten strands have resulted in nooses. But, as in my telling of Kikuchi's life, I believe in what's possible. If interracial alliances existed in the trauma of the incarceration era, even if for a brief, fleeting moment, they can exist again. If a young Filipino who didn't see any role models who looked like him in school can listen, learn from, and love a towering African American intellectual and pedagogue, then there's always hope. Through Toni Morrison and James Baldwin, Cornel taught me the *letter* of the love ethic. From specific acts of compassion toward my family and me, Cornel has shown me the *spirit* of the love ethic. When my mother was losing her short but excruciating struggle against pancreatic cancer in 2008, he called me nearly every day, just to talk when I needed him to, and just to listen when I asked him to. Five years later, as I sleep-walked through an ugly and painful divorce, Cornel was there once more, hugging my daughters Cadence and Ella West (named after him) in Rockefeller Chapel in Chicago when I could barely stand up.

It shouldn't come as a surprise: his love for Cliff and Zeytun demonstrates to me how one can and should balance the emotional with the intellectual, the personal with the political, and the human with the scholarly. Thanks to him, I harbor a deeper understanding of how the ineffable love I feel for my daughters inspires me to be a better man. Thanks to Cornel, I appreciate how one's passion for teaching young people can indeed stimulate both their intellect and their humanity.

Especially during this most tragicomic chapter of our history, I tell my daughters—young Asian American women well aware of what they face—and my students that compassion, hope, knowledge, and love can triumph over the specter of fear, nihilism, ignorance, and grievance. Although he was referring to the turn of the twentieth century, Du Bois had apt advice for our current moment, writing: "Only by a union of intelligence and sympathy across the color-line in this critical period of the Republic shall justice and right triumph" (*Souls* 136).

I, do, however, prefer the words of my examiner, my teacher, and my brother who taught me about the tragicomic sorrow songs in that small seminar room nearly two decades ago, when he exhorted: "Let us hope and pray that the vast intelligence, imagination, humor, and courage of Americans will not fail us. Either we learn a new language of empathy and compassion, or the fire this time will consume us all" (*Race Matters* 8).

Notes

1. See Novick, especially his "Introduction: Nailing Jelly to the Wall," for further explication of this mythical, objective aim.

2. See Omi and Winant for further explication of racial formation theory, especially ch. 4, pp. 105–36.

3. Lee credits Kim and Sakamoto, ". . . Asian American Men . . . Labor Market Parity."

4. See Kim and Zhao, "Are Asian American Women Advantaged?"

5. In 2012, 75 percent of Asian Americans supported affirmative action, while in 2016, the number dipped to 65 percent. Excluding Chinese Americans, however, the number was 73 percent. See Ramakrishnan and Wong, "Survey," for the data; see as well Lee, "Asian Americans," pp. 190–195, for the arguably exceptional case of relatively recent Chinese immigrants, their conservative politics and their push against affirmative action.

6. See the Stop AAPI Hate report, *The Rising Tide of Violence*. . . . Also see Hoang on the history of spas and sex work, and the Atlanta shootings.

Works Cited

AALDEF (Asian American Legal Defense and Education Fund). "AALDEF Deplores the Supreme Court's Decision Upholding the Muslim Ban." *aaldef.org*, 4 July 2018, www.aaldef.org/press-release/aaldef-deplores-the-supreme-court-s-decision-upholding-the-muslim-ban/.

———. "Over 160 Asian American and Pacific Islander groups file amicus briefs in U.S. Supreme Court in support of affirmative action." *aaldef.org*, 3 Nov. 2015, www.aaldef.org/press-release/over-160-asian-american-and-pacific-islander-groups-file-amicus-briefs-in-support-of-affirmative-act/.

Banerjee, Rupa, et al. "Do Large Employers Treat Racial Minorities More Fairly? An Analysis of Canadian Field Experiment Data." *Canadian Public Policy*, vol. 44, no. 1, 2018, pp. 1–12.

Bell, David A. "The Triumph of Asian-Americans." *New Republic*, 15 July 1985, pp. 24–31.

Brand, David, et al. "The New Whiz Kids: Why Asian Americans Are Doing So Well, and What It Costs Them." *Time*, vol. 130, no. 9, Aug. 1987, p. 42.

Bridge Initiative Team. "Fact Sheet: the NYPD Muslim Surveillance and Mapping Program." *bridge.georgetown.edu*, 11 May 2020, bridge.georgetown.edu/research/factsheet-the-nypd-muslim-surveillance-and-mapping-program/.

Briones, Matthew M. *Jim and Jap Crow: A Cultural History of 1940s Interracial America*. Princeton UP, 2012.

Dawson, Michael C. *Behind the Mule: Race and Class in African-American Politics*. Princeton UP, 1994.

Du Bois, W. E. B. *Dusk of Dawn: An Essay Toward an Autobiography of a Race Concept*. 1940. Kraus-Thomson Organization, 1975.

———. *The Souls of Black Folk*. 1903. Vintage Books/Library of America, 1990.

———. *W.E.B. Du Bois: A Recorded Autobiography, Interview with Moses Asch*. Smithsonian Folkways Recordings. Catalog number FW05511, Liner notes, p. 3. 1961.

"A Formula for Success." *Newsweek*, 23 April 1984, p. 77.

Gates, Henry Louis, Jr., and Cornel West. *The Future of the Race*. Knopf, 1996.

Gayle, Caleb. "Supreme Court pick could put 40 years of affirmative action precedent at risk." *Guardian*, 7 July 2018, www.theguardian.com/law/2018/jul/07/supreme-court-pick-affirmative-action-precedent.

Hoang, Kimberly Kay. "How the history of spas and sex work fits into the conversation about the Atlanta shootings," *vox.com*, 18 March 2021, www.vox.com/first-person/22338462/atlanta-shooting-georgia-spa-asian-american.

Hsu, Hua. "The Rise and Fall of Affirmative Action." *newyorker.com*, 15 Oct. 2018, www.newyorker.com/magazine/2018/10/15/the-rise-and-fall-of-affirmative-action.

JASC (Japanese American Services Committee). "Japanese American Service Committee Statement on Forced Separation of Migrant Children and Indefinite Family Detention." *jasc.org*, 22 June 2018, www.jasc-chicago.org/wp-content/uploads/2018/07/2018.06.22-JASC-Press-Release-Child-and-Family-Detention.pdf.

Kim, ChangHwan, and Arthur Sakamoto. "Have Asian American Men Achieved Labor Market Parity with White Men?" *American Sociological Review*, vol. 75, no.6, Dec. 2010, pp. 934–957.

———, and Yang Zhao. "Are Asian American Women Advantaged? Labor Market Performance of College Educated Female Workers." *Social Forces*, vol. 93, no. 2, Dec. 2014, pp. 623–652.

Kramer, Paul. "Not Who We Are." *slate.com*, 3 Feb. 2017, slate.com/news-and-politics/2017/02/trumps-muslim-ban-and-the-long-history-of-american-nativism.html.

Lee, Jennifer. "Asian Americans, Affirmative Action and the Rise in Anti-Asian Hate." *Dædalus*, vol. 150, no. 2 (Spring 2021), pp. 180–198.

———. "Ending Affirmative Action Will Hurt Us All." *nbcnews.com*, 28 June 2017, www.nbcnews.com/think/news/opinion-ending-affirmative-action-will-hurt-us-all-ncna777751. Accessed 21 June 2021.

———. "Harvard Likes Legacies: The Children of Alumni Have Too Great an Advantage." *Los Angeles Times*, 22 June 2018, p. A11.

MPI (Migration Policy Institute). "Deferred Action for Childhood Arrivals (DACA) Data Tools." *migrationpolicy.org*, www.migrationpolicy.org/programs/data-hub/deferred-action-childhood-arrivals-daca-profiles. Accessed 22 June 2021.

Novick, Peter. *That Noble Dream: The "Objectivity Question" and the American Historical Profession*. Cambridge University Press, 1988.

Omi, Michael, and Howard Winant. *Racial Formation in the United States*. 3rd edition. Routledge/Taylor and Francis Group, 2015.

Petersen, William. "Success Story, Japanese-American Style." *New York Times*, 9 Jan. 1966, pp. 21–43.

Pew Research Center. "Key Facts About Asian Origin Groups in the U.S." *pewresearch.org*, 29 April 2021, www.pewresearch.org/fact-tank/2021/04/29/key-facts-about-asian-origin-groups-in-the-u-s/.

Ramakrishnan, Karthick, et al. "National Asian American Survey (NAAS) 2016 Pre-Election Survey." Riverside, CA: National Asian American Survey, 5 Oct. 2016. naasurvey.com/wp-content/uploads/2016/10/NAAS16-Fall-Oct5-slides.pdf.

Ramakrishnan, Karthick, and Sono Shah. "One Out of Every Seven Asian Immigrants is Undocumented." *aapidata.org*, 8 Sept. 2017, aapidata.com/blog/asian-undoc-1in7/.

———, and Janelle Wong. "Survey Roundup: Asian American Attitudes on Affirmative Action," *AAPI Data*, 18 June 2018, aapidata.com/blog/asianam-affirmative-action-surveys/. Data Bits.

Sotomayor, Sonia. Dissenting opinion. *Trump v. Hawaii*, No. 17–965, 585 US ___, 26 June 2018, pp. 1–28. *Supreme Court of the United States*, www.supremecourt.gov/opinions/17pdf/17-965_h315.pdf.

Stop AAPI Hate. "The Rising Tide of Violence and Discrimination Against Asian American and Pacific Islander Women and Girls." *stopaapihate.org*, 20 May 2021, stopaapihate.org/aapi-women-and-girls-report/.

"Success Story of One Minority Group in the U.S." *U.S. News & World Report*, 20 December 1966, pp. 73–76.

"Success Story: Outwhiting the Whites." *Newsweek*, 21 June 1971, pp. 24–25.

West, Cornel. *Race Matters*. Boston: Beacon Press, 1993.

Woodward, C. Vann. *The Strange Career of Jim Crow*. New York: Oxford UP, 1955.

CHAPTER 8

Soulful Kenosis in Narcissistic Times

Farah Jasmine Griffin

In the past, when asked to deliver a brief tribute or to introduce Cornel before he speaks, my words have come easily, flowing like the lyrics of a cherished song. Not this time. Instead, I found myself stuck in a morass of thoughts, images, and sound-bites. They came like an assault, barreling forth even in my sleep—an anxious cacophony, interrupted by an occasional breakthrough, which I rushed to jot down in fear of losing.

Surely part of my anxiety might be attributed to the times in which we were living. At the time that we gathered to celebrate the twenty-fifth anniversary of *Race Matters*, every day seemed to bring a new outrage that either kept us on edge or numb. The television, which in a rush for ratings and profits helped to create the moment, kept us captive with daily reports of new assaults: images of babies torn from their mothers, families separated, entire countries banned, white supremacists marching through the streets. Sometimes so-called news shows with pundits screaming at each other seem to have been inspired by various real housewives snatching wigs and throwing drinks. The twenty-four-hour news cycle competed with "reality television" to showcase our basest impulses. Social media emerged as a forum where black death was documented at every turn, and images of police and vigilante violence against black people seemed to have been replaced with clips of pursed-lipped whites calling the police on black people who were simply living their lives. The police continued to assault and kill black and brown people, but until the 2020 murder of George Floyd, for a while it seemed social media moved on; it found this new genre. At the same time, social media was (and continues to be) dominated by selfies, hostile, mean-spirited declarations, a culture of "take down" and shallow pronouncements.

Such narcissism, such cruelty.

Jean Twenge and W. Keith Campbell, in *The Narcissism Epidemic: Living in the Age of Entitlement* (2009), describe the conditions that have given rise to the "cultural narcissism" of our times. Since that book's publication, the epidemic seems to have become a permanent state of our culture. Dennis Shen also explored the rise of narcissism on societal conditions. He writes that "at extremes, narcissism undermines institutions that underpin a strong society, with links to shallow values, less intellectual interest and value on hard work, aggression and relationship complications, and lack of empathy and concern for others."[1] Although Shen does not mention rampant consumerism, neoliberal policies and practices, and market values run amok, surely these contribute to the rise in narcissism as well.

When communities and families fail to provide support networks, the lack of real connection reinforces a focus on "me," further damaging the ties of family and community. Shen writes this context "encourages divisive and antisocial short-term behavior over long-term decision making."[2] Significantly, the conditions that give rise to cultural narcissism are also the conditions that gave rise to the crises that Cornel West warned about in *Race Matters*. Especially in the chapter on nihilism.

Some part of my inability to think clearly certainly came from my consumption of social media and the distractions that come with it. Another came from the task. How to pay tribute to a man who means so much to me, to us, to our struggle, to our history? How to talk about the legacy of this book, *Race Matters*, in this moment of crisis, in a way that speaks to an informed audience that includes his colleagues, friends, and former students? Just thinking of it I experienced another malady of our time—anxiety. Like Morrison's Baby Suggs withdrawing to her bed to contemplate color, I too wanted to withdraw—to look at Instagram posts of pretty pictures: cute babies . . . kittens . . . sunsets . . . (and oops! A selfie!!).

And then, I stopped. Stepped away. Went to visit and spend time with my ninety-year-old mother and my beautiful niece, Karen, a bride-to-be in the midst of planning her wedding. Together, Karen and I walked the streets of South Philadelphia where I had been nurtured and loved. I took her on a tour of the various homes occupied by my immediate family members during the years when I grew up: my maternal grandmother lived two blocks away from my paternal grandparents. Cousins around every corner it seemed, because like most black communities, we claimed cousins far and wide. The tour ended at the small row house where I was raised, and that we still own, though the area is rapidly gentrifying. While in Philly, I spent days listening to Luther, Donny Hathaway, Trane, Roberta Flack, and Geri Allen . . . Perfection. Ensconced in the geographical and musical contexts that gave birth to and nurtured me, I returned to a sense of proportion and perspective. And then, instead of thinking about my task, I thought about my dear, dear friend of over thirty years, Cornel. To think about him is to be pulled back from the brink of despair. To think about him evokes warmth and laughter, to be inspired and dazzled by his brilliance, to witness compassion take shape in his actions—to experience Love.

Given the occasion, as I have done so often, when I don't know what to think, I read what he has written. In this instance, I returned to *Race Matters*. In the past I have written books and essays informed by sentences Cornel has written. (His words have provided epigraphs for two of my own books.) This time was no different. Except it wasn't a sentence. It was a phrase. Two words, in fact: *Soulful Kenosis*.

In the introduction to the twenty-fifth anniversary edition of *Race Matters*, Cornel reiterates the significance of the Black Freedom Struggle and of the black musical brotherhood tradition and elaborates on the relationship between the two. He writes: "The greatest tradition of black prophetic fightback in the American Empire is the Black Freedom Struggle. The greatest tradition of moral and spiritual fortitude in the American Empire is the Black musical tradition. . . . The artistic excellence in the best of Black music, including the magnanimity and majesty of the sound—sets the standard for the Black freedom struggle."[3]

These standards include freedom, love, and truth-telling. There is little to argue with here. And those of us who have followed Cornel over the years have heard him say this. There is a deep familiarity in these words. But just as I settled in and felt comfortable, there at the bottom of the page and continuing to the next, he writes: "The distinctive benchmark of Black music is soulful kenosis—the courageous and compassionate styles of genuine self-emptying that give all one is and has to empower, enable and ennoble others. In this metaphoric way, the greatest black musicians and black freedom fighters are the truth in that they embody and enact a radical love (especially for an unloved people) by freely giving all they are and have to inspire and encourage others."[4]

Soulful. Kenosis. Self-Emptying.

The concept of kenosis finds its origins in the New Testament. Specifically, in Paul's letter to the Philippians. Kenosis from the Greek KENOO, meaning to empty. (Here it helps to be married to a New Testament scholar). Philippians 2:5–8 reads:

> 5 Let the same mind be in you that was[a] in Christ Jesus,
> 6 who, though he was in the form of God,
> did not regard equality with God
> as something to be exploited,
> 7 but emptied himself,
> taking the form of a slave,
> being born in human likeness.
> And being found in human form,
> 8 he humbled himself
> and became obedient to the point of death—
> even death on a cross.

This is the New Revised Standard Version. In other translations it variously appears as "he emptied himself," "he made himself nothing," "he gave up all he had." But it is the language of "emptying" that most resonates.

Not since having learned of the concept of Grace, which quickly became my most cherished spiritual concept, have I been as taken by a principle. In religious terms (and I resist religion although I am vulnerable to it), this means: unequal to God, humble to the will of God, obedient to God. But might it also mean unequal to the traditions that shape us, humbled in the face of the best of that tradition, that collective genius, that collective will toward freedom (as Kendrick says, "Be Humble"). Obedient to the task of furthering it. I read the state of self-emptying as having resonance with that brilliant phrase of the black vernacular: "It ain't about you!" The call to self-emptying, as a call to rid oneself of self-aggrandizement, ego, competition, and to identify with the least of these, to be humble in their presence and the presence of those who came before, to be disciplined and obedient in pursuit of justice, freedom, and love. To allow suffering to speak, bear witness to it. Can one empty oneself, live in the knowledge that "it ain't about you"—leader, artist, entertainer, politician, intellectual. It's about something bigger than you—a relay race, or a wave in the vastness of the ocean, a struggle of which you are a part. I see it as an aspiration and a practice, not a permanent state of being. And I believe that this moment of Kenosis or in the practice of Kenosis, one may touch upon Genius, your own yes, but a collective genius to which you contribute. Think Martin Luther King Jr. of the "I've been to the mountaintop" sermon in Memphis, on the eve of his assassination; think John Coltrane, "Peace on Earth," recorded in Japan in July 1966, found on the *Live in Japan* recording; think Toni Morrison on the pages of *Beloved*. Might each of these masterpieces indeed be the result of the individuals self-emptying in order to become a vessel for a larger purpose?

Cornel modifies kenosis with the adjective soulful. Soulful is defined as expressing feeling or emotion. But it is so much more than that. It is also "unapologetically black" as in one definition of soul—"characteristic of, or for, Black Americans and their culture."

What might Soulful Kenosis, a metaphor of kenosis, as a feature of black music, look like? The tradition is full of examples. I immediately thought of Coltrane, but after the immense pleasure of sorting through numerous examples, I kept returning to one.

In 1974 Al Green appeared with a full band on *Soul Train*, the nationally syndicated music/dance show founded and executively produced by Don Cornelius. The dancers were local teens, many of whom became celebrities in their own right. Most often performers lip-synced because of the prohibitive cost of producing live music. However, on occasion Al Green, Stevie Wonder, Sly Stone, Barry White, and others appeared live. America watched, but for black Americans watching it became a collective ritual, one that produced other rituals in turn, most notably the Soul Train Line, which Cornelius described as giving "everybody a chance to style a while," demonstrating once again the deep democratic practice that informs much of black culture. On this day Al and his band shared the program with the Impressions.

Al, dressed in Oshun Yellow,[5] bearing a rose in one hand, while the other arm was cradled in a sling (a stylish silk scarf). His arm was broken, but as with Toni Morrison's Baby Suggs, "who decided that because slave life had 'busted her legs, back, head, eyes, hands, kidneys, womb and tongue' she had nothing left, but her heart, which she put to use at once," Al, despite his broken arm, gives all of himself in and for this performance, his audience, and the tradition of which he is a part. He first sings the recognizable melody over the horn line, funky bass, guitar, and the trademark gospel organ: "Here I am Baby, Come and Take Me." I stand before you, open, vulnerable, available.

An offering and an invitation, the song was written by Al Green and Mabon "Tiny" Hodges, with whom he penned a number of hits including "Love and Happiness." It appeared on the 1973 release *Call Me*. It reached number ten on Billboard's Hot 100 and number two on the Soul Singles Chart. At the time of this performance, he was at the peak of his artistic powers and his commercial success. After the initial statement of the lyrics, he appears to empty himself to near exhaustion, allowing himself to become a vessel. Filled with a new spirit, he now takes the music and those of us listening to a higher plane, by slowing the tempo down, and moving up into his falsetto range. In Nathaniel Mackey's *Bedouin Hornbook*, the character N muses that the falsetto: "bears the weight of a gnostic, transformative desire to be done with the world. By this I mean the deliberately forced, deliberately 'false' voice we get from someone like Al Green creatively hallucinates a 'new world,' indicts the more insidious falseness of the world as we know it. (Listen, for example, to 'Love and Happiness.')"

Mackey continues: "What is it in the falsetto that thins and threatens to abolish the voice but the wear of so much reaching for heaven? . . . . Like the moan or the shout, I'm suggesting, the falsetto explores a redemptive, unworded realm—a meta-word, if you will—where the implied critique of the momentary eclipse of the word curiously rescues, re-stores and renews it: new word, new world."[6]

As Green's voice moves into the falsetto range—moving into that new world as he builds it for us, he reaches toward heaven, aspiring toward a better place—his body moves across the stage and he begins the Holy Dance, an indication that he has invoked a spirit, that he is overcome, and words give way to a rhythmic repetition: "Love me, love me, love me." It is more chant than song, an affirmation, a meditation, an instruction, both a demand and a request. At this point he is so moved, with love and generosity, he begins to distribute roses. And his lyrics give way to a floating lyric: "The way you do the thing you do." I always think of floating lyrics as the moment when the tradition enters into the song lyrically. . . . It is there free for the taking, it comes to the singer, performer like an ancestral visitation, like a gift. It makes sense in the context of the song, it expresses a collective yearning, longing, state of being.

At this point the dancers become aware of the transformation. They come closer and some turn to the stage, dancing still, but in place. The middle part of the song has carried him to a spiritual space where he is now ready to deliver the sermon. "This evening" signals the sermonic nature of the performance. The dancers respond to his call with "Well!!," encouraging him, acknowledging the power and the generosity of his performance. "Get on board. . . . It don't take no money. It doesn't take no ticket. Just get on board." The Soul Train joins the tradition of freedom trains in black culture, the Underground Railroad, all those trains that appear in the blues, in Romare Bearden's paintings, the train that takes you out of the Jim Crow South, the trains that cross the Mason-Dixon Line. Freedom trains, bound for glory or just for a place where the white folk ain't so mean. And he is the conductor, he has taken us somewhere else. By the end, he is spent, "Bye" he says. He blows kisses. He has emptied himself. A Soulful Kenosis.

In the days following my encounter with Cornel's use of this phrase I have read a great deal about kenosis. It is clear that I have much to learn from the philosophers and theologians in our midst; and I look forward to doing so. I am aware of Alex Dubilet's recent book *The Self-Emptying Subject: Kenosis and Immanence, Medieval to Modern*,[7] in which he argues: "Self-emptying is intimately tied to one of the key preoccupations of continental philosophy and critical theory in the twentieth century—the critique of the subject, its autonomy and consistency, its self-possession and mastery, its self-enclosure and self-identity—it carries with it a distinctly theological lineage."

Perhaps unsurprisingly, it is this theological lineage that speaks most to my understanding and interpretation more than the philosophical, except as they come together in the work of Simone Weil, a thinker to whom Cornel introduced me many years ago. For Weil writes: "The soul empties itself of all its own contents in order to receive into itself the being it is looking at, just as he is in all his truth" (*Waiting for God*).[8] Similarly, the Franciscan monk Kevin Cronin writes of kenosis as an emptying of oneself, laying down one's life, letting go.[9] Informed by Cronin and Weil, I see this as a call to those of us who are activists, artists, and intellectuals, to empty ourselves of ego and the impulse toward narcissism, to lay down our bodies, if not our lives, to give all that we have to give. Might that be the level of commitment required of this historic moment? Might it be a fitting response to these desperate and narcissistic times? It need not only inform our activism, our intellectual and creative work, but also our interactions with each other. To step outside of ourselves and care for others. To comfort a sick person, to visit the lonely, sit with the dying, or gently quiet a child in distress. To give of oneself for the benefit of another. Toni Morrison calls upon us to meet the disorder of our times with our "own humanity." In a 2011 commencement address at Rutgers, she warned against a media designed to change us from citizens to consumers or "taxpayers," from "a community of engaged civic life, to individuals with hundreds of electronic friends."[10] (This is the work of neoliberalism.) For this reason, her last two novels, *Home* and *God Help the Child*, each turn on the ability of individuals, couples, and communities to care for the weak and the vulnerable. In the process of caring for others we find integrity and meaning in our own lives.

In 1993, Cornel described the conditions that have led us away from this sense of community and commitment, the conditions of selfishness, greed, and lack of meaning that we see today. In part, because we as a nation did not heed the advice he offered there to eschew market values for empathy and compassion, we find ourselves today in a viscous, raw, extreme version of what he described then. The hateful one who occupied the White House from 2017 to 2021 was not the cause of this; he was one of its consequences. This in no way diminishes the harm and devastation he wrought and continues to wreak, but it is to say that he exists in a lineage that directly leads to his fascistic aspirations.

By the time *Race Matters* appeared in print, Cornel had already established himself as a thinker of great gifts who was on the verge of becoming an important public figure, one who was as at home in the classrooms of our most prestigious universities as he was in pulpits of churches large and small, prisons, stages he shared with musical artists, and street corners where he engaged countless unknown individuals. And, like Miles Davis, he is always the same in whatever setting he finds himself, rising to the occasion to communicate truths in a variety of contexts, without sacrificing his integrity or the tone, tenor and timbre of his voice. There is no code-switching, no slip into and out of the vernacular. His references range from the Western philosophical and literary traditions (of which the Black American literary tradition is a part), to the Bible and black expressive culture, and he shows the deep wisdom they all share. Those of us who knew him before *Race Matters* met a man for whom the life of the mind and the path of the public intellectual was a calling, a vocation, not a choice driven by career or professional concerns. The academy was but one site of his contribution to struggle, an important, but certainly not the only one. For many of us Cornel has been a pathbreaker long before the publication of *Race Matters*. He was an all too rare example of intellectual generosity and brilliance, inviting and welcoming us with affirmation and assistance. He was unafraid to acknowledge his love for black people, willing to affirm black intellectual, political, and cultural traditions. But he was never provincial, narrow, or liberal. With Cornel we read deeply and widely from the Western Marxists to Frantz Fanon, from James Baldwin to Richard Rorty, Anton Chekov, Oliver Cox, and Toni Morrison. As we came to know him, we came to love him and because of him we gained faith that our side could win. And he reminded us that if we did not win, we must "go down fighting."

By 1993 he had already produced a body of scholarship that helped to establish him as an important figure in philosophy, political thought, African American studies, religion and theology.

In *Prophesy Deliverance! An Afro-American Revolutionary Christianity* he reads the African American intellectual/literary tradition for its prophetic dimensions while also insisting that Black Theology engage Marxism as a means of underscoring the centrality and significance of class to the black American experience. In *The Ethical Dimensions of Marxist Thought* (1991) West reveals the ways that ethics are central to Marx's thinking and demonstrates how later interpretations by figures such as Georg Lukás and others narrowed the project so that it appeared solely motivated by the economic dimension of social life at the expense of the ethical. The text has much to teach us about Marxism and about the relationship of Marx's view to questions of the good and the just. *The American Evasion of Philosophy: A Genealogy of Pragmatism* (1989) is perhaps his academic masterpiece. Here he charts the development of American Pragmatism through sustained attention to Emerson, Dewey, Du Bois, and others. A masterful work arguing for the importance of American Pragmatism to ongoing efforts to reform and transform American society.

Race Matters, published after these three, is his most popular work, written for a non-academic audience, yet it builds upon the foundation of this earlier work. Like the figures about whom he writes in *American Pragmatism*, with *Race Matters* Cornel West entered fully into the public square, seeking to inspire reasoned thought and dialogue amongst fellow citizens. Within these pages, readers encounter a philosopher who believes philosophical thinking has something to offer citizens of a democracy. Much of the book is a critique of faulty logic and reasoning and an attempt to offer alternative ways of thinking about how we live together in a multiracial society, with attention to matters of class as well.

As with all of his work, *Race Matters* is a text that is deeply historical and broad in its sense of the world it occupies. Each edition opens with a new preface or introduction that situates it in the current moment. Consequently, race matters are always understood as matters of history in dialogue with contemporary struggles of oppressed peoples worldwide. In 1993 the urgency was to strip "white supremacy of its authority and legitimacy" in the face of its seeming intransigence. By 2001 he insists that we understand race matters in the context of the need for workers', environmental, and consumer protections. (His book of that title, *Democracy Matters: Winning the Fight Against Imperialism*, was published in 2004). By the new introduction to the twenty-fifth anniversary edition, *Race Matters* exists in the context of "imperial meltdown": American Empire in "decline and decay." He writes that in 2018, "We live in one of the darkest moments in American History," and cautions: "The deep denial of race matters in American history . . . is an example of the more profound denial of empire matters in the emergence and sustenance of America."[11] So things have not gotten better since the initial publication of *Race Matters;* in many ways they've gotten worse. They are cruder, more virulent and violent, but they are not new or unique.

In 1993 Cornel warned us about the "Pitfalls of Racial Reasoning" that regulated black thought and action, arguing for the replacement of racial reasoning with moral reasoning. Racial reasoning invokes the "undeniable history of racial abuse and struggle" and can be used to manipulate black people's support for figures such as Clarence Thomas. Cornel called for a moral assessment that selects "views based on black dignity and decency over claims to racial authenticity."[12] Furthermore, in "Crisis of Black Leadership" he identified so called race transcendent leaders who try to reach a large white constituency while keeping a black one. Such leadership silences prophetic voices in the black community by "casting the practical mainstream as the only game in town."[13] Might not racial reasoning and this crisis of leadership have shaped the moment that gave us our first black president, certainly a moment of progress and change, but one which found too many of us unwilling to offer challenging, constructive critique of him. Certainly many kept silent out of understandable concern for the very real vitriol and threats of violence on his life and did not wish to contribute to the environment of hatred that surrounded him; others did so because they were convinced that the "practical mainstream" was indeed the only game in town. Others opportunistically marketed the ascent to the White House as the culmination of our centuries-long freedom struggle. Finally, I think most were thrilled and proud to see an image of dignity, intelligence, and elegance projected by America's first black family. So few were willing to be openly critical of paternalistic speeches about black behavior, false equivalencies between justified black anger and white resentment, policies of immigrant detention and deportation, and the use of excessive military force in the form of kill lists and drone strikes. Even in those instances where President Obama acknowledged black suffering and his concern and identification with it, the backlash was swift and harsh. He often said nothing publicly out of concern for garnering white hatred. Many whites hated him anyway. They were driven insane by his very existence. And, they ushered in a backlash so vicious that it has opened the gates for the would-be fascists and barbarians.

In 1993, Cornel warned about a growing nihilism in poor black communities and caught a lot of flak for doing so. He highlighted the failures of those who only consider structural constraints on the lives of black people or only on their behavioral impediments, arguing instead that the two are inseparable. Furthermore, he called our attention to growing levels of "dread and despair" that flood black America such that a basic issue facing black communities was the nihilistic threat to its very existence. Much of black life up to that point had been a struggle against nihilism, a fight against the loss of hope and meaning. At the time, younger radical thinkers found the discussion of nihilism conservative, leaning in the direction of blaming the victim and yet today it seems the threat of nihilism is even stronger. The near daily witnessing of police killings of innocent black people, the refusal to penalize those who murder them, the profound consequence of two-plus decades of mass incarceration and unfair sentencing amid growing rates of poverty lend to this understandable sense of despair. It is not only poor black youth who experience it. In my upper-level undergraduate seminar on African American Novelists and the Conception of Justice where I teach Chesnutt, Hurston, Wright, Ellison, Morrison, and Gaines, my students, recipients of an elite education, many of them enchanted by the theories of Afropessimism, asked for more text on black nihilism and vigilantism. They wanted more of Morrison's Seven Days and less taking the moral high ground.

Even Cornel, author of *Hope on a Tightrope*, writes in the twenty-fifth anniversary edition of *Race Matter*, that while he reached "heartbreaking yet hopeful" conclusions twenty-five years ago, today "in our times heartbreak cuts much deeper and hope has nearly run out."[14]

Yes, we gathered to celebrate this landmark text in dark times. The election of the 45th president represented the triumph of the worst version of America. Ignorance, violence, hatefulness, racism, misogyny, anti-immigrant animus. He sat atop a vile lineage of slavery and Indian removal, of the Klan and the Dixiecrats, of base sexual aggression and rampant, crude capitalism, anti-intellectualism and shallow opportunism. This IS America.

But as Cornel has told us in books like *Democracy Matters* and countless speeches and interviews, there is another America, and it has not died. It is the America of King, Baldwin, Dorothy Day, Ella Baker, and Caesar Chavez. This too, is America.

Personally, although daily I too found myself on the brink of the abyss, confronting despair, I nonetheless hold onto hope that this version of America is finding a new birth, is alive and striving to fight the good fight. It erupted in global, multiracial protests following the police murder of George Floyd in June 2020. In spite (or perhaps because) of the fact that we were living in the midst of a global pandemic that disproportionately took the lives of black, brown, and poor people, millions took to the streets. It is smarter, equipped with the critical insights of black feminism and with a recognition of the value of queer lives. It demonstrated the spiritual fortitude that sustained generations past. The courageous souls who emerged in the moment gave me hope and inspiration as well as the courage to continue the pursuit of justice.

What might soulful kenosis, our political and intellectual work, look like in these times? I see it in numerous guises:

I see it in people willing to put their bodies on the line, willing to empty themselves as they confront evil.

I see it in the young people who took to the streets of Ferguson, Missouri, within hours of Mike Brown's murder by Darren Walker, who continued to do so night after night, who faced down tanks of a militarized police force. I see it in those who picked up the fight after the murders of Ahmaud Arbery, Breonna Taylor, and George Floyd. I see it in those who are part of Black Lives Matter and the BYP100, who very well may be among the only generation of black activists who put a black feminist analysis at the center of their theorizing, organizing, and praxis. I see in in Heather Hayer, murdered by a white supremacist in Charlottesville as she stood with others to challenge the hatred that descended upon that city, and in her mother who courageously maintains her daughter's legacy with integrity. I see it in the immigrant rights activists, who were engaged in struggle under the Bush administration and the Obama administration, and who under their successor, were joined by others inspired by a disdain for him or by an awakening to what is being done, in their name, to immigrant families. I see it in a figure like Rev. William Barber who in his life, words and actions insists that "We've got to hold up the banner until every person has health care, we've got to hold it up until every child is lifted in love, we've got to hold it up until every job is a living-wage job, until every person in poverty has guaranteed subsistence."[15] I see it in all of those who gathered in my hometown, Philadelphia, during the summer of 2020 as votes were counted to decide the next president of the United States. I see it in the work of The Brotherhood/Sister Sol, an organization that is dear to my heart that provides long term, holistic support to youth ages eight to twenty-two in areas like Leadership development, educational achievement and political education. It is a locally based institution that welcomes queer youth, immigrant youth. According to the leaders and staff, "Our theory of change is to provide multi-layered support, guidance, education and love to our membership, to teach them to have self-discipline, form order in their lives, and then to offer opportunities and access so that they may develop agency." The young staff is the most self-sacrificing group of people I know. They are available to our young people 24/7 and always provide unconditional love for them.

I see it on the pages of Darnell Moore's beautiful memoir, *No Ashes in the Fire; Coming of Age Black and Free in America,* who challenges the heteronormative master narratives of black history with beauty and compassion, bearing witness to the communities that name him and in whose name he wages his struggle.

I see it in all of you.

Soulful kenosis can exist in large, grand gestures and meaningful action. But it can also exist in our everyday interactions with each other. It might be as simple as giving every shred of your dignity to coax a baby's smile, holding the hand, rubbing the feet, kissing the forehead of an ill person, listening without judgment to the fears of an anxious teen or elder. It might look like a daily ritual of love and care for someone other than you and yours.

While we fight, struggle, beat back despair, build a new world together, let us also stop, be still, offer gratitude to God (if you believe in God), to the Universe, to the Ancestors, to the communities and families that birthed and/or sustain us, to each other, let us say thank you for the privilege of being part of something bigger than ourselves, for allowing us to be a vessel, to be one in the number, to be what Cornel calls "a hope." In the closing pages of the twenty-fifth anniversary introduction, he writes: "Since the prophetic fire lit by hope has been so damped by neoliberal chatter about 'hope,' I prefer to be ***a*** hope rather than talk about hope. Being *a* hope is being in motion, on the move with body on the line, mind set on freedom, soul full of courage, and heart shot through with love. Being a hope is forging moral and spiritual fortitude, putting on intellectual armor, and being willing to live and die for the empowerment of the wretched of the earth."

Sounds like *Soulful Kenosis* to me. Thank you, Cornel, for being ***a*** hope, for inviting us to join you, and for earnestly and sincerely striving to model the way with style, love, and soul.

Notes

1. Dennis Shen. "A Rise in Narcissism Could Be One of the Main Causes of Americans' Political and Economic Crises." London School of Economics, United States Politics and Policy, Phelan US Center. https://blogs.lse.ac.uk/usappblog/2017/06/28/a-rise-in-narcissism-a-root-of-americas-crisis/.

2. Shen, "Narcissism."

3. Cornel West. *Race Matters.* Twenty-fifth anniversary ed., Beacon Press, 2017, 15.

4. *Race Matters*, twenty-fifth anniversary ed., 16.

5. Oshun is the Yoruba deity of sweet waters, love, beauty, sensuality, and creativity. Her colors are yellow and gold.

6. Nathaniel Mackey. *From a Broken Bottle Traces of Perfume Still Emanate: Bedouin Hornbook, Djbot Baghostus's Run, Atet A.D.* New Directions, 2010, 50.

7. Alex Dubilet. *The Self-Emptying Subject: Kenosis and Immanence, Medieval to Modern.* Fordham UP, 2018.

8. Quoted in Dubilet, 10–11.

9. Kevin M. Cronin. *Kenosis: Emptying Self and the Path of Christian Service.* Continuum International Publishing, 2005.

10. Toni Morrison, Commencement Address, 25 May 2011, Rutgers University. https://www.youtube.com/watch?v=yh0cyb8kVMI.

11. *Race Matters*, 12.

12. *Race Matters,* 41.

13. *Race Matters,* 49.

14. *Race Matters,* 11.

15. Rev. William Barber, https://www.oldwestchurch.org/core-values.

AFTERWORD

Race Matters: Philosophy in the Funk

Cornel West

This serious and substantive book focused on my work and witness is a result of the vision and determination of my dear sister Associate Dean Barbara Will, now the vice provost (and aided by the highly capable Sarah M. S. Coulter) of Dartmouth College. The profound spiritual decay and pervasive moral decrepitude of American capitalist civilization often prohibit an unflinchingly honest understanding of Race Matters in our times. This volume plunges into the depths of the catastrophic preconditions—settler colonialism and slavery—of American democracy. Unlike popular narratives about white supremacy and caste with no capitalism and settler colonialism, the voices in this text confront the complex dynamics of Race Matters that keep track of the relations of the economic and existential, social and spiritual, political and personal.

Barbara Will's introduction provides a superb background for this kind of multi-dimensional inquiry into Race Matters. Paul Bové lays bare the overlooked effects of academic professionalism and celebrity journalism—both market-driven and selected by white neoliberal establishments—on race discourse. The mainstream obsession with diversity and inclusion—though better than homogeneity and exclusion—easily slides down a slope of narrow multicultural careerism and opportunism that simply make myopic power centers more colorful yet still oppressive. Lucius Outlaw continues our twenty-year battle over the legacy of the great W. E. B. Du Bois. And despite our deep brotherhood and undeniable disagreements, we reside in a zone far removed from superficial race talk. Brandon Terry's essay is a masterpiece—definitely the best treatment I know of my influential writings on nihilism. And given the emerging popularity of the Afropessimist movement, Terry brilliantly teases out my own deep respect for what motivates this movement and my deep disagreement with where this movement leads us.

Andrew Prevot's original reflections on my views on Black Nihilism are refreshing. I applaud his attention to my own prophetic Christian sensibilities. Susannah Heschel's magnificent essay on my work and witness in relation to my soul-companion, Abraham Joshua Heschel, brought tears to my eyes. Susannah Heschel is a distinguished scholar and prophetic figure who has done more than anyone to keep alive the rich legacy of her world-historical father. I hope and pray my lifework can even approximate the respect and confidence she invests in me! Nkosi Anderson rightly and wisely links me to one of my Black Pastor heroes—Rev. George Washington Woodbey. His name should be known across the nation and world.

Of all of my thousands of students and mentees, Matthew Briones stands out as the most humble, steadfast, and reliable. His spiritual maturity and personal integrity are implacable. And of all my thousands of colleagues and fellow professors, Farah Jasmine Griffin stands out as the most wise, soulful, and trustworthy. She indeed is one of the few great intellectuals in our time.

Between 1982 and 1993, I published nine books (and coedited two books). *Race Matters* appeared in 1993. And although this text remains my most best-known book, I would never have thought it so. It was Deborah Chasman's vision to put together the various essays that constitute *Race Matters*. The only original piece was "Black Sexuality: The Taboo Issue." The Rodney King verdict catapulted my work and witness in an extraordinary manner. I quickly became the darling of the white liberal establishment. For months my image and figure surfaced incessantly. Only my work for the Million Man March shattered this position. I welcomed the shattering given my past and present work with revolutionary communists, revolutionary Black Nationalists, democratic socialists and Pan-African anti-imperialists. In other words, my approach to Race Matters has always been informed by a particular philosophical orientation—an orientation rooted in my own experiences and shaped by my own intellectual choices and existential commitments.

Race Matters (1993) was a unique and singular moment in my forever evolving journey. Race Matters in the twenty-first century is a complex form of catastrophe caught between the massive neglect and pervasive betrayal of poor and working-class peoples by the power elites in the USA—this includes the Black middle and professional classes' neglect and betrayal of Black poor and working people in Hoods shot through with indecent housing, low quality education, inadequate health care and few jobs with a living wage. The militarism and materialism, greed and graft, ignorance and indifference are squeezing the democratic life out of an American Empire with domestic ruins and global debris. American-style fascism harkens even as some of us heed prophetic voices and legacies—and prepare to bear any burden and pay the ultimate price!

For me, philosophy is a creative and courageous reckoning with catastrophe. This reckoning—led by a fallible and fierce practical wisdom—confronts forms of death, despair, dogma, and domination. From Plato's monumental dethroning of poetry in the name of philosophy to Richard Rorty's historic dethroning of philosophy to make the world safe for poetry, great philosophers have embodied original cries for help and enacted grand attempts to find a way out of our trapped predicaments. Intellectual discontent and existential defiance sit at the very core of philosophy.

Every philosophy presupposes a metaphilosophy—a conception of the role and function, style and form, content and character of philosophy. My own catastrophic philosophy began with my early encounters with the existential angst of Soren Kierkegaard, the political rage of Karl Marx, and the prophetic witness of Martin Luther King Jr. These earthshaking encounters transformed my adolescent focus on biblical responses to the problem of evil to philosophic wrestling with the catastrophes of death and dread, dogma and cowardice, domination, and exploitation. Arthur Schopenhauer and Friedrich Nietzsche became my intellectual ancestors just as Antonio Gramsci and W. E. B. Du Bois became my political comrades. All of them taught me to take history seriously, to philosophize in my space and my time, and to contextualize my voice and the voices of others.

I entered Harvard in 1970, during the last years of its second Golden Age. The philosophic genius of W. V. Quine, Nelson Goodman, John Rawls, Stanley Cavell, Hilary Putnam, and Robert Nozick cast large shadows over my philosophic education. And I reveled in their midst. Yet it was the pragmatism class taught by the adorable Israel Scheffler that sparked my deepest interest. To put it quite crudely, William James became my American Kierkegaard and John Dewey my American Marx. I left for Princeton in 1973 as a self-styled pragmatist—obsessed with fallibilism over skepticism, contextualism over sentential atomism, experimentalism over dogmatism, anti-foundationalism over Cartesianisms—yet driven by a catastrophic consciousness tied to imperial, class, racial, and gender domination as well as death and despair.

The first Golden Age of Princeton—of David Lewis, Gil Harman, Thomas Nagel, Thomas Scanlon, Paul Benacerraf, Walter Kaufmann, Margaret Wilson, Gregory Vlastos, Carl Hempel, Thomas Kuhn, and Richard Rorty—awaited me. And I was overjoyed. Yet, ironically, my biggest influence turned out to be Sheldon Wolin—the greatest theorist of radical democracy in America, who had written his MA thesis on John Dewey under Henry David Aiken (with whom I had studied at Harvard). My PhD dissertation, "Ethics, Historicism, and the Marxist Tradition," was written with Wolin and the inimitable Raymond Geuss (though Nagel, Vlastos, Scanlon, and Rorty were also on my committee).

Needless to say, my years in graduate school shaped my conception and practice of philosophy in timely and untimely ways. I was very much a child of my age, trained in and conversant with analytic philosophy, yet highly mindful of its blind spots and limitations. After serving as a teaching assistant in classes taught by the ever supportive G. A. Cohen (a Marxist analytic philosopher) at Princeton, the magnificent Stanley Cavell, and the young and brilliant Martha Nussbaum at Harvard, as well as taking classes from the great Hans-Georg Gadamer at Boston College and the creative Alasdair MacIntyre and the idiosyncratic J. N. Findlay at Boston University, I was constantly crossing the fragile bridge between analytic and continental philosophy. I also was very much a child against my age because the insurgent voices of my teacher, mentor, and friend Richard Rorty, the French voices of poststructuralists and postmodern figures (Jacques Derrida, Michel Foucault, Gilles Deleuze, Jean-François Lyotard, Julia Kristeva, and others) and the marginalized voices of Blacks, women, and queers (towering figures such as Stuart Hall, Judith Butler, and Hortense Spillers) meant much to me.

When I moved to New York to teach philosophy at Union Theological Seminary (the place of giants such as Paul Tillich and Reinhold Niebuhr, James Cone, and Beverly Harrison), I was a battered iconoclastic pragmatist with a catastrophic consciousness and Christocentric temperament. Upon my meeting and eventual deep friendship with the great Edward Said, I rightly sensed a fellow highbrow humanist—he secular, me Christian—in critical allegiance to the Socratic legacy of Athens and the prophetic legacy of Jerusalem. His secular criticism left little room for philosophy but much focus of critical engagement with catastrophe by poets (such as Gerard Manley Hopkins and Charles Baudelaire) and critics (like R. P. Blackmur and C. L .R. James). My prophetic pragmatism left room for philosophy with a strong emphasis on theoretical and practical engagement with catastrophe by poets (like T. S. Eliot and Muriel Rukeyser), critics like (Georg Lukács and Fredric Jameson), sociologists (like C. Wright Mills and St. Clair Drake), or philosophers (such as Theodor Adorno and Simone de Beauvoir).

My prophetic pragmatism has deep elective affinities to the two most important and profound fellow travelers of pragmatism of our time—Jeffery Stout and Roberto Mangabeira Unger. I am blessed to have known and taught with both of them for over twenty years at Princeton and Harvard. Both are grounded, in part, in Ralph Waldo Emerson's experimental quest for excellence and justice motivated by a profound sense of integrity and vocation. Though influenced by Emerson, my prophetic pragmatism is more shaped by Herman Melville's tragic preoccupation with the calamitous and monstrous in the American grain and Anton Chekhov's tragicomic fusion of catastrophe and compassion in the everyday lives in the Russian grain.

Hence, my philosophical development began with an early biblical sense of evil to a middle pragmatic wrestling with the problematic—always informed with a catastrophic consciousness—then to a full-blown prophetic vision wedded to a tragicomic expectation. My late prophetic pragmatism—radically democratic in content, sadly tragicomic in character, and joyfully jazz-like in style—has become so disillusioned with philosophy and so disappointed with pragmatism that it nearly ceases to be either. Like my fellow philosopher and intimate mate in the republic of letters—George Santayana—my love of wisdom yields a mature skepticism and uncynical bleakness. For him, Lucretius and Spinoza yield a haunted humanism with no illusions. For me, a blues-soaked prophetic pragmatism leads toward a dark humanism—P almost all the way down.

To put it bluntly, the centrality of temporality and historicity on the existential front in Kierkegaard and on the institutional and structural front in Marx resulted in my embrace of a pragmatism that held onto wrestling with existential angst and exploitative capitalist economics—all in my lived experience as a Black man in a white supremacist civilization.

It is no accident that nihilism remains a master-term in my corpus—from my early essay on Nietzsche in 1981 to my chapter on black nihilism in *Race Matters* in 1993 to my discussion of imperial nihilism in *Democracy Matters* in 2004, and my essay on hope and despair in Martin Luther King Jr.'s philosophy, in 2018. My developing conceptions of nihilism—not to be confused with René Descartes' methodological skepticism, Schopenhauer's deep pessimism, Nietzsche's passive or active nihilism, Ivan Turgenev's rich depiction of the nihilism of Bazarov in *Fathers and Sons* or Jean-Paul Sartre's stunning rendition of nihilism of Roquentin in *Nausea*—are corporeal and conceptual, economic and existential, personal and political.

My prophetic pragmatism begins with soul-shattering encounters with an indescribable monstrosity, centuries-long criminality, and an unfathomable catastrophe (then and now). In this sense, my prophetic pragmatism is a philosophy in the funk. This funk is, in part, what the greatest European writer in the barbaric twentieth century—Samuel Beckett—deemed the "mess." To wrestle with this funk and mess with Socratic energy and prophetic witness with little possibility of change or transformation—with only a "perhaps" (Beckett's favorite word), wedded to one's soulful kenosis, one's willingness to push one's self to the edge and end of self-giving and self-emptying with style and a smile in community. To be a blues man in the life of the mind and a jazz man in the world of ideas has always been my aspiration as a philosopher and person. To embrace one's own fallibility and acknowledge one's own inadequacy without paralysis or anomie; to see unflinchingly into the darkness of the past, present, and future without a faltering of one's own fire or a fading of one's own fight; and to keep alive the best of those grand exemplars of mind, heart, and soul who are no longer alive but have afterlives, in part, in the lives we live—this is the historical raw stuff, the temporal primordial background ingredients for prophetic pragmatism.

Another master-term of my discourse is democracy. Like the grand Hilary Putnam (with whom I taught his last course at Harvard on pragmatism), I claim that pragmatism is inseparable from democracy. Philosophy should be part of a larger conversation in which critical voices are raised with vision, argument, and narrative in a flexible and fluid manner to enable and enhance a communal quest for truth, beauty, and goodness. Like death, despair, and dogma, domination is an unavoidable reality of our world. Democracy is a way of life and mode of being in the world that tries to strip domination of its legitimacy and operation by rendering dominators accountable and answerable to those who are dominated. The aim is to overcome domination, yet every revolutionary effort must itself be accountable to democratic practices. The democratic aim is to affirm the dignity of ordinary people by ensuring their voices shape their destiny in civic, public, and private sectors. Courage and compassion, experimentation and improvisation, humility and empathy are inseparable in prophetic pragmatism. The anti-idolatrous strand in any form of philosophy or pragmatism—relentless self-criticism and self-correction—must remain vigilant in the face of any form of domination that may impede the quest for truth, beauty, or goodness. Arrogance and hubris, indifference and callousness always stand in the way of democratic ways of being in the world. Do not the best jazz quartets, quintets, or orchestras exemplify democratic symbolic action—critical voices raised from free and unique personalities in order to reach high forms of soulful excellence and common good?

Yet even democracy must never become a mere idol or fetish. Every democracy in human history has been either a patriarchal democracy, capitalist democracy, racist democracy, homophobic democracy, or imperial democracy (or some combination of all of the above)—all falling far short of a radical democracy. So far democracy in history is a tragicomic phenomenon. Like the blues, it is a sad yet sweet interplay of courageous agency and historical constraints, a melancholic yet melioristic movement of free peoples against severe limitations that identify and confront catastrophic misery only to see such efforts fall short of their mark. It is tragic because it is heroic action that is neither sentimental nor cynical—yet it runs up against overwhelming obstacles. It is comic in that the incongruity, mendacity, and hypocrisy of the systems of domination are revealed and disclosed. Democratic practices must be relentless and resilient—shot through with courage and compassion—yet usually yield disappointment.

In this broad sense, my tragicomic version of prophetic pragmatism (wrestling with but never triumphing over catastrophe or pushing back but never winning over nihilism) goes hand in hand with my tragicomic conception of democracy in history. Just as the ecstasies and erosions of the body constitute the body, so the breakthroughs and the backlashes of the body politic constitute the body politic. The rise and fall of empires, the ebb and flow of civilizations, the emergence and collapse of democratic regimes are neither natural nor seasonal—yet the heroic efforts of freedom-loving peoples and movements tend to be fugitives so far in human history. Sheldon Wolin's profound theory of fugitive democracy remains a formidable challenge to all of us willing to live and die for truth and justice for poor and working people.

Like my two teachers, Richard Rorty and Sheldon Wolin, my prophetic pragmatic philosophy is, in part, a historical interpretation, full of dialogical moments and democratic ends—that attempts to illuminate the past and present in order to inspire courageous action for a better future. To prophesy is not to predict an outcome but rather to identify, analyze, and confront concrete evils. No matter how dark and bleak my catastrophic version of prophetic pragmatism becomes, I refuse to predetermine the future, foreclose unpredictable breakthroughs, or trump the present only to give way to a neofascist world to come. Our human cries for help and grand efforts to find a way out of our trapped predicaments rest on a groundless mystery: why and how the weak armors of love and democracy—in a long history of hatred and domination—have not yet been snuffed out, eliminated, or forgotten. The thin reeds of Socratic energy and prophetic witness, critical consciousness and steadfast love, subversive memory. and sacrificial praxis have kept a flickering candle kindled in the dark tunnel of human history.

As the wise Howard Thurman and Donald MacKinnon have noted, the Christian story of the cross is one way of keeping track of and living in the midst of this groundless mystery: the kenosis of a God who takes on our flesh and blood in the form of a prophetic Jew who enacts and embodies a love and justice that leads to a bloody and humiliating crucifixion as a political criminal at the hands the greatest empire of the day. And even his cry for help—the blues line of Jesus on the tree at Calvary—seems to go unanswered. Yet this catastrophe does not have the last word. The drops of blood shed by the Christian exemplar of unarmed truth and unconditional love yield small seeds that grow to yield more works of love in a world overrun with hatred and domination (aided by Constantinian Christendom of past and present). My Christian version of prophetic pragmatism—with its embrace of tragicomic elements, blues-soaked sentiment, and catastrophic temperament—puts a premium on intellectual, existential, and political combat: to go down fighting with all and everything one has to keep alive the highest standards of excellence and integrity, courage and compassion, sacrifice and generosity for all peoples, especially the wretched of the earth. As long as "perhaps" we can see, love, laugh, and live better to create a better world, prophetic pragmatism and radical democracy survive—and maybe thrive, at least for a moment!

CONTRIBUTORS

Nkosi Du Bois Anderson received his PhD at Union Theological Seminary.

Paul A. Bové is Distinguished Professor of English at the University of Pittsburgh.

Matthew M. Briones is an associate professor of American history and the College at the University of Chicago.

Farah Jasmine Griffin is the William B. Ransford Professor of English and Comparative Literature and African American Studies at Columbia University.

Susannah Heschel is the Eli M. Black Distinguished Professor of Jewish Studies at Dartmouth College.

Lucius T. Outlaw Jr. is the W. Alton Jones Professor of Philosophy at Vanderbilt University.

Andrew Prevot is an associate professor in the Department of Theology at Boston College.

Brandon M. Terry is the John L. Loeb Associate Professor of the Social Sciences at Harvard University.

Cornel West is the Dietrich Bonhoeffer Chair at Union Theological Seminary.

Barbara Will is the A. and R. Newbury Professor of English and vice provost at Dartmouth College.

INDEX

Aaron, Daniel, 161
Absalom! Absalom! (Faulkner), 20–21
academic professionalism, 25, 27, 47, 193
"Across 110th Street" (Womack), 70
Adamic, Louis, 164
Adorno, Theodor, 85–86, 197
affirmative action policies: African Americans and, 168–69; Asian Americans and, 167–72, 175n5; Black humanity and, 3; race and, 50, 53, 149; West on, 172
African Americans: affirmative action policies and, 168–69; conservatism and, 3, 5; historiography and, 79–80, 85; interracial coalitions and, 11, 165–67, 170, 172, 174; mass incarceration of, 4; mattering and, 1; nihilism and, 9, 65, 68–70; police murder of, 2, 4, 96, 154–55, 173, 178, 189; struggle against white supremacy, 3, 137, 139, 141, 147, 197
African Methodist Episcopal Church, 137, 156n2
Afropessimism: antiblackness and, 80, 109–10; on Blackness and negation, 77–80; Black nihilism and, 78–82, 86, 94, 98–99, 102, 111, 188, 193–94; Black pathology and, 81, 92n79; failure of progressivist movements and, 9, 80–81, 87; ironic narratives of African American history and, 79–81, 84, 86–87; philosophy of personal conduct and, 81; prophesy and, 87; stability thesis and, 80; time-consciousness and, 78–80; West's rejection of, 109–12
Afropessimism (Wilderson), 19
Aiken, Henry David, 196
Alexander, Elizabeth, 111
Alexander, Michelle, 4
American democracy: authoritarianism and, 115, 125; Black agency and, 24; Blues and, 109, 123–24, 126–27; capitalism and, 115; challenges to well-being and, 36–37; civil rights movement and, 126; equality for Black folk and, 52; liberal individualism and, 55; militarism and, 115; multiracial, 54; racial justice and, 2; settler colonialism and slavery in, 135, 193; white supremacy and, 4, 36–39, 54–55, 58n7, 129
American Evasion of Philosophy, The (West), 26–27, 50, 186
American society: antiblackness and, 118; decline of social institutions and, 66, 69–70; disavowal and, 116–20; economic inequality and, 7, 23, 66, 119, 151; ghetto poverty and, 67, 89n12; group-based inequalities in, 66, 89n12; narcissism and, 179; spiritual blackout and, 7, 135–36, 149, 152; West critique of, 115–16
Anderson, Nkosi, 10, 194
Anderson Cooper 360, 155
Angelus Novus (Klee), 74
antiblackness: Afropessimism and, 80, 109–10; conservative politics and, 167; domination and, 80–81; emancipatory attempts and, 80; nihilism and, 65; racism and, 93n92, 95, 97–99, 102, 110; withdrawal and, 87
antiblack violence: blackness and, 77–80, 96, 109–10; Black nihilism and, 96; disavowal and, 116–17; performances of, 80; police brutality and, 82, 96, 154–55, 178; rates of, 70; self-destruction and, 30
antiracism, 19–20, 103, 124
antisemitism, 110, 119–20
Appeal (Walker), 15

Appiah, Kwame Anthony, 51
Arbery, Ahmaud, 5, 96, 155, 173, 189
Arendt, Hannah, 9, 76, 84–85, 88
Armstrong, Lisa, 4
Asian American Coalition for Education, 168
Asian American Legal Defense and Education Fund, 172
Asian Americans Advancing Justice, 170
Asian Americans/Pacific Islanders (AAPIs): affirmative action policies and, 167–69, 172, 175n5; discrimination and, 169–70, 173–74; immigration exclusion laws, 167, 172; internment of Japanese Americans, 165, 172–73; interracial coalitions and, 11, 164–67, 170, 172, 174; Los Angeles uprising and, 166; model minority myth and, 166–67, 169–70; Muslim Americans, 173; personality ratings in admissions, 169, 171; poverty rates and, 170; undocumented immigrants and, 170; violence against, 173, 175n6. *See also* Chinese Americans; Japanese Americans

Ba'al Shem Tov, 121
Bad Faith and Antiblack Racism (Gordon), 109
Baker, Ella, 189
Baldwin, James: on crisis in Harlem, 30; critique of disavowal and, 116–18; intellectual tradition and, 8, 10, 113, 185; love ethic and, 30–31, 174; on "New Jerusalem," 114; "Notes of a Native Son", 29–30; politics of conversion and, 27; prophetic tradition and, 120, 130; race-transcending prophecy and, 25–26; social justice and, 189
Bannon, Steve, 170
Barber, William, 189
Baudelaire, Charles, 197
Bay, Mia, 163
Bearden, Romare, 184
Beauvoir, Simone de, 197
Beckett, Samuel, 198
Bedouin Hornbook (Mackey), 183
Beloved (Morrison), 11, 17–18, 20–21, 32, 98, 102, 182
Benacerraf, Paul, 196
Benhabib, Seyla, 85
Benjamin, Walter, 9, 74, 84–85, 115, 125
Berger, Peter, 51
Bible and Socialism, The (Woodbey), 153
Biden administration, 23–24, 168
Bielik-Robson, Agata, 126
Black Aliveness (Quashie), 111
Black Church: Black community and, 137–39, 145–46, 148–50; Black suffering and, 137, 139, 145, 147, 150, 152; Black women and, 140; Christianity and, 108, 113–14, 136–40; diversity and, 136–37; elevation tradition in, 138–40; eschatology and, 145; freedom and, 144–45; human equality and, 137–38, 142; independent churches in the North, 137, 140, 156n5; as invisible institution, 137, 156n4; liberation tradition in, 139, 146; market culture and, 150; mystical theology and, 100, 103–4; prophetic tradition and, 10, 108, 114, 136–38, 142, 144–49, 155; prosperity gospel movement, 151–52; racial justice and, 148–49; radicalism and, 139–40, 142; religious ethics and, 137–38, 156n2; social gospel and, 140–42; social justice and, 10, 136–42, 145, 155–56; survival tradition in, 138; West and, 136, 142–45; white rhetoric on, 127; younger generation and, 156n7. *See also* Black religion; Christianity
Black death, 19, 178
Black feminism, 98, 189
Black folk: conservation of raciality, 53, 56, 58n6; cultural production and, 41, 50, 52–53, 58n6; Du Bois and everyday, 41–47, 164; imposed ignorance and, 44–46; peoplehood of, 51–53, 56; responsibility of Talented Tenth to, 40–43, 45, 56; Sorrow Songs and, 44; West and historic conditions of, 46; white supremacist oppression and, 45–46, 52
Black freedom struggle, 69, 136–38, 156n1, 180
Black intellectuals: Afropessimism and, 4, 9; creativity and, 17; Du Bois as, 40, 43, 47; insurgency and, 18–20; legacy of, 6–8; love ethic and, 8, 25; prophetic tradition and, 6, 25–26; race-transcending prophecy and, 25–27; responsibilities as Talented Tenth, 40–43, 45, 56; self-criticism and, 19–20; Talented Tenth and, 40–43, 45

Black leadership: Black women and, 57n2; collective, 98; crisis of, 50, 69, 150, 152, 187; ideal qualities for, 8; race-transcending prophecy and, 152–54, 187; shift to elected officials, 147–48
Black literature: cultural production and, 52; ghetto poverty and, 70; insurgency and, 18, 21–22; nihilism and, 66, 70; resistance and, 139–40; social change and, 8
Black Lives Matter (BLM), 23, 96, 155, 189
Blackmur, R. P., 197
Black nationalism, 52, 140–41
blackness: Afropessimism and, 77–80, 109; antiblack violence and, 77–80, 96, 110; associations with abjection, 77–79, 86; Black theologians and, 146; denial of Black life and, 97, 109; disavowal and, 117–18; humanity and, 110; mystical traditions and, 103; racism and, 110–11
Black nihilism: Afropessimism and, 78–82, 86, 94, 98–99, 102, 111, 188, 193–94; annihilation and, 104–5; antiblack violence and, 96; Black insurgency and, 20; Black literature and, 66, 70; Black self-regard and, 3; Christianity and, 100–101; defining, 18, 63; denial of Black life and, 97; despair and, 102; divine love and, 104–5; eclipse of hope and, 8–9, 65–66; expressive culture and, 9, 68–73, 90n36; ghetto poverty and, 65–67, 70–72, 90n37, 97; lived experience and, 18, 63, 78; loving critique and, 16–17; market culture and, 4, 150; meaninglessness and, 78; modernity and, 78; Movement for Black Lives and, 96; neoliberalism and, 67–68, 95; political conservatism and, 5; politics of conversion and, 19, 68, 87–88, 95, 97–98; pursuit of pleasure and, 150, 156n8; as result of white supremacy, 18; sense of history in, 78; social fragmentation and, 66; West struggles against, 7–9, 16–17, 188. *See also* nihilism
Black Panthers, 166
Black peoplehood, 51–53, 56
Black Power movement, 69, 146
Black prophetic tradition: Black freedom struggle and, 156n1, 180; challenge of prosperity gospel to, 152; challenge to white supremacy, 147; critique of institutional racism, 146; critique of slavery, 146; critique of US capitalism, 147; critique of white Christianity, 146; decline in, 147–48; freedom and, 145, 147; justice and, 147; liberation tradition in, 136, 139, 146–47, 156; love ethic and, 147, 149, 156; racial uplift and, 136; social justice and, 10, 145; West and, 10, 142–47; Woodbey and, 153–54. *See also* prophetic tradition
Black radicalism, 139–40
Black rage, 3, 29, 50, 127, 149
Black register, 111
Black Register, The (Sithole), 109
Black religion: activism and, 127, 136, 139; Blues and, 109; elevation tradition in, 138–39, 149; liberation tradition in, 139; racial justice and, 148–49; radical politics and, 139–40, 142; relevance of, 148–49; social issues and, 148, 150; survival tradition in, 138; white assumptions of innate, 127. *See also* Black Church
Black Religion and Black Radicalism (Wilmore), 138
Black sexuality, 3, 50, 149
Black strivings, 52, 58n7
"Black Strivings in a Twilight Civilization" (West), 39–40, 47–49, 52, 75, 83
Black theology, 140, 146–48, 186. *See also* Black Church; Black religion
Bland, Sandra, 96
Bloch, Ernst, 124
Blues: American democracy and, 109, 123–24, 126–27; Black humanity and, 32n3; Black religious aesthetics and, 109, 127; disavowal and, 123; ghetto poverty and, 70; hope and, 124; literate creation and, 18, 20–21; modernity and, 20–21, 32n3, 124; prophecy and, 123–24, 126; prophetic pragmatism and, 197; redemption and, 127–28; as response to catastrophe, 18, 21–22, 123; West and, 18, 20, 113, 123–24. *See also* music
Boggs, Grace Lee, 39
Boggs, James, 39
Bové, Paul, 8, 193
Breaking Bread (hooks and West), 19, 21, 32n2
Briones, Matthew, 10–11, 194
Brotherhood / Sister Sol, The, 190

Brown, James, 58n4
Brown, Michael, 82, 96, 189
Buck-Morss, Susan, 125
Burden of Black Religion, The (Evans), 127
Burroughs, Nannie H., 140–41
Bush administration, 167, 189
Butler, Judith, 196
BYP100, 189

Call Me (Green), 183
Campbell, W. Keith, 179
Camus, Albert, 73
capitalism: American imperialistic, 37; American racial, 7, 95; Black nihilism and, 63, 150; Black theology critique and, 147; Christianity and, 151; impact on community, 185; individualism and, 149; Marxist social theory and, 80; politics of conversion and, 68; predatory, 95, 135; prosperity gospel and, 151–52; racism and, 119, 147; religion and, 125; resistance of prophecy to, 115; white supremacy and, 119, 193
"Capitalism, Immigration, and the Prosperity Gospel" (Machado), 151
Carlebach, Shlomo, 121
Carrasco, David L., 32n6
Carter, J. Kameron, 110, 130n
Castille, Philando, 96
catastrophe: Blues as response to, 18, 21–22, 123; economic, 149, 152; history and, 84, 193; nihilism and, 69, 78; philosophy and, 195–98; poor and working-class, 194; prophetic pragmatism and, 198–200; tragedy and, 82, 86; white culture and, 21–22
Cavell, Stanley, 133n77, 195–96
Cayton, Horace, 165
Chasman, Deborah, 194
Chauvin, Derek, 154–55
Chavez, Caesar, 189
Chekhov, Anton, 20–21, 99, 128, 185, 197
Chinese Americans, 167, 170, 172, 175n5
Christianity: annihilation and, 100; antisemitism and, 110; Black Church and, 108, 113–14, 136–40; Black nihilism and, 100–1; Black social gospel, 140–42; Black theology critique and, 146–47; capitalism and, 151; Chekhovian, 58n4, 144, 156n6; Hebrew prophets and, 108; Judaism and, 109, 111; liberation theology and, 100; love ethic and, 15–16, 23, 144; mystical theology and, 9, 94, 99–104; nihilism and, 64; prophetic tradition and, 108, 111, 124–26, 144; prosperity gospel movement, 150–52; redemption and, 127; revolutionary, 144, 156n6; Socialism and, 154; whiteness and, 109, 146. *See also* Black Church
civil rights movement, 80, 93n92, 121, 126, 141
Clark, Kenneth, 67
Clark, Stephon, 96
Cleaver, Eldridge, 92n79
Clinton, George, 58n4
"Coalition Politics" (Reagon), 130n
Coates, Ta-Nehisi, 119
Cohen, Cathy, 92n78
Cohen, G. A., 196
Cohen, Hermann, 108, 130n1
Coltrane, John, 99, 182
Combs, Sean "Puff Daddy," 72
Cone, James, 196
"Conservation of Races, The" (Du Bois), 50–51, 53, 56
conservatism, 3, 5, 65
conversion: hope and, 19; human struggle and, 27; love ethic and, 9, 15–16, 19, 27; nihilism and, 87–88; self-criticism and, 20; spiritual, 140. *See also* politics of conversion
Cooke, Willie P., 143
Cornelius, Don, 182
Cornel West (Yancy), 6
Cornel West Reader, The, 40
Coulter, Sarah M. S., 193
Cox, Oliver, 185
creativity: Black insurgency and, 21; Black resistance and, 16, 20; Blues and, 21; crossed traditions in, 20–21; love ethic and, 15–18, 31–32; suffering and, 75
"Crisis of Black Leadership, The" (West), 25, 187
Cronin, Kevin, 184
Crouch, Stanley, 127
Crummell, Alexander, 83, 141
Cullors, Patrisse, 96

Dakota Access Pipeline Protests, 136
Damn (Lamar), 22

Darkwater (Du Bois), 76–77
Darsey, James, 125
Davis, Angela, 92n79
Davis, David Brion, 161
Davis, Miles, 185
Dawson, Michael, 172
Day, Dorothy, 126, 189
Day, Keri, 151
"Day Without A Woman" protest, 136
"Death Come to My House He Didn't Stay Long" (J. W. Johnson and J. R. Johnson), 100
Debs, Eugene V., 153
Deleuze, Gilles, 196
democracy: Athenian, 36; authoritarianism and, 125; corruptibility of, 37; hope and, 124; pragmatism and, 198–99; prophetic tradition and, 114–15; radical, 8, 27, 196, 199–200; Tocqueville on, 54; West and, 7, 112–14. *See also* American democracy
Democracy in America (Tocqueville), 54
Democracy Matters (West), 4, 37, 112, 187–88, 197
Derrida, Jacques, 196
Descartes, René, 198
Dewey, John, 26–27, 77, 98, 186, 195–96
Dienstag, Joshua, 79
disavowal: American society and, 116–19; blackness and, 117; Blues challenge to, 123; defining, 117; neoliberalism and, 119; prophetic tradition and, 117–19; racism and, 117–20; West critique of, 116–20
Distribution of Wealth, The (Woodbey), 153
Dorrien, Gary, 137, 140–42
Drake, St. Clair, 197
Drug Use for Grown-Ups (Hart), 89n20
Dubilet, Alex, 184
Du Bois, W. E. B.: on Black leadership, 57n2; Black social gospel and, 141; critical engagement of West with, 8, 37–57, 57nl, 58n4, 83, 112, 163–64, 193; death of infant son, 75–76, 83, 163; everyday Black folk and, 43–47, 164; immortality and, 76; on interracial alliances, 175; move to Ghana, 58n4; on preservation of Black culture, 41, 50, 58n6; on progress, 83–84; prophetic tradition and, 26; as public intellectual, 49; on race and racism, 2, 44, 58n6, 75–77; social thought and, 92n79; Sorrow Songs and, 162–64; West and legacy of, 8, 25, 27, 36, 113, 163–64, 195; on white supremacy in American democracy, 36–39, 48, 55
Du Bois, W. E. B. *Works*: "Conservation of Races, The," 50–51, 53, 56; *Darkwater*, 76–77; *Dusk of Dawn*, 50, 163; *Philadelphia Negro, The*, 43; *Souls of Black Folk, The*, 43–44, 46, 48, 75, 83, 164; "Talented Tenth, The", 40–42, 47, 49; "Talented Tenth Memorial Address, The," 40; "Whither Now and Why", 50, 52–53
Dusk of Dawn (Du Bois), 50, 163

economic inequality: American society and, 7, 23, 66, 119, 129, 188; Asian Americans and, 170; education and, 23; ghetto poverty and, 67, 89n12; social fragmentation and, 66; structural, 151. *See also* ghetto poverty
Edelman, Marian Wright, 2
Eliot, T. S., 197
Emerson, Ralph Waldo, 186, 197
Ethical Dimensions of Marxist Thought, The (West), 186
Evans, Craig, 127
existentialism, 7, 73, 100, 145, 147, 193

faith-keeping, 9, 84
Fanon, Frantz, 26, 31, 109, 185
Fathers and Sons (Turgenev), 198
Faulkner, William, 20
feminism, 19–20, 98, 141, 189
Ferguson, Jeff, 161
Fields, Bruce L., 146
Findlay, J. N., 196
Fire Next Time, The (Baldwin), 27
Fisher v. University of Texas, 170
Floyd, George, 2, 5, 96, 154–55, 173, 178, 189
Foner, Philip S., 156n9
Forman, James, 66
Foucault, Michel, 196
Franklin, Aretha, 58n4
Frazier, Darnella, 155
freedom: Black Christianity and, 144–45; Black radicalism and, 139–40; cultural solidarity and, 145; existential, 145; natality and, 76; prophetic tradition and, 145; radical love and, 144–45; religious beliefs and, 139–40. *See also* Black freedom struggle

Freud, Sigmund, 116
Future of the Race, The (Gates and West), 40–41, 49

Gadamer, Hans-Georg, 196
Garner, Eric, 96
Garnett, Constance, 20
Garvey, Marcus, 140, 146
Garza, Alicia, 96
Gates, Henry Louis, Jr., 40–42, 49, 137
Gaye, Marvin, 70
Geuss, Raymond, 196
"Ghetto, The" (Hathaway), 70
ghetto poverty: Black expressive culture and, 70–71; Black nihilism and, 65–67, 70–73, 90n37, 97; decline of social institutions and, 70; drug economy and, 70; economic inequality and, 67, 89n12; need to smash, 30; violence and, 71–72
Gilmore, Ruth Wilson, 119
Gilroy, Paul, 25
Gitlin, Todd, 125
God Help the Child (Morrison), 185
Goodman, Nelson, 195
Goodson, Jacob, 124, 133n77
Gordon, Lewis, 109, 111
Graham, Billy, 125
Gramsci, Antonio, 27, 29, 115, 195
Green, Al, 182–83
Griffin, Farah Jasmine, 11, 194

Habermas, Jürgen, 78
Hall, Stuart, 25, 196
Hannah-Jones, Nikole, 23, 32n6
Harlem Renaissance, 127
Harman, Gil, 196
Harris, Fredrick C., 151–52
Harrison, Beverly, 196
Hart, Carl L., 89n20
Hartman, Saidiya, 5, 80, 109
Harvard University: admissions process, 169, 171; affirmative action policies and, 167–71; denial of tenure to West, 23, 31, 32n6, 130n; legacy admissions and, 171; public attack on West, 133n64
Hathaway, Donny, 70
Hayer, Heather, 189
Hebrew prophets, 10, 108–9, 113
Hegel, Georg Wilhelm Friedrich, 122
Heidegger, Martin, 122
Heimert, Alan, 162
Hempel, Carl, 196
Heschel, Abraham Joshua: on divine need (*zorech gavoha*), 128; Hasidic Judaism and, 121–22; influence on West, 113–14, 120, 122, 128, 194; King and, 107–8, 129; prophetic tradition and, 2, 10, 109, 111, 113–15, 120, 124, 126, 128–30, 133n64; *Prophets, The*, 113; public critiques of, 122, 124, 133n64; reception of, 113–14, 131n35; social critique and, 114–16, 122; whiteness and, 121, 124
Heschel, Susannah, 6, 10, 130n, 194
Higginbotham, Evelyn Brooks, 163
Himes, Chester, 70
historical discourse, 79, 82, 162–63
Hitler, Adolf, 108, 130n2
Hodges, Mabon "Tiny", 182
Holly, James Theodore, 141
Home (Morrison), 185
Hong, Grace Kyungwon, 119
hooks, bell, 19–21, 32n2
Hope on a Tightrope (West), 188
Hopkins, Gerard Manley, 196
Hoq, Laboni, 170
Horton, Willie, 167
Hose, Sam, 83, 163
Hsu, Hua, 169
Huggins, Nathan, 163
Hughes, Albert, 71, 90n37
Hughes, Allen, 71, 90n37
Hughes, Langston, 127
Hunter, Tera, 163
Hurston, Zora Neale, 127, 162
Hussman, Walter E., Jr., 32n6

If He Hollers Let Him Go (Himes), 70
Ignatieff, Michael, 118
individualism, 5, 55, 66, 149, 152
In My Father's House (Appiah), 51
"Inner City Blues" (Gaye), 70
interracial coalitions: Asian and African American, 11, 165–66, 174; crisis in Black leadership and, 69; racial formation theory and, 166, 175n2; structural impediments to, 166–67

Jackson, Zakiyyah Iman, 110–11
James, C. L. R., 24–25, 197
James, William, 195

Jameson, Fredric, 197
Japanese Americans, 164–67, 172–73. *See also* Asian Americans/Pacific Islanders (AAPIs)
Japanese American Service Committee (JASC), 172
Jews and Blacks (Heschel and Lerner), 120
Jim and Jap Crow (Briones), 164
Johnson, James Weldon, 66
Johnson, Mordecai, 141
Jones, Aiyana, 96
Judaism: antisemitism and, 119–20; Black church and, 122; challenges to, 122; Christian antisemitism and, 110; Christianity and, 109, 111; Hebrew prophets and, 10, 108–9, 113; prophetic commitment to justice, 131n36; prophetic tradition and, 108, 111, 114–15, 131n36; as religion of dissent, 122; whiteness and, 121

Kafka, Franz, 47–48
Kant, Immanuel, 84, 122
Kaufmann, Walter, 196
kenosis. *See* soulful kenosis
Kierkegaard, Soren, 119, 195, 197
Kikuchi, Charlie, 164–65, 174
King, Martin Luther, Jr.: Afropessimism and, 80, 82; hope and despair in, 197; influence on West, 113, 143; intellectual tradition and, 6, 92n79; "Letter from Birmingham City Jail," 91n50, 95; prophetic tradition and, 10, 107, 109, 126, 130, 146, 195; Rabbi Heschel and, 107–8, 129; religious/political leadership of, 140; social justice and, 2, 141, 189; soulful kenosis and, 182
King, Rodney, 2, 29, 194
Klee, Paul, 74
Kochiyama, Yuri, 166
Kramer, Paul, 173
Kristeva, Julia, 196
Kuhn, Thomas, 196

Lamar, Kendrick, 22
Laplanche, Jean, 117
Latinx, 166, 168, 172
Lawson, James, 113, 115
"Learning to Talk of Race" (West), 2–3
Least of All Possible Evils, The (Weizman), 118
Lee, Jennifer, 169, 171
Lee, Swan, 168
Lerner, Michael, 120
Lesser Evil, The (Ignatieff), 118
"Letter from Birmingham City Jail" (King), 95
Levine, Lawrence, 163
Lewis, David, 196
liberal individualism, 55
Linnaeus, Carolus, 97
"Living for the City" (Wonder), 70
Long Civil Rights movement, 86, 93n92
Lorde, Audre, 2
Lott, Eric, 24–25
love ethic: agency and, 17; Black freedom movement and, 136; Black intellectuals and, 8, 25; Black resistance and, 15–16; celebration and, 16; Christian humanism and, 19, 23; Christianity and, 15–16, 23, 144; conversion and, 9, 15–16, 19, 27; creativity and, 15–18, 31–32; defeat of nihilism and, 100; politics of conversion and, 8–9, 15–16, 19, 27, 94, 98, 104; prophecy and, 10
Luckmann, Thomas, 51
Lukács, György, 31–32, 186, 197
Lyotard, Jean-François, 196

Machado, Daisy L., 151
MacIntyre, Alasdair, 196
Mackey, Nathaniel, 183
MacKinnon, Donald, 200
marginalization, 81, 92n78
Martin, Trayvon, 96, 104
Marx, Karl, 195, 197
Marxism, 26, 69, 115, 147, 185–86
mattering, 1, 11
Mawewera, Thobile, 5
Mayfield, Curtis, 58n4, 70
Mays, Benjamin E., 141
McWilliams, Carey, 164
Melville, Herman, 197
Menace II Society (1993), 71–72, 90n36, 90n37
Mendieta, Eduardo, 124
Men in Dark Times (Arendt), 88
#MeToo, 23
Metropolitan Baptist Church, 142
Metz, Johannes Baptist, 124
Miller, Arthur, 85

Mills, C. Wright, 197
Mirror of Simple Souls, The (Porete), 101
modernity: Afropessimism and, 78; Black body as adversary in, 97; Black nihilism and, 78; Blues and, 20–21, 32n3, 124; Christian antisemitism and, 110; collapse of utopian dream, 125; disavowal and, 117; market culture and, 102; neoliberalism and, 78; nihilism and, 65; racism and, 110; rationality and, 102; time-consciousness of, 78
Moore, Darnell, 190
Morgan, Edmund, 161
Morrison, Toni: *Beloved*, 11, 17, 20–21, 28, 32, 98, 102, 182; despair and, 102; *God Help the Child*, 185; *Home*, 185; humanity and, 184–85; intellectual tradition and, 185; literary style of, 17, 20–21, 28, 32n3; love ethic and, 174; on music as healing, 126
Mount Zion Missionary Baptist Church, 142
Movement for Black Lives, 4, 94–96, 103–4, 136
Muhammad, Elijah, 29–30
Murray, Charles, 171, 174
Murray, Pauli, 141
music: *Beloved* and, 11, 20–21; Black resistance and, 21–22, 137, 180; cultural production of, 52, 58n4; ghetto poverty and, 70–73; hip-hop, 70–71; moral fortitude in, 156n1; nihilism and, 70–73; slave spirituals and, 100, 137; Sorrow Songs and, 44, 162; soul and, 11, 52, 58n4, 182; soulful kenosis and, 180, 182–84. *See also* Blues
Muslim Americans, 172–73
Myrdal, Gunnar, 127, 165
mysticism: antiracism and, 103; Christianity and, 9, 94, 99–104; divine love and, 103–4; Porete and, 9, 94, 100–4

Nagel, Thomas, 196
narcissism, 179, 184
Narcissism Epidemic, The (Twenge and Campbell), 179
narrative form, 82
natality, 76–77, 86
National Black Baptist Convention, USA, 137, 156n2
Native Son (Wright), 30, 70
Natural System (Linnaeus), 97
Nausea (Sartre), 198
necropolitics, 111, 119
neoliberalism: academic professionalism and, 193; authoritarianism and, 24; Black nihilism and, 67–68, 95; collapse of left/independent Black politics, 68; disavowal and, 119; individualism and, 5; market culture and, 95, 155, 179; modernity and, 78; prosperity gospel and, 151; university systems and, 22–24, 28–29
Nesbitt, Raleigh, 5
New Thought Movement, 150
Newton, Huey, 92n79
Niagara Movement, 141
Niebuhr, Reinhold, 116, 128, 196
Nietzsche, Friedrich: expressive culture and, 69, 75; hopelessness of suffering and, 64, 87; influence on West, 195; on nihilism, 64, 68–69, 75, 197; pessimism and, 9, 65; on romantic notions of progress, 73–74
nihilism: Christian doctrines and, 64; conceptions of, 197–98; decline of social institutions and, 66; defining, 18; despair and, 64–68, 75, 102; epistemic humility and, 86, 88; failure of moral ideals and, 3, 64, 68; lovelessness and, 63; meaninglessness and, 67–68, 78; modernity and, 65; pessimism and, 65, 73–77, 99, 111; politics of conversion and, 9, 19, 87–88; possibility of, 66, 89n14; prophetic tradition and, 9–10; revision and reformulation of, 67, 89n20; time-consciousness and, 78; undeserved suffering and, 64, 74, 88n1. *See also* Black nihilism
"Nihilism in Black America" (West), 63, 66, 73, 94
Nishi, Setsuko, 165
No Ashes in the Fire (Moore), 190
"Notes of a Native Son" (Baldwin), 29–30
Notorious B.I.G., 72–73
Novick, Peter, 162
Nozick, Robert, 195
Nussbaum, Martha, 196

Obama, Barack, 4, 23, 117, 129, 187–89
Omi, Michael, 166, 175n2
On the Genealogy of Morality (Nietzsche), 64
oppressed: agency and, 17; enslavement and, 41, 44–45, 48; humanity and, 16;

meaningfulness and, 68; permanent state of emergency and, 84; resistance and, 67, 73, 90n39; white supremacy and, 26, 45–46, 52
Oshun, 182, 191n5
Outlaw, Freida, 35
Outlaw, Lucius T., Jr., 8, 35, 193

Pacific Islanders. *See* Asian Americans/ Pacific Islanders (AAPIs)
Paris, Peter J., 137–38, 142, 156n2
Parker, William, 166
Patterson, Orlando, 109
Pentecostalism, 150
Perry, Imani, 161
pessimism: eclipse of hope and, 9; intellectual tradition and, 9; nihilism and, 65, 73–77, 99, 111; politics of conversion and, 98; progress and, 74; racial identity and, 119; West rejection of, 111, 124, 144. *See also* Afropessimism
Petersen, William, 166
Petry, Ann, 70
Philadelphia Negro, The (Du Bois), 43
"Pitfalls of Racial Reasoning" (West), 187
Plato, 36–37
police violence, 5, 96, 154–55
politics: Afropessimism and, 9, 81, 87; anti-Black propaganda, 167; apostasy and, 81; crisis of the American Left and, 68–69; interracial coalitions, 165–66; Jim Crow policies and, 23; loving conversion and, 27, 30–31; multiracial democracy and, 25, 54, 68; postwar Black, 68–70; public intellectuals and, 56–57; Rightist action against universities, 22–23, 32n4; secondary marginalization and, 81, 92n78
politics of conversion: Black cultural and religious traditions in, 98; Black nihilism and, 19, 68, 87–88, 95, 97–98; love ethic and, 8–9, 15–16, 19, 27, 94, 98, 104; nihilism and, 19, 68, 87–88; pessimism and, 98
Pontalis, Jean-Bertrand, 117
Porete, Marguerite: divine love and, 95, 101–4; execution of, 100–101, 104; *Mirror of Simple Souls, The*, 101; mystical theology and, 9, 94, 100–3; nothingness and, 101–3, 105
Powell, Adam Clayton, Jr., 141
Powell, Adam Clayton, Sr., 141
pragmatism: democracy and, 198–99; historical reflection and, 82; prophetic, 6–7, 9, 114, 126, 197–200; tragic, 87; West and, 7, 87
"Pragmatism and the Sense of the Tragic" (West), 98
Prevot, Andrew, 9, 194
Price of the Ticket, The (Harris), 151
progress: Afropessimism on, 79–81; critique of narratives on, 74, 84; cultural production and, 53; Du Bois on, 83–84; epistemic humility and, 86; Nietzsche on romantic notions of, 73; Talented Tenth and, 45
prophecy: Afropessimism and, 87; Blues and, 123–24, 126; Hebrew, 10, 108–9, 113; race-transcending, 25–27, 120, 152, 154; resistance to capitalism and, 115
Prophesy Deliverance! (West), 69, 97, 113, 186
prophetic pragmatism, 6–7, 9, 114, 126, 197–200
prophetic tradition: Black Church and, 10, 108, 111, 136–38, 144–48; Black intellectuals and, 6, 25–26; Black leadership and, 8; Black theology and, 146–47; counter-theological tradition and, 113; critique of disavowal and, 116; democracy and, 114–15; disavowal and, 117–19; Heschel and, 2, 10, 109, 111, 113–15; hope and, 124–25; Judaism and, 108, 114, 131n36; justice and, 114, 128, 130, 131n36; radicalism and, 125–26; redemption and, 111–12, 114–16; as response to disenfranchisement, 6; social critique and, 115; speaking truth to power, 155; West and, 6, 109, 111–16, 119–20, 124, 126–30. *See also* Black prophetic tradition
Prophets, The (Heschel), 113
prosperity gospel movement, 150–52
Prosser, Gabriel, 140, 146
Pryor, Richard, 58n4
public intellectuals: contestation of white supremacy, 49; Du Bois as, 49; engagement with "race"/*race*, 51, 56; responsibilities of, 56–57; West on role of, 38, 45–46, 48, 57n1
Putnam, Hilary, 26–27, 29, 195, 198
Putnam, Robert, 66

Quashie, Kevin, 111
Quine, W. V., 195

Race in North America (Smedley and Smedley), 51
Race Matters. See West, Cornel. *Race Matters*
racial formation theory, 166, 175n2
racial justice: biracial coalitions and, 11, 18, 20, 68; Black Church and, 148–49; social rage and, 2–3; transfiguration of Black suffering and, 77
racial reasoning, 50, 187
racism: antiblack ideology and, 79–81, 99; antiblackness and, 93n92, 95, 97–99, 102, 110–11; Black nihilism and, 99; Black oppression and, 29, 44, 58n6, 78; Black religious opposition to, 149; Black reproduction and, 75–76; capitalism and, 119; disavowal and, 116–20; hopelessness and, 66; institutional, 146; modernity and, 110; persistence of, 78–79, 81, 95; symbolic annihilation and, 97; voting rights and, 118
radical critique, 25, 141
radical democracy, 8, 27, 196, 199–200
radical politics, 15, 24–25, 27–29, 125–26
Ransom, Reverdy, 141
Rauschenbusch, Walter, 126
Rawls, John, 195
Ready to Die (Notorious B.I.G.), 72
Reagon, Bernice Johnson, 130n
redemption: Blues and, 127–28; Christianity and, 127; critique of disavowal and, 116; mystical theology and, 103; nihilism and, 64; prophetic tradition and, 111–12, 114–16, 128
Rice, Tamir, 96
Riley, Enrico, 4–5
Roberts, John, 168
Robertson, Katie, 32n6
Roe v. Wade, 168
Rorty, Richard: academic professionalism and, 26–27, 32; indeterminate hope and, 77; influence on West, 196, 199; intellectual tradition and, 185; on irony and democratic maturity, 124; pragmatism and, 87, 111; on prophetic pragmatism, 126; on social and political philosophy, 82; on West, 26–27, 32
Roumain, Daniel Bernard, 4
Royce, Josiah, 82, 98–99
Rukeyser, Muriel, 197

Said, Edward W., 25, 31–32, 196
Santayana, George, 197
Sartre, Jean-Paul, 198
Scanlon, Thomas, 195–96
Scheffler, Israel, 195
Schopenhauer, Arthur, 9, 64, 75, 87, 88n1, 98, 195, 197
Seeskin, Kenneth, 128
Self-Emptying Subject, The (Dubilet), 184
Sexton, Jared, 110
Shange, Ntozange, 110
Shen, Dennis, 179
Shiloh Baptist Church, 142–43
Shulman, George, 120
Sithole, Tendayi, 109–11
Slater, George W., Jr., 141
Smedley, Audrey, 51
Smedley, Brian D., 51
Smith, Henry Nash, 161
Social Construction of Reality, The (Berger and Luckmann), 51
social gospel, 140–42
Socialist Party, 153–54
social justice: absence from prosperity gospel, 151–52; American failures and, 128; Black Church and, 10, 136–42, 145, 155–56; coalition-building and, 11; prophetic tradition and, 145; West and, 1, 7, 10–11
social media, 178–79
Social Teaching of the Black Churches, The (Paris), 137
Socrates, 114
Socratic tradition, 112–13, 127, 144, 196, 198, 200
Sollors, Werner, 163–64
Sommer, Benjamin, 131n35
Sorrow Songs, 44
Sotomayor, Sonia, 172
soulful kenosis: Black music and, 180, 182–84; collective genius and, 182; in everyday actions, 190; in political and intellectual work, 189–90; self-emptying and, 181–82, 184; West and, 11, 180, 182, 184
Souls of Black Folk, The (Du Bois), 43–44, 46, 48, 75, 83, 164

Soul Train, 182
Spillers, Hortense, 21, 80, 109, 196
Spinoza, Baruch, 122
Springsteen, Bruce, 21
Standing Rock Sioux Tribe, 136
Stone, Sly, 182
Stop AAPI Hate, 173
Stout, Jeffery, 197
Strange Career of Jim Crow, The (Woodward), 166
Street, The (Petry), 70
"Strength in the Blues" (West), 22
Students for Fair Admissions (SFFA), 168
Summers, Lawrence, 133n64
Superfly (Mayfield), 70

Takada, Michael, 172
"Talented Tenth, The" (Du Bois), 40–42, 47, 49
"Talented Tenth Memorial Address, The" (Du Bois), 40
Taylor, Breonna, 5, 96, 155, 173, 189
Terrell, Mary Church, 66
Terry, Brandon, 9, 194
"Theses on the Philosophy of History" (Benjamin), 74
Thomas, Clarence, 187
Thomas, Dorothy Swaine, 164
Thomas, Norman, 165
Thomas, W. I., 164
Thurman, Howard, 141, 200
Tillich, Paul, 196
Tocqueville, Alexis de, 54
Tolstoy, Leo, 47–48
Tometi, Opal, 96
Transcendentalism, 133n77
traveling theory, 25, 31–32
"Traveling Theory Reconsidered" (Said), 31
Troeltsch, Ernst, 108, 130n1
Trotter, Joe, 163
Trump administration, 23, 32n4, 168, 171–74
Trump v. Hawaii, 172
Truth, Sojourner, 100, 126
Turgenev, Ivan, 198
Turner, Henry McNeal, 140–41, 146
Turner, Nat, 140, 146
Twenge, Jean, 179

"Uncompleted Argument, The" (Appiah), 51
Unfinished Business (Day), 151
Unger, Roberto Mangabeira, 197
Union Theological Seminary, 1, 130n, 196
universities: academic professionalism and, 25, 27, 47, 193; affirmative action policies and, 167–72, 175n5; diversity and, 22; legacy admissions and, 171; loving critique and, 32; neoliberalism and, 22–24, 28–29; persistent criticism in, 29; racial discrimination in, 23, 32n6; radical thinking and, 24–25, 27, 29; Rightist action against, 22–24, 32n4; speaking truth to power, 22; traveling theory and, 25; underrepresentation of Blacks in, 23

Vesey, Denmark, 140, 146
violence: antiblack, 30, 70, 77–78, 80, 109; ghetto poverty and, 71–72; Los Angeles uprising and, 166; neoliberalism and, 119; police and, 155, 178; white, 23, 30. *See also* antiblack violence
Vivian, C. T., 113
Vlastos, Gregory, 196
Voting Rights Act of 1965, 22, 118

Walker, Darren, 189
Walker, David, 15–16, 140
Wall, Cheryl, 161
Walters, Alexander, 141
Warren, Calvin, 77–78, 80–82, 86–88, 92n79
Washington, Booker T., 140–41
Weil, Simone, 184
Weizman, Eyal, 118
Wells, Ida B., 141
West, Cheryl, 143
West, Cliff, 143, 175
West, Clifton L., Jr., 142–43
West, Clifton L., Sr., 142–43
West, Cornel: admiration for Russian writers, 20–21, 47–48, 58n4, 128; on African American mattering, 1; on American democracy, 36–37; bell hooks and, 19–21; on Black nihilism, 63, 188; on Black strivings, 52, 58n7; as bluesman, 18, 58n4, 109, 123–25, 127–28; Chekhovian Christianity and, 58n4, 144, 156n6; Christianity and, 19, 99, 120, 128, 142–45; critique of disavowal and, 116–19; critique of Du Bois and, 8, 37–57, 57n1, 57n2, 58n4, 83, 112, 163–64, 193; critique of Obama, 117, 129; on culture and

West, Cornel (*continued*)
language, 20–21, 32n3; democracy and, 7, 112–14, 127, 198–99; denial of tenure, 23, 31, 32n6, 130n; education and influences on, 195–200; elitism and, 42–43, 45, 47; evasion in engaging with "race" / *race*, 50–56; on expansion of universities, 24–25; on faith-keeping, 9, 84; on George Floyd's funeral, 155; as Hasidic rebbe, 120–23; Heschel and, 120–21, 129; historical consciousness and, 85; humanism and, 19, 21, 93n87; influence of Heschel, 113–14, 120, 122, 128, 194; intellectual tradition and, 3–10, 16, 20, 25–27, 29, 32, 40, 113; on Jewish prophetic commitment to justice, 114, 131n36; lack of self-awareness, 56; love ethic and, 8–9, 15–19, 23, 29, 99, 174–75; on Malcolm X, 29, 31; neo-Marxist analysis and, 65–66, 69, 89n11; on nihilism, 63–69, 73–75, 78, 81, 87–88, 99, 102, 197–98; as organic intellectual, 27, 29; philosophy and, 195–200; prophetic fightback and, 136, 156n1; prophetic pragmatism and, 6–7, 9, 114, 126, 197–200; prophetic tradition and, 6, 10, 109, 111–16, 119–20, 124, 126–30, 133n64, 142, 144–47; public attacks on, 133n64; as public intellectual, 1–3, 7, 18, 38, 57n1, 124–25, 156, 185–86; race-transcending prophecy and, 25–27, 120; rejection of Afropessimism, 109–12; on role of public intellectual, 38, 45–46, 57n1; social critique and, 114–16; social justice and, 1, 7, 10–11; Socratic questioning and, 112–13, 127; speaking truth to power, 6, 22, 38; on spiritual blackout, 135–36; on tragedy/tragicomic, 82–83, 98–99, 112, 162, 164, 175, 199; on urtext of Black culture, 111; on white supremacy, 110–11, 129

West, Cornel. *Race Matters*: catastrophe and, 194–95; "Crisis of Black Leadership", 25, 187; crisis of the American Left and, 69; Du Boisian challenge and, 8, 37–38, 44, 50–51, 55; evasion in, 50–56; faith-keeping and, 9; impact of, 2–7, 10–11, 35–36; intellectual tradition and, 8, 186; love ethic and, 8, 15–17, 27; "Nihilism in Black America", 63, 66, 73, 94; "Pitfalls of Racial Reasoning", 187; politics of conversion and, 27, 97–98; racial justice and, 2–3; soulful kenosis and, 11, 180, 182, 184, 190

West, Cornel. *Works*: *American Evasion of Philosophy, The*, 26–27, 50, 186; "Black Strivings in a Twilight Civilization," 39–40, 47–49, 52, 75, 83; *Breaking Bread*, 19, 21, 32n2; *Democracy Matters*, 4, 37, 112, 187–88, 197; *Ethical Dimensions of Marxist Thought, The*, 186; *Future of the Race, The*, 40–41, 49; *Hope on a Tightrope*, 188; "Learning to Talk of Race," 2–3; "Nihilism in Black America", 63, 66, 94; "Pragmatism and the Sense of the Tragic," 98; *Prophesy Deliverance!* 69, 97, 113, 186; "Strength in the Blues", 22

West, Cynthia, 143

West, Irene B., 142

West, Zeytun, 175

What to Do and How to Do It (Woodbey), 153

Wheatley, Phillis, 57n2

White, Barry, 182

White, Hayden, 82

white privilege, 171

white supremacy: Afropessimism and, 9; American democracy and, 4, 36–39, 54–55, 58n7; antiblack racism and, 97; Black nihilism as a result of, 18; Black radicalism and, 139–40; Black struggle against, 3, 137, 139, 141, 147, 197; Black theology critique and, 147; capitalism and, 4, 119, 193; coalition-building against, 18; dehumanization of Blacks and, 18, 45–46, 52; individualism and, 55; pseudo-Christianity and, 100; public intellectual contestation of, 49; social realities of, 51; speaking truth to power against, 38; West on, 110–11

"Whither Now and Why" (Du Bois), 50, 52–53

Wieseltier, Leon, 133n64

Wilderson, Frank, 19, 98, 109–10

Will, Barbara, 32, 193

Williams, Delores, 140

Williams, Fannie Barrier, 140

Williams, Tennessee, 21

Wilmore, Gayraud S., 137–40, 142

Wilson, Margaret, 196

Winant, Howard, 166, 175n2

Wittgenstein, Ludwig, 87
Wolin, Sheldon, 196, 199
Womack, Bobby, 70
womanist ethicists, 98, 141, 147
Wonder, Stevie, 70, 182
Woodbey, George Washington, 10, 141, 153–54, 156n9, 194
Woodward, C. Vann, 166
Woolf, Virginia, 20, 32n3
Wright, Richard, 30, 70, 162
Wright, Richard R., Jr., 141

X, Malcolm: Black nihilism and, 67; Black rage and, 29; as crisis figure, 29–31; race-transcending prophecy and, 8; racial justice and, 2; religious/political leadership of, 140; self-criticism and, 20, 28; West on, 29, 31; Yuri Kochiyama and, 166

Yale University, 167–68
Yamamoto, Hisaye, 166
Yancy, George, 6–7, 124
Young, Andrew, 113
Young, Robert Alexander, 140

Zafar, Rafia, 161
Zimmerman, George, 96